Speeding the Net

Speeding the Net

The Inside Story of Netscape and
How It Challenged Microsoft

*Joshua Quittner and
Michelle Slatalla*

Atlantic Monthly Press   New York

Published simultaneously in Canada
Printed in the United States of America

FIRST EDITION

Library of Congress Cataloging-in-Publication Data
Quittner, Joshua.
    Speeding the Net : the inside story of Netscape and how it challenged
Microsoft / Joshua Quittner and Michelle
Slatalla.
        p.   cm.
    ISBN 0-87113-709-7
    1. Netscape Communications Corporation—History.   2. Microsoft
Corporation—History.   3. Internet software industry—United States—
History.   I. Slatalla, Michelle.   II. Netscape Communications
Corporation.   III. Title.
HD9696.65.U64N477   1998
338.7'61005713769—dc21   98-9805
                                                                    CIP

Design by Laura Hammond Hough

Atlantic Monthly Press
841 Broadway
New York, NY 10003

98 99 00 01   10 9 8 7 6 5 4 3 2 1

To Zoe, Ella, and Baby Clementine, as always

Contents

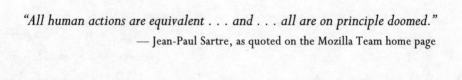

"All human actions are equivalent . . . and . . . all are on principle doomed."
— Jean-Paul Sartre, as quoted on the Mozilla Team home page

Prologue

A young software engineer named Jamie Zawinski arrived at his desk at Netscape Communications Incorporated at the ungodly early hour of eight-thirty in the morning on August 9, 1995. He was there to document history, in all its Kodachrome splendor. Netscape was going public, so Zawinski brought his Nikon FM2 camera in to work to capture the shocked, giddy expressions on his colleagues' faces as they calculated the worth of their stock options. Forgive them if their big grins made them look like lottery players who finally had won the big one.

For months, they had routinely worked 120 hours a week to write an elegant software program called a browser that enabled anyone, anywhere, using any desktop computer, to navigate the unfamiliar terrain of the Internet's World Wide Web. During that time—as they snatched naps on futons in a back room and went home only when ordered to take a shower—they had believed that the software they were writing was *cool*, that it was *fun*, that it was *useful*.

But not until today did they prove it also was big business. On the other side of the continent, hysteria had gripped Wall Street, creating a frenzy to buy Netscape at any price. The stock (which Netscape's chief executive officer, Jim Barksdale, had been a little nervous about pricing at a lofty $28 a share) was in such demand that it opened at an unheard-of $71 a share. Investors were fighting for a chunk—please, please, please, just a few shares!—and traders at Morgan Stanley were screaming themselves hoarse in the pit as they tried to place orders.

By the close of trading that day, the market would set Netscape's value at $4.4 billion.

Not bad, considering the fifteen-month-old company had yet to show a profit.

The shares owned by the company's cofounders, Dr. James Clark and wunderkind Marc Andreessen, would be worth $583 million and $59.4 million, respectively. Barksdale would have $253 million in stock.

How did the Silicon Valley start-up achieve success so quickly? It started with a crude but effective program that Andreessen had thought of as an undergraduate at the University of Illinois. Andreessen and his friend, Eric Bina, had written the original code for the browser in a matter of weeks during the winter of 1992–93; their program was university property and subsequently was distributed free over the Internet to anyone in the world. But building on the collective memories of Andreessen and his friends, Netscape Communications had created a new version. It was a fantastically popular product that people all over the world would be willing to pay for.

Or, at least, Netscape had convinced investors that this was a realistic business proposition; Wall Street's reaction was an amazing endorsement for a Silicon Valley start-up so green that it had not yet earned a profit. It was the best opening day ever for an issue of that size.

The idea that you could actually sell Internet software was novel to most of the programmers who wrote the Netscape browser as well. Most of them had come from a very different environment at the University of Illinois, where you wrote a useful application and then posted the program in its original form on the Internet for others to use or tinker with as they wished.

Netscape seemed to have put an end to that more idealistic tradition—and made its programmers into paper millionaires. They hooked up a big electronic ticker display in the engineering department at company headquarters on Middlefield Road in Mountain View, California. It looked like a smaller version of the Times Square Zipper, with news bulletins scrolling by. They could type a message on their computers at their desks and send it to the sign to display. They rigged the sign to flash back and forth between two messages: ARE WE RICH YET? and BLACK WEDNESDAY?

That day, the programmers sat around trying to decide what to do with all their money: . . . buy a house? . . . buy a boat? . . . buy two boats? Zawinski figured he'd buy a bigger TV.

The success of Netscape's initial public offering raised bigger questions for the rest of the world. The event officially ushered in a new golden era for California's Silicon Valley, which since the 1970s had incubated most of the exciting new ideas that caused the shift away from mainframes to the more accessible, affordable world of the desktop computer. Thank Netscape for spawning overnight a new industry devoted entirely to the creation of software for the Internet. Netscape's client browser, consisting of a few hundred thousand lines of code, carried the flag for a technological future whose products didn't need to be manufactured. Or boxed. Or shipped. Internet software was compact, just a few bits, really. But that didn't stop it from being revolutionary; it needed only to be copied from a site on-line to be distributed to a worldwide audience.

Most important, the Netscape browser, by creating a bridge to the new on-line world, had legitimized the Internet as a commercial medium and ensured that the worldwide network of computers would become firmly established as the information highway. The old hippie-ethos days of the Internet seemed to be over. Companies in most any line of business you can imagine began scrambling to expand onto the Internet; a few lines of computer code had toppled old ways of thinking about publishing, commerce, banking, and communications. The evolution occurred so quickly that three years later the dictionaries lying around in most households didn't even have an entry for the word *Internet*.

Do you remember a time before you heard of the Internet? Most likely your children won't. Thank Netscape for that, too, and for the fact that even people who don't own computers, who wouldn't know a modem from a cold-fusion reactor, have accepted the Net as a ubiquitous cultural and economic phenomenon. Soon after Netscape went public, it became impossible to walk down the street or through an airport, impossible to turn on the TV or radio, without seeing or hearing an advertisement for someone's page on the World Wide Web. Who could have imagined, before Netscape, that the complicated phrase "h-t-t-p-colon-backslash-backslash-w-w-w-dot" would become as familiar to us as the Campbell's soup slogan?

The photos that Jamie Zawinski took of his stunned colleagues on August 9, 1995, left no doubt that he was witnessing the triumph of a company that had broken all the rules.

But what no one yet realized on that marvelous, optimistic, over-the-top day when the company went public was this: Sometimes success can be as bad for a start-up as failure.

In Netscape's case, success was dangerous. By transforming that great democratizer, the Internet, into a commercial entity, Netscape had unleashed powerful forces it could not hope to control. The enormous amount of attention that the tiny company attracted with its ingenious new product also had an unwanted—but inevitable—side effect: It put the Internet right in the middle of the radar screen of the most ambitious software company in the world— Microsoft.

On the day Netscape went public, Bill Gates's company did not have any Internet software on the market—but that would change within a matter of weeks. And Netscape's wide lead in the race to provide Internet software would diminish within months, as Microsoft focused the full force of its attention on winning control of the emerging Internet software industry.

It was inevitable, from the day Netscape turned the Internet into a valuable commodity, that the two companies would become locked in one of the great corporate battles of the century, the first fought entirely in the new landscape of cyberspace. As the most powerful software company in the world, Microsoft had a long list of advantages to leverage: more money, more programmers, more experi-ence, and a firmly entrenched monopoly over the operating systems of personal computers.

Netscape had Marc Andreessen's team of idealistic hackers— and speed.

In a fight like that, who would you bet on?

PART ONE

Birth of a Browser

CHAPTER ONE

Bored at Work

For at least a week before Marc Andreessen's new, totally fabulous Silicon Graphics Indigo workstation arrived on his desk at the National Center for Supercomputing Applications in 1992, that machine was all he talked about. Who needed a Cray if you had one of these suckers? The Indy was the ultimate toy. What a box! It was real eye candy. The highly pixelated, denser-than-granite resolution of the monitor made everything look so crisp and clean. It rendered three-dimensional graphics with liquid grace and handled video beautifully. It even had a little NTSC tuner with a coaxial cable attachment inside, so you could watch cable TV in the corner of your screen while programming—if you had access to cable TV.

It had taken Andreessen about three minutes to realize, after the Indy was unpacked and plugged in, that he desperately needed cable. For some reason, he felt the urge to watch CNN.

Now, while *he* didn't exactly have cable access, the building itself had a cable drop. The Gulf War had played out a few months back, and the NCSA computer jocks had vowed not to miss the next conflict. Hence, the cable drop. It ran from the roof of the Oil Chemistry Building (the name was a holdover from the premicroprocessor days when engineers worshiped a different kind of energy) down into the Fishbowl, a big windowless boil that protruded from the building's exterior. The cable was attached to the big overhead projector that was used in the Fishbowl, which was the conference room on Andreessen's floor.

The Great Cable Caper

Of course, Andreessen couldn't go up to his bosses and say he wanted
to order cable dropped down to his desk, now, could he? He was
just a student, after all, a faceless undergrad drone in comp sci at the
University of Illinois in Urbana-Champaign. On a campus where as
many as fifteen hundred other undergraduates competed for limited
access to mere PCs, the fact that he got to use the latest tools—like
fancy $20,000 workstations—was luxurious enough. Had the di-
rector at the supercomputer center, Larry Smarr, even been aware
of him, he would have tagged young Andreessen as just another
conscriptee in what Smarr liked to refer to as the Children's Crusade. Cable? Come on.

But Andreessen had another, less orthodox option. His name
was Eric Bina. Bina was a salaried full-timer and had his own little
office with two windows that gave him a splendid view of the parking
lot. The thing about Bina was that he could do—well, just about anything. Bina, like the rest of the crew in the Oil Chemistry Building,
was there to write computer code. But unlike most computer programmers, he hacked code with the same simple elegance that
Hemingway had brought to prose. He understood the big picture in a
way few programmers do; his code could cover all possible inputs and
every permutation that you hit it with. Not only was Bina a natural
who could churn out an incredible amount of highly creative and bug-
free code in an eight-hour period if he was fueled by the proper amount
of Mountain Dew and junk food, he had hidden non-computer-
related talents as well.

1. He knew all the species of striped roses and what caused those
   dark spots on their leaves.
2. He could fix TVs.
3. He liked to climb trees and buildings.

These last two skills put him on Andreessen's shortlist. But
Marc would have to be careful: Bina had no patience for fools. He

could be savagely sarcastic, and if you suggested something he thought made no sense, he had no compunctions about telling you it was the stupidest thing he'd ever heard.

It was one of the more courageous acts of Andreessen's young life, then, the night he went over to Bina's chaotic office—piles of paper spilling everywhere, awaiting the twice-annual cleanup their owner imposed whether the place needed it or not—and cleared his throat. "Hey, do you know anything about splicing cable?"

Before Bina could come back with "Well, duh, who doesn't?" Andreessen laid out the plan. It wasn't a grand sort of proposition, but it was definitely a new idea. And sometimes all you had to do to set into motion the incredible whirlwind of competence and efficiency that was Eric Bina was to suggest doing something that hadn't ever been done before.

Better yet, they could do it right now! After months of slogging away on the same project at work, Bina was happy to be able to accomplish something *tonight*.

It turned out that when Eric had worked for a summer at a TV repair shop during high school, he had spliced a lot of cable. Unlike Andreessen, who was completely inept at anything mechanical—well, he could set up a stereo and hook the speakers to the receiver, the birthright of all American males—Bina viewed the job as a simple thing to accomplish. Anyone with a hankering to splice coaxial TV antenna cable can just buy the connectors at Radio Shack and follow the directions on the back of the box. We're not talking brain surgery here, Marc.

Still, the logistics were somewhat intriguing. They went outside the building to do some field reconnaissance. The challenge of the operation would be to get to the cable itself. The connection was up on the roof of the two-story building. To Andreessen, the climb looked like Mount Everest, but Bina had enough caffeine and sugar coursing through his young veins to find the up-wall assault stimulating.

He armed himself with the necessary implements of splicing: screwdriver (check), pliers (check), a pocketknife (always carried it— check), and the necessary Radio Shack supplies (check).

Then he hoisted himself up to the one-story roof over the building's entrance. From there, he could survey the situation. The best route, the most logical and bug-free route, would be to climb onto the one-story overhang that connected the main part of the building to the Fishbowl and, from there, move up to the roof with the cable connection.

Bina expected to have to cut the cable and put a splitter in. But whoever had run the wire to the roof had joined two short pieces with a connector already. It was a simple job to replace the connector with a splitter and drop the new line down the side of the building.

Together, he and Andreessen widened an existing gap at the edge of a window near Andreessen's desk and ran the wire through. Hello, CNN!

Bina and Andreessen made a good team.

Portrait of the Artist as a Young Hacker

Actually, the cable caper was the second thing Andreessen did with his new toy. The first thing he did, about five minutes after figuring out how to work the built-in camera on the new Indy, was take his own picture.

It was a snapshot of a big-faced, well-fed Scandinavian boy from the middle of Nowhere, Wisconsin. If you could interpret it the way that handwriting "analysts" read signatures at state fairs, you'd look at this face and say, Here is a kid in pursuit of success. Of course, knowing the lad would only reinforce that notion: Andreessen had always pursued success in that objective way that people do who end up making a lot of money. Guys like Bill Gates and Warren Buffett aren't interested in money for what it can buy, but for what it means. Money as points. Money as power. Money as ratification.

Also, in Andreessen's case: Money as nitro-charged rocket fuel blasting you out of here to somewhere better.

The first "here," Andreessen's hometown, was New Lisbon. He loathed it. It was boring! It was isolated and tiny (population 1,491) and, worst of all, it was slow. Some people love small-town life. He didn't; he doesn't even like to talk about it years later.

Andreessen lived on the outskirts, if a town that small can be said to have outskirts. His house was at least ten miles out, on the backwaters of Castle Rock Lake—as if such a lake had anything other than backwaters. His dad was a salesman for Pioneer Seed and his mother worked for a catalog company. His only sibling was a brother, five years his junior.

He always knew he would leave.

He measured out his days in after-school jobs and summer earnings. He was a bag boy at the grocery store. He slaved in a restaurant at the golf course. Mostly, he mowed lawns. That gave him enough money, by the time he was eleven, to at least leave intellectually. With his parents pitching in, he purchased a Radio Shack computer, a TRS-80. History will surely remember the Trash 80 as the Stone Age ax of a whole dispersed tribe of budding young hackers and computer tyros. It was a simple machine, cheap and functional, nothing sexy or crunchy about it. No color screen, no hard drive. A generation of hackers cut their eyeteeth on the TRS-80 in the late 1970s when the Apple II was an awe-inspiring rich kid's machine. If the Amish used computers, the TRS-80 would be the buggy you'd be stuck behind on the info superhighway. In short, it was the ideal vehicle to learn the basics of BASIC, the ABCs of programming.

Andreessen taught himself to write little programs, the Tinkertoys that most kids learn: calculators and sorting routines, the either-or exemplars of Boolean logic (IF B (I) > HI THEN HI =B (I)). He also spent some of his lawn-mowing profits on software magazines. With names like *Byte* and *Compute!,* they functioned as correspondence courses in computing. He found in computers what so many before him had discovered. The computer was an endlessly energetic teacher. It was never boring, and it was always there for you. It was a tool that would always be valuable.

Not like, say, phys ed. Andreessen was a tall kid, big and with the raw materials to play football or baseball. But he didn't see the point. And if he didn't see the point of something, forget it. He was candid; he told his high school principal, Ken Adams, how he felt about gym class: I don't like this, and I don't know why I'm here. Of course, it being school, that inflexible institution, he said the same thing continually for four years. Even after he retired, years later, Adams could still picture that gangly, earnest kid, launching a philosophical argument against compulsory physical education.

But then, Marc was not the kind of student you forget. It wasn't just that he excelled in his studies, he did it effortlessly. It became obvious to the teachers at New Lisbon High School that his computing skills went far beyond the modest parameters of the curriculum in the school's business department. They let him design his own projects; anytime the doors to the computer lab were unlocked, Marc was likely to be inside, hacking one project or another.

Once he wrote a dating program for a school dance. It was a fund raiser. All the students who filled out the questionnaire got matched up with a date. You'd think Andreessen would have tampered with the formula a bit, matched himself up with the head cheerleader or something. But no, it would have never worked—the class was too small and the fix would have been too apparent. This was the 1980s, after all, before it was cool to be a nerd. Geeks were not yet chic. So he never even tried (though the idea occurred to him). Better to bide your time and then jump the wall.

The worst part of New Lisbon High School's computer lab was that none of the computers even had a modem. Since they weren't connected to anything, what he could do on them was limited. You couldn't really go anywhere on them; you couldn't get away from New Lisbon.

So how did he land in college in Urbana-Champaign, surrounded by miles and miles of flat cornfields, in the heart of downstate Illinois, tornado territory? Since he was a National Merit Scholar in high school, he could have gone just about anywhere, and certainly the University of Wisconsin, with its in-state tuition, would have been most affordable. But Madison was too close to home. During his junior year in high school, in the typically logical way of budding young engineers, Marc methodically combed through an annual *U.S. News & World Report* article that ranked colleges. He saw that the top salary you could get that year with a bachelor's degree was in electrical engineering, and one of the top three schools offering that major was the University of Illinois. It seemed far enough away from New Lisbon— for a while.

Business 101: How Not to Run One

At college, he had to pay the bills, which was how Marc Andreessen became an unwitting enlistee in Larry Smarr's Children's Crusade. He found a programming job at the university's National Center for Supercomputing Applications. Even though the job only paid $6.85 an hour, there were hundreds of computer science undergrads who would have killed for it. Even having your own reserved carrel to work in would have been enough to make the average comp-sci student salivate.

He had one of the few desks in the Cave, a dark open area on the first floor of the Oil Chemistry Building. The Cave itself was sort of the shantytown of NCSA; it was defined by random pieces of dismantled cubicles, leaning up against filing cabinets and precariously held together by twisted paper clips. To see that, though, required squinting, because one of the other geeks who sat there had long ago removed the overhead fluorescent bulbs.

The darkness had another salutary effect. A lack of light, natural or otherwise, made the environment stable, homogeneous, and calm. It made it impossible to tell whether it was night or day—some people call it the Las Vegas casino effect—and made it feel as natural to hack at 2 A.M. as at 2 P.M. What light there was came grudgingly from computer monitors and a few low-wattage lamps scattered here and there on desks.

Ah, the cheery raster glow of his SGI! The importance of workstations had been evident to him during his first internship, freshman year, when he toiled in one of the physics research labs that were informally attached to the supercomputer center. In the lab, all these top researchers who were running extremely high-end simulations supposedly had all the supercomputers at their disposal. After all, many had been attracted to the university for that very reason. Yet they were buying their own desktop workstation computers and using them instead. Forget about the Cray in the computer. These guys were sidestepping the Cray altogether.

It occurred to Andreessen then that this whole supercomputer thing would never work out. He thought the mighty metronome of Moore's Law (which decrees that the power of the microchip doubles every year and a half) was beating too fast. Chips were getting exponentially more powerful while becoming ever more cheap. The time of the supercomputer was rapidly passing. The researchers in the physics lab were an object lesson. So what if you could remotely access a supercomputer from your desktop? There was still a bottleneck: processing time. Your project might be queued up for hours until it was your turn to grab Cray processing cycles.

He observed how the smartest researchers were figuring out how to use their ever-more-powerful workstations simply to hack their problems on the desktop. The irony here was that, yes, a Cray could execute hundreds of millions of operations per second—but what good was that if you had to wait until Christmas for your turn? It was faster just to run problems day and night on your workstation.

Besides, Andreessen had come to believe that the Silicon Graphics workstation sitting on a desk was becoming just as functional as the supercomputer. Both machines ran the Unix operating system; they both handled complex tasks. Indeed, the main difference between the two machines seemed to favor the cheaper workstation. The SGI machine, with its high-end graphics capabilities, could make pretty pictures, and the Cray couldn't. It was yet another example of how the information revolution favored the small over the large, the local over the central, the individual over the group. He first learned this lesson during an internship at IBM, down in Austin, Texas. That really caused the bigger-isn't-always-better epiphany. It took about two days to figure out that IBM looked like it was starting to—well, collapse, not to put too fine a point on it. But this was the autumn of 1990, and the situation was a shock after all those decades of unmitigated success, not only to the honchos at IBM but to corporate America and Wall Street. The stock price dropped to *what*? Layoffs at IBM? Come on.

But the truth was, after all those years on top, IBM was falling behind in almost all the different product categories in which the company had competed—been dominant—for so long. That was the downside. The silver lining, at least for Andreessen, was the opportunity to see on a local level how the problems plaguing a big corporation trickled down to all levels of the company.

Andreessen was just a co-op student. He might as well have been invisible, because nobody seemed to care when he sat in on high-level meetings where managers were screaming at each other. Nobody bothered to sugarcoat the bad news, nobody noticed he was sitting there thinking, Oh, my God, what's wrong with this place?

He was assigned to the RS6000 project, IBM's big push into the world of Unix workstations. A small and committed group of people had been working on designing the machine, and now it was time to create a graphics board for it. The code name for the project was Pedernales (for the river in Texas), and the goal was to seamlessly incorporate three-dimensional graphics into the RS6000. In fact, the goal was to create a product that would blow the reigning king, Silicon Graphics, off the map.

But the result, at least as Andreessen saw it, was catastrophic. As near as he could sort it out, the problem stemmed from an internecine rivalry between the Austin division and the IBM arm in New York. The New York division did IBM's graphics work for mainframe computers. So now the Austin project was supposed to incorporate all the same architecture into the RS6000 project. That, Andreessen thought, was a big mistake. Mainframes aren't workstations; they process information in dramatically different ways. The architecture for rendering three-dimensional graphics was not going to map to the more tightly integrated world of workstations—that was clear to Marc and lots of other people in Austin. But they couldn't convince the folks in New York. After numerous delays, IBM shipped a new machine in 1991, but it was four times slower at seven times the price when compared to the competing Silicon Graphics computer.

The tragedy, Andreessen believed, was that IBM had the raw materials to achieve its goal. A lot of really bright people worked on the Austin team. They knew what the problems were, since they were closest to them. Left alone, they would undoubtedly have solved them. But the top-down bureaucracy of the huge corporation stifled their creativity.

By the time he got back to the University of Illinois and started work at the supercomputer center, Andreessen had absorbed a powerful lesson about the nature of corporate quagmires. And he had developed a certain cynicism. What he had learned, he was happy to tell anyone who cared to listen to him declaim, months later in his coffeehouse hangout, Espresso Royale, was that it's impossible to run large engineering organizations in such an autocratic manner. Operations like that don't allow for innovation. They can't run with new and radical ideas in the unlikely event that their engineers somehow hack them.

It was as if the whole essence of the computer revolution translated from the machine to the organization. Technology as praxis. Smaller was better. The power of a network was at its end points, not in the middle. Smaller was faster, and faster was better.

Andreessen had vowed never to forget those lessons.

And yet here he was at NCSA, working in a place that seemed to him to make the same mistakes. Bigger wasn't better (who needed supercomputers?). Everyone was hacking away at projects to nowhere, mired in bureaucracy, while the truly great ideas—Marc's ideas!—never got airtime. Instead, he had to toil on the dread PolyView project.

Fan Mail from Some Flounder

The Cave felt like a good hiding place. Except that E-mail could find you anywhere.

One day, Andreessen was sitting there in the raster gloom when he got an E-mail from a new hire named Chris Houck. Houck was a real employee, a full-timer who made $40K a year plus benefits; he had his own office.

Houck wanted Andreessen to do some work for him. The gall!

Andreessen sat staring at this arrogant E-mail on his screen, trying to conjure up an image of this Houck dude. He'd seen him in the halls: thin, with curly brown hair and the kind of wholesome face that smiles reflexively rather than frowns. Good way to hide what you're really thinking. He was assigned to work on a project called HDF, which stood for Hierarchical Data Format, essentially a library and data format that allowed researchers around the world—environmental scientists, aerospace engineers, physicists—to store and exchange data. Houck was writing a suite of tools to let scientists move data between supercomputers, workstations, and even PCs, for researchers (like oceanographers) who had such small budgets they couldn't afford workstations.

Anyway, it turned out that both Houck and Andreessen were working on projects that used the same kind of data files. As the offending E-mail on Andreessen's screen pointed out, "It might be useful to have an identical data structure as well." Well, duh, of course that might be useful. But the message implied that creation of such a structure might be a job for Andreessen. Was this Houck guy nuts? Like Marc didn't have enough to do on his own project, PolyView.

Andreessen fired back an E-mail: "Yeah, that would be cool to do. Why don't you do it?" Snicker, snicker.

By the time Houck read the rejoinder, sitting in his office in the basement, Marc had left the building. The message had its intended effect: It made Houck angry. Where did this pissy little undergrad— an employee who belonged to the infrequently working, unreliable

ranks of those who disappeared during finals week for days at a time—
get off?

A different kind of person might have been so steamed that he
fired off angry E-mail in response, sparking a flame war and who knows
what. But Houck was a pragmatist; he tested the waters before he
drew conclusions. That was probably because he believed any undertaking was predestined to failure and should be entered into only with
the greatest of caution and the lowest of expectations.

Houck thought of himself as an "antivisionary." Consider how
he had tested graduate school at Illinois two years back, after he'd
graduated from Cornell University in upstate New York, where his
dad was an astronomy professor. Houck gave grad school a year and a
half before he decided that it wasn't for him—the politics, the hard
work, just so you could get a good grade and then throw it all away in
the trash can at the end of the semester.

So he dropped out. He figured if he was going to work that
hard all the time, he might as well be working to get to a place that
looked like it would be fun once he arrived. That's why he had applied
for the job at NCSA, but he was still too new there to understand the
politics. He hadn't developed a sixth sense about who it was OK to
scream at and who you were supposed to steer clear of in the halls.

Houck went to his boss and asked him what to do. "About this
Marc Anderson," Houck said.

"Andreessen," his boss corrected.

Whatever. Houck told his boss about the insolent E-mail.
His supervisor thought, yes, it might be a good idea to talk to Marc
about it.

"So where does Anderson sit?" Houck asked.

"Andreessen."

"Andreessen. Where does he sit?"

A couple of days later, Houck found himself in the timeless
light of the Cave. Andreessen sat hunched over the computer at his
desk, wearing jeans and a T-shirt even though it was March and therefore still technically winter. That wasn't unusual here. The heat was

turned up so high in the building that the employees could work in short sleeves even if there was a blizzard outside. Most of the programmers traded in their long pants for shorts as soon as the first signs of spring appeared. It was efficient: T-shirts worked fine, year round.

Houck introduced himself. "What's up with this E-mail?" he asked. "Do you have any code to do this?"

"No," Andreessen said. "And I'm not going to have any time to do it either."

Andreessen looked up from his monitor, unmovable. Not yelling, not screaming, not throwing a fit. Just implacable, in a blond, blue-eyed, larger-than-life kind of a way.

It probably says more about Houck than it does about Andreessen that somehow, after that, they became friends.

The View from PolyView

Anyone who knew Andreessen was aware that he was bored by the work and spent most of his time trying to find ways to get out of it. This was not too hard to get away with at the supercomputer center, where the full-timers were resigned to the fact that the part-time students kept irregular hours, depending on class schedules and the proximity of finals week.

PolyView, the project that Andreessen had been detailed to, was a software program that would run on high-powered Silicon Graphics workstations and enable an elite cadre of researchers around the world to do three-dimensional modeling of complex data sets. The idea was to visualize data points, to transform numbers into meaningful graphics. The program could run on NCSA's Thinking Machine supercomputer and accomplish, among other things, "finite element analysis."

This goal did not grab Andreessen. How many people in the world needed to do finite element analysis? he wondered. It was yet another example of keeping high-end computers safely contained within the dull reaches of academia and big science.

No, what interested Andreessen—and this was no secret; how many nights a week was he spouting off about it to his friends, arms waving, booming voice promising a coming economic revolution?— was *mass* appeal. Often, these discussions occurred at the Espresso Royale. Marc and his friends from NCSA would sit at a table in the back, the only ones in the place in shorts and T-shirts. The rest of the late-night crowd made a different kind of fashion statement, wearing black and carrying copies of alternative newspapers.

Houck would order lemonade, even at midnight, because he didn't like coffee. Marc wasn't there for the food; he came to Espresso Royale because he needed a convenient (read: open in the middle of the night) place to talk. From the back of the long tunnel-shaped shop, they could look out the plate-glass windows at the late-night sidewalk scene. Frat boys were stumbling home from the bars, and you could place bets on which ones would puke before they made it to the corner. On weekends, Marc and his friends sometimes went to the Blind Pig instead, a bar where you could drink a lot of beer and hear pretty decent jazz and blues. But the Blind Pig was too loud for the kinds of important conversations that the computer programmers regularly engaged in: complaints about their bosses, gossip about ex-girlfriends, laments about the lack of eligible women. Marc was as predictable in what he ordered—something big and greasy, make that two; I'll take an espresso to wash it down—as he was in his philo-sophical rants about what was wrong with his job, what was wrong with PolyView, and how Larry Smarr's supercomputing center was too bureaucratic and slow-moving.

CHAPTER TWO

On Giants' Shoulders

It was ironic that Marc said he was stifled at work. He was working in an atmosphere that had been created precisely to *foster* the creativity of talented young hackers who wanted to break the rules and change the world. The supercomputing center had, over the years, developed into the sort of free, unstructured work environment where, for instance, a part-time undergrad programmer could cadge cable without fear of reprisal. The reason is simple. The boss wanted the kids to have room to maneuver, to brainstorm . . . and to throw themselves full-speed into a grand idea, even if the endeavor hadn't been assigned and approved and rubber-stamped by management.

Since its creation in the mid-1980s, the supercomputing center had built a reputation for groundbreaking work that put the power of massive supercomputers at the fingertips of researchers around the world who were using desktop computers. For one thing, NCSA's top programmers (many of whom were students) had recognized—and capitalized on—the shift from mainframe to desktop computers during the early 1980s, creating essential software tools to connect the masses to the muscle machines. NCSA also enjoyed a worldwide reputation as a leader in building visualization tools that transformed data into images.

Part of the reason that NCSA stayed at the forefront was that the center's director, Larry Smarr, had learned long ago that the best ideas often come from kids who want greater access, faster, to the world's wonderful trove of information. Smarr had learned that lesson from his own experience as a smart midwestern kid with big ideas about how to cut through bureaucracy. Like Andreessen, the youthful Smarr had wanted to democratize the computer, to share its power with the masses. The main difference between them in that regard had to do with the era in which each grew up. While Andreessen was seduced by the power of the desktop, back in the 1970s Smarr had been preoccupied with a different problem: how to connect computer users to the awesome supercomputers that sat locked away in climate-controlled rooms. The problem that had consumed Smarr in the early days had been how to transform those powerful machines from hoarded prizes into everyday tools.

Was Smarr the only long-haired antiwar activist ever to get a top-secret military clearance? Probably not. Still, it makes sense that one of the Net's progenitors would be a hearty hybrid: a sixties-style war hater funded by Defense Department Cold War bucks.

Smarr's folks ran a florist shop in the family's Columbia, Missouri, home. A prodigy of sorts, young Smarr went to the nearby University of Missouri and studied math and physics. By the time he was a senior he was doing original research on Einstein's general theory of relativity; at twenty-two, he delivered his first international paper on the discovery of black holes.

Smarr began noodling around with computers at his father's urging, grudgingly at first. As he became increasingly intrigued with cosmic phenomena, he came to appreciate the computer as a potential tool for helping visualize the unseeable.

There was only one problem: In the 1970s, the only machines capable of cosmic number crunching were supercomputers—multimillion-dollar machines that were beyond the reach of most universities and certainly the great majority of graduate students. In those days, the Defense Department had a virtual lock on Crays and other supercharged iron—war room–sized machines that were perfect for simulating how a thermonuclear bomb was engineered. So Smarr's doctoral adviser at the University of Texas at Austin (his thesis: "The

Structure of General Relativity with a Numerical Illustration: The Collision of Two Black Holes") offered a wacky idea: Why not get a security clearance from the Department of Energy? That way you can get into the facilities that have the machines you require.

Smarr did, and he found a research position at Lawrence Livermore National Laboratory in California, doing relativity research alongside the bomb makers and sneaking in supercomputer time whenever he could get it. While there, researchers showed him something that proved he was on the right track: a simulation of the detonation of a hydrogen bomb. If you could get a computer to reproduce that primordial chaos, what couldn't you do? Smarr's dream—that supercomputers were finally getting powerful enough to hack the level of complexity you find in outer space—seemed as if it might actually pan out.

He wanted more access to supercomputers. You'd think a scholar like that—a disciple of the great Stephen Hawking—would get whatever he desired. Smarr's résumé read like a road map to the best schools. He got his M.S. in physics at Stanford and, after his Ph.D., lectured in astrophysics at Princeton, was a research affiliate at Yale, and capped it off in 1979 as a junior fellow at Harvard. But Smarr came to realize he was spending far too much time just trying to get access to his beloved tools. During his summers at Livermore, for instance, he was "living between the cracks," working a hundred hours a week running computations whose green printouts he'd then take back to Harvard and pore over for the rest of the year.

He decided to take a faculty position at the University of Illinois, which was renowned for its role in developing the Illiac series, some of the earliest high-speed computers. The first Illiacs relied on electronic devices called vacuum tubes to perform computations. By the early 1970s, the Illiacs were by far the fastest in the world, and the university continued to have an excellent reputation for advancing computer technologies. Unfortunately, it did not have a real supercomputer when Smarr arrived. So, like the bootstrappers who built the Illiac before them, Smarr and some associ-

ates hacked together their own minicomputer, using off-the-shelf
mainframe components.

Now, finally, Smarr could do what he had planned all along:
He wrote a program that modeled black holes. He could hardly wait
to run it. The homemade University of Illinois machine sped through
the program—in slightly more than eight hours. Still, it was better
than nothing.

That summer, Smarr got to go to Munich, to the Max Planck
Institute for Physics and Astrophysics, where he had the chance to run
his program on a powerful Cray supercomputer, the first of Seymour
Cray's prodigal machines to be exported to Europe. Smarr's host in
Germany was Karl-Heinz Winkler, a top computational astrophysi-
cist whose work was on the leading edge of the German post–World
War II scientific renaissance. Smarr felt like a young American artist
expatriate in Paris circa 1925; all the best and brightest U.S. researchers were overseas, and many of them had gravitated to the Cray as if it
were a silicon Gertrude Stein. When at last Smarr got to run his black-
hole simulator, the Cray sped through it, running the simulation in
two minutes flat.

Smarr remembered Winkler's coming up to him one night
and saying, "Aren't you guys ashamed of yourselves, coming over to
my occupied country? You know, we scraped together all our money
to buy one little supercomputer, and you're over here using it up!
How did you guys ever win the war?"

It was true. The most powerful country in the world treated
its academics and scientists like charity cases. What's wrong with this
picture? wondered Smarr. No one in the United States, apparently,
thought there was anything dubious about its top scientists living fur-
tively behind barbed wire at military labs or sneaking off to foreign
countries to do computational science.

What could be dumber? Clearly, supercomputers ought to be
made available to researchers in the United States. There had to be
federal money available somewhere to fund such a project. Smarr

became obsessed with the idea of creating supercomputing centers at academic institutions. He began to evangelize, telling his peers and fellow researchers that the situation was desperate. America needed to put supercomputers at its universities!

Back to America he went, so caught up in the project that he recalled, It's like that line in the Blues Brothers movie, we're on a mission from God. Smarr quickly marshaled his forces, documenting case after case of science stalled for want of supercomputer time. His timing was perfect. Another scientist, it turned out, was doing the same thing in San Diego, and a number of reports were beginning to surface suggesting that the state of advanced research in the United States was hitting a critical computational bottleneck.

Smarr argued that universities needed supercomputers immediately. Along with Nobel Laureate Ken Wilson and others, he testified before Congress. "We've got to put into the hands of the people the means of production!" he told people. He wrote a $43 million proposal—and to his surprise Congress passed a measure to fund five national supercomputer centers.

The National Science Foundation was to be allowed to conduct leading-edge experiments in hooking up the computers at the five centers—in California, New York, New Jersey, Pennsylvania, and Illinois. In 1985, Smarr became the director of the National Center for Supercomputing Applications at Urbana-Champaign.

That was just the beginning of his crusade. The year Smarr assumed the directorship of the Illinois center, perhaps one hundred academics had access to the powerful machines nationwide; within five years, thirty thousand professors, research fellows, and graduate and undergraduate students in the fields of physics, chemistry, astronomy, biology, ecology, and engineering could get supercomputer time.

This isn't meant to suggest that supercomputers were suddenly as ubiquitous as blackboards. Far from it. Resources were scarce. There was only one supercomputer per national center. How, then, did so many people gain access?

Through a network, of course. A network was needed to tie all those machines together and to the people who needed access to them, a high-speed backbone. The national centers adopted the TCP/IP standard of moving data across the ARPANET, creating a production network in support of scientific endeavors. It looked like a continent-sized oval racetrack stretching from Boston to San Diego. It was an interstate of sorts, and it came within reach of a dozen metropolitan centers, where smaller networks grew up around it and got permission from the NSF to connect to that sprawling high-speed backbone. The U.S. government's decision in 1985 to invest in the national supercomputing centers, through funding from the National Science Foundation, turned out to be the birth of the commercial Internet.

A Cray in Every Mac

Smarr had long ago realized that the best way to get his people to create truly revolutionary ideas—software that would push the boundaries and make it suddenly possible to use computers in wholly new and useful ways—was to create an environment where they could experiment, make wild mental leaps, and land on the far side of a problem that had at first seemed insurmountable. "I hung with guys who were the youngest tenured professors ever, at Harvard and Stanford and Cornell and all these places," Smarr said. "So I'm used to working with the very best people in the world. I'm used to this crowd of really smart superachievers. The goal of NCSA, to a certain extent, was to create an organization that was like a home for these people. I tried to collect the best young talent I could find and then give them the opportunity to do things they couldn't have done if they were by themselves."

Almost immediately, he created a division to develop desktop—not supercomputer—software. That division eventually would become the Software Development Group for which Andreessen and the rest of his friends worked. The idea was to come up with a way for everyone to have access to the vast computing resources of the center through their desktop PCs. Smarr thought of it as "the Cray inside the Mac."

The Development Group originally was run by Larry White and later by Joseph Hardin, a graduate student in the communications department who shared Smarr's concern that nuclear arms were proliferating during the Reagan years. As it turned out, Smarr was co-director of the Illinois Alliance to Prevent Nuclear War. After Smarr stepped down, Hardin took over the alliance's leadership.

Hardin wasn't a classic computer guy. His interest was in communications, one of the softer sciences. He had some experience using the machines, though, in the social sciences, mainly for cluster analysis—trying to find patterns in the surveyed behavior of large groups of people. He was especially interested in group behavior. For instance, among people opposed to the war, why did some groups align along, say, moralistic lines (war is bad) and others along technical lines (nuclear war is unwinnable), and how did that affect their ability to solve a common problem? After Hardin spent some time teaching at the University of Georgia, in Athens, and returned to Urbana, Smarr told him he absolutely had to help with the new supercomputing center.

"What in the world for?" Hardin asked.

Smarr explained that giving people access to supercomputers would help all the sciences—researchers like Hardin as well as people in physics and chemistry. Besides, the two men fundamentally agreed that technology, especially computer technology, ought to be used for the common good.

When Hardin agreed to help, he began to organize the hundred or so universities who were the early NCSA collaborators. This was during the mid-1980s, and Hardin soon found he was becoming something of an Internet evangelist, going from regional network to regional network, arguing for interoperability and introducing people to the open protocols and standards that are the lingua franca of the Net.

Then Smarr asked Hardin to head up the Software Development Group, a division that was founded on the assumption that the desktop computer was the most important computer out there. "I don't know that much about software development," Hardin pointed out.

Smarr said it didn't matter. "You believe in a lot of the goals here."

Technology ought to be used for some good—but what? The thing to do was get this powerful stuff into as many hands as possible, both men agreed. We're democrats of technology, Hardin thought. And as Smarr pointed out, the desktop computer was the one machine that most researchers had access to around the world. So the mission, from the beginning, was to write programs that personal computer users and workstation users could run to get access to supercomputers. Indeed, right alongside the Cray XMP that was NCSA's first supercomputer—with an imposing bank of red blinking lights, living in a climate-controlled environment—were PCs. Truckloads of some of the earliest IBM PCs and the first Macintoshes were uncrated and set up on desks throughout NCSA.

The idea was to use all those resources as "portholes to supercomputers" and figure out a way to make it easy enough for all scientists—not just computational jocks—to tap into them. Smarr believed that Hardin was perfect for the job, since he was focused on the nontech end-user.

The Children's Crusade

One of the earliest software programs that NCSA programmers wrote—NCSA Telnet—remains one of the Net's most popular applications to this day precisely because it delivers so much power to virtually anyone who needs it. It created the porthole to the supercomputer that was so integral to the master plan.

In fact, a graduate student named Tim Krauskopf worked with an undergraduate named Gaige Paulsen to write the software with PC and Macintosh users in mind. Telnet already existed in Unix, and its function was extremely useful: It enabled researchers using workstations to hook up remotely, over the Internet, to supercomputers at academic centers. The genius of NCSA Telnet was that it allowed the vast number of DOS and Macintosh users to do the same thing—to use the Internet, a world ruled by an arcane thicket of Unix commands, to reach any computer on the network, up to and including supercomputers.

Created at AT&T's Bell Labs in 1969, the Unix operating system had become by the early 1990s a familiar staple on the powerful workstations that acted as gateways to the Internet. But, with NCSA Telnet, a user could hook up remotely to as many as five different computers at once and see simultaneously on the screen what all five connections were accomplishing. One connection might be to a mainframe on a college campus, another to a remote supercomputer at a research center, a third to a VAX mail server, and so on.

These days, it's hard to image the impact a simple program like that could have, but back in 1986 and 1987, when NCSA Telnet debuted, it changed the world. Before NCSA Telnet, scientists working on desktop computers with dial-up modem connections who needed access to a supercomputer were out of luck. Now, it was as if they were right there at the supercomputer center themselves. They were empowered.

Virtually overnight, almost every researcher in the world who used the Internet started to use NCSA Telnet routinely, as unconsciously as they breathed. Within mere months after its creation, the program had become one of the standard tools enabling hundreds of thousands of Internet users to navigate an arcane on-line landscape.

Over time, as the government began opening up the Net to commerce and private use, NCSA Telnet became so popular that Gaige Paulsen went on to help establish a company called InterCon Systems to create a commercial version of the software. Business people, after all, typically want immediate hands-on technical support and are willing to pay for it, rather than participate in what was then the prevailing communal culture of the Net. InterCon was there for them.

That marked the start of another NCSA tradition: propelling smart young programmers into the private sector to create commercial versions of successful NCSA software products. Smarr was particularly proud of that aspect of the center.

In 1990, in fact, programmer Tim Krauskopf also left NCSA and founded a start-up called Spyglass, headquartered in Urbana-Champaign. The mission of Spyglass was to create a commercial version of another popular NCSA program that Krauskopf had worked on, after NCSA Telnet, called Image. In its own way, Image was as radical as Telnet had been. The program enabled a user to manipulate images as easily as words. It looked as if Spyglass's business might grow substantially—though clearly the company would eventually have to expand its product line. By 1993, Spyglass was earning a profit selling a commercial package of programs based on the original NCSA code—while the supercomputing center itself enjoyed a worldwide reputation for being in the vanguard of bringing images to desktop computers.

Another enterprise that enjoyed a similar reputation in those days was Silicon Graphics, the computer maker founded by a former Stanford professor named James Clark who brought three-dimensional computer graphics to workstations. As far back as the mid-1980s, Smarr and Clark knew each other because both regularly attended the visualization community's version of the Academy Awards, the annual SIGGRAPH conference. Later, when Clark wanted to persuade Silicon Graphics CEO Ed McCracken of the importance of developing a new desk-top machine called the Iris (a predecessor to the Indy machines that Andreessen so loved), Smarr flew out to California to help make the case. Smarr told McCracken, "From where we sit at NCSA, Jim is right on target. The desktop is everything. If you bring the cost of a machine down to around five thousand dollars, you'll put the ability to do these beautiful graphics into the hands of so many people."

Clark prevailed, the Iris got built, and Clark later donated a million dollars' worth of the new machines to NCSA as "sort of a thank-you," Smarr remembered. In those early days of desktop visualization, Smarr and Clark were "good for each other," Smarr remembered. "By around 1992, Jim and I called an impromptu press conference at SGI to talk about the importance of the network and the coming information highway. Jim and I were like a team." It was no accident, therefore that a youth culture pervaded NCSA. The best computer programmers are typically the youngest ones. They have the freshest ideas, the least exposure to time-entrenched traditions, the most open and curious approaches to writing code. Krauskopf, one of NCSA's first star programmers, had started writing his Volks- wagen version of NCSA Telnet when he was a graduate student. Smarr remembered that when the center's deputy director turned forty, somebody looked around at the staff of about two hundred employees and said, "Gee, forty. How many other people here are that old?" (Answer: six.)

Smarr made a conscious effort to recruit young staffers from the ranks of the university's computer science majors, both under- graduates and graduates. He called this policy the "Children's Crusade," and it was under its auspices that another small-towner, whiz kid, and paradigm smasher, Marc Andreessen, came to work at NCSA.

CHAPTER THREE

Making Mosaic

Marc arrived at NCSA at a perfect moment in time. That lovely academic backbone for which Smarr and others had compaigned for only six years before had begun to take on a life of its own. Not that he used it to connect to supercomputers. No, Andreessen, like tens of thousands of others, was exploring the frontier outposts of people and the repositories of wildly diverse stuff springing up all over the growing Internet.

Even by 1992, there was a lot to see out there. You could read text files archived in a computer in Australia, download pornographic pictures from a computer in Denmark, get copies of software programs that did nonsensical things like make the monitor of your Unix machine look like into a giant aquarium. You could search enormous libraries of documents on any subject that interested you or tap into Usenet, the thousands of newsgroups where people from around the world were arguing about esoteric topics ranging from computer graphics visualization to which pet food was best for golden retrievers.

The more Andreessen looked around, the more excited he got. The Net could be a whole new way for people all around the world to communicate. It could be, frankly, the most lucrative medium ever, bigger than TV. In the glow of his monitor, the possibilities seemed endless. Banks could do financial transactions! Salespeople in overseas offices could send messages back to headquarters and bypass long-distance phone charges! Businesses could sell things over the Net! Advertisers could buy space! Newspapers and magazines could sell nonpaper versions of their products over the Web! It had the potential for mass appeal.

Not that there was anything like that out there now. The Internet remained, for the most part, a private playground for academics and savvy computer programmers, the people most likely to have fast connections and ready access to the on-line world. But it didn't take a huge amount of imagination to extrapolate the growth curve and see that critical mass was approaching.

You could explore for hours, days, weeks on-line. You could get lost out there—if you knew Unix.

That was the main drawback of the Internet, Andreessen thought. The software you needed to use to travel the Net was out-of-date. It wasn't really accessible to the average joe. For instance, while Andreessen could scour huge archives of images and download, for free, an image of the Grand Canyon to use to create a background image on his monitor, it required him to invoke a bunch of arcane Unix commands to get around. To upload or download a file, he had to execute a command called ftp—Unix-speak for file-transfer protocol. Then he had to use other commands to navigate up and down until he found the file he wanted. Depending on the file, he might have to uncompress it or toggle it to other files in order to view it. It wasn't hard for a computer science guy, but it was pretty much beyond the reach of laypeople—the mass market.

That was entirely understandable. For decades the Net had been the jealously guarded baby of academia, nursed by federal grants and researchers but not designed or optimized for public consumption. The typical home computer user out there was running a Windows PC or a Macintosh on the desktop in the den. The average citizen didn't know anything about Unix or how to use its arcane commands. Shell prompt—huh?

There had to be a better way to navigate the Net, Andreessen concluded, a way to interact with the arcane world of ftp sites and tar files and uuencodes as seamlessly as Mac users found and copied files. In an age of graphical user interfaces—at a time when the Indy could render exquisite objects in three dimensions on the fly—it made no sense for a user to have to rely on a Pravda-dull command-line interface as rarefied as Unix.

Lots of people were hacking around with building better mousetraps, of course. The most interesting work Andreessen stumbled across was being done on something called the World Wide Web. It was a research project that some physicists were doing at CERN, a high-energy physics lab in Switzerland.

Using a new kind of software program called a browser, he got his first glimpse of the horizons of a new world.

Bina Meets Web

One night in late 1992, Marc asked Eric if he had ever seen the Web.

"No," Eric said, unaware that the tour on which he was about to embark would represent a shoulder-surfing eureka moment that would change history.

Andreessen had been noodling around with a piece of software called WWWMidas, using it to look at text documents on the World Wide Web. The Web, as most comp-sci guys knew, was a confederation of computer sites that used a set of common protocols to link to each other. Tim Berners-Lee had originally conceived of the Web in 1989 as a networked environment that used hypertext links for high-energy physics research. Berners-Lee had wanted to create a worldwide database that would make it easier for physicists in remote locations to tap into a central archive of information. He created a trove of documents that anyone in the world could access. All documents on the Web were assigned addresses based on a single system. If a user typed in an address, a file would appear on the screen. Addresses for other useful related documents were embedded in files and linked by hypertext. The way hypertext worked, all a user had to do was point and click on a linked document and be instantaneously transported to the additional material.

But the Web project grew to encompass much more than that, and now dozens of researchers, graduate students, and undergraduate students were hacking away at pieces of the grand design. Computers that processed requests from computer users around the world, patiently responding to thousands a day, were called servers. Servers that handled the hypertext transport protocol (or http, which was written by Berners-Lee) had come on-line, and people were publishing pages written in the so-called hypertext markup language, HTML (a simple, open language for laying out pages, also written by Berners-Lee). The Midas browser, which was written by Tony Johnson and Chung Huynh at Stanford University and had just been uploaded to a public ftp site, was one of the first browsers that actually allowed people to navigate among those hypertext-linked "pages" on the nascent Web.

Let me show you how it works, Andreessen said to Bina, clicking here, clicking there.

While a stranger to the Web, Bina had spent a lot of time snooping around on the Net. Most of the programmers at NCSA did, not only for their work but for their fun. If you knew where to look, and if you knew how to get around, you could find vast repositories of games and screensavers and dirty pictures and utilities to make your computer run better. You could also find reams of documents on everything from computer manual pages to genetic research. Bina, though, confined his Net meanderings mostly to reading the public postings on a long list of Usenet newsgroups, including alt. graphics.pixutils, comp.graphics.animation, comp.graphics. visualization, comp.windows.x.intrinsics, comp.windows.x.motif, and, for something completely different, rec.humor.funny. He liked to read the jokes people posted.

But the browser Andreessen was using looked a lot different from the standard Internet interface Bina used. For one thing, Andreessen didn't need to type any Unix commands to get around; it was just point and click. His screen was filled with a display window, which showed the text of whatever Web document he was reading at the time. And the text wasn't standard, ugly ASCII stuff, either; it was displayed in lovely (or at least moderately more interesting) fonts. More important, words in the documents were underlined; if you double-clicked on them with your mouse, you could automatically follow hyperlinks to other pages, sometimes on other computers across the Net.

At the top of the screen there was a button that said BACK and a button that said FORWARD. When you clicked on one of the buttons, you moved from document to document over the Web.

The browser also had a big picture of a house, and if you clicked on that you automatically went back to the document you'd started from. It was sort of a home base that you could always return to when you were disoriented.

That's the home page, Andreessen said. *Point, click, point, click.* Bina was intrigued by the simplicity; here was something unlike anything he'd ever seen.

Andreessen mentioned that there were a few browsers already out there. A student named Pei Wei, at UCal-Berkeley's Experimental Computing Facility, had hacked together a hypertext browser called Viola; a team of Finnish undergrads at Helsinki Technical University was working on a web browser called Erwise; and of course there was Midas. While the browsers were a great way to link text—you could follow an idea from page to page—so far they couldn't handle pictures or other images. If you wanted to see a picture, you had to download it separately and run it through another program, which was a drag.

Still, the browsers and the browser makers were on the right track: All of them used graphical user interfaces that were supposed to make getting around the Net (or the Web, as it were) easy.

Marc pointed out an obvious flaw: The browsers themselves weren't easy to get—at least not for the masses. Here was yet another example of the best minds building something that only a select few could use. It was like PolyView. What irony! Browsers were supposed to make the Net easy to use, but you had to be a genius like Alan Turing to run one! For instance, setting one up would be beyond the abilities of many folks. The browsers all used large custom "toolkits"— software that had to be installed on the hard drive. Also, none of them ran on garden-variety desktops; they ran on Unix boxes and NeXT machines and other powerful computers that home users were unlikely to have.

Andreessen figured the accessibility problem was fatal; that was his breakthrough idea. Most programmers don't like to worry about how the ground-zero computer user is going to react to a particular program. Most programmers are more interested in the elegance of their code than in dumbing it down to make it accessible to everyone. But Andreessen wasn't a typical programmer. At heart, he was a businessman. Make it easy to use and they will come! So the thing to do is—Wait a minute. *Do?*

The thing to do is write a browser that everybody can use easily, Marc said. He sounded absolutely sure of this.

Bina, despite himself, was listening.

Mission Impossible

Bina was the man, Marc was sure of it. Bina would be able to push the browser to new heights of usefulness and accessibility. Bina would make the thing really work, make it do things no one else had thought of, fix it so that images would flow right into pages and be rendered automatically. It was a relatively simple idea. But it was the right idea at the right time. If they succeeded, a page on the Web could look exactly like a page in a book.

It was a simple vision; the execution would be less so. Marc knew Bina could do it, though. The key to Eric Bina, the muse that would force him to work for four days on end with no sleep, was this: All one had to do was convince him that the task at hand was impossible. Only then, fueled constantly by Snickers bars, Suzie-Qs, Skittles, and Mountain Dew, could he set to work disproving himself.

The project he was currently undertaking, for instance, NCSA Collage, was so far-reaching, so ambitious, so beyond anything that had been conceived before that the mere mention of its name would cause more cynical programmers to roll their eyes with head-slapping sarcasm. Yeah, right, that'll work—in about fifty years.

Not that there was anything wrong with the idea. The purpose of NCSA Collage was to create an environment where researchers scattered across the globe could fully collaborate over their computers. Say you were a radiologist working in a rural town in Maine, and you had some questions about an X ray of a broken bone that was up on your screen. NCSA Collage was supposed to be the tool that would link you up with a top-tier radiologist at a big urban teaching center in Boston. Both of you could be using the program at the same time, simultaneously looking at the X ray and typing notes to each other about diagnosis and potential treatment.

With NCSA Collage, researchers in all kinds of fields would be able to collaborate; the software was supposed to incorporate audio and video conferencing as well as shared virtual whiteboard space. Andreessen, frankly, thought the idea was (to put this kindly) ahead of its time. He figured it would be another decade, at least, before either the scientific community or the software caught up to those lofty goals.

Bina also thought NCSA Collage was impossible. That was why he was working on it. The hacker could really crank himself up into a tizzy, thinking about how it was the stupidest thing he had ever heard of; he could toss off a few insults in the direction of the person who suggested such a ridiculous undertaking; he could stew about it until he was so worked up that there was only one possible outcome. Then he would disappear into his office and emerge a few hours later with a solution. The joke was that it took Bina, on average, about eight hours to do the impossible.

Bina grew up in a Chicago suburb called Arlington Heights. He loved to blow things up. He loved to dissolve things in acid. He figured he'd be a chemist. But after the glory days of blowing things up and dissolving them in acid in high school chemistry class were behind him, Bina took stock of his situation. As an undergrad at the University of Illinois with a few semesters under his belt, he noticed that while he was sweating chem classes to earn A's, he was coasting in comp sci. After he changed his major, he used to joke that—*da-dum!*—he'd chosen the path of least resistance.

The code he was most proud of writing? Xfishtank. It was a screensaver, modeled on one that the company After Dark had created to run on Macintosh and DOS computers. The After Dark screensaver made a computer monitor look like an aquarium, with beautiful tropical fish swimming languidly across a watery screen. Bina wrote his own version of it so he could run it on Unix computers and anything that could run X Windows. It had one notably humorous difference from the After Dark program: Instead of swimming against an uninterrupted background of water, the fish in Bina's screensaver swam under all the windows that had been left open on the user's computer, gracefully navigating past the blinking cursor. Xfishtank became a cult favorite.

Bina posted the program on a site on the Internet where other X Windows users could copy it for free. To avoid infringing on After Dark's copyright, he had drawn his own images of fish freehand, so the program only had a few images to choose among at first. But aquarium owners around the world who liked xfishtank obligingly photographed some of their more colorful fish, scanned in the images, and sent them to Bina to incorporate into subsequent versions. The last time he updated xfishtank, Bina had more than fifty different fish to choose from. People online were cool like that.

This Web thing that Marc was going on and on about was kind of cool too, Bina thought.

The New and Improved Children's Crusade

At the same time that Andreessen and Bina were exploring the Web, talking about writing a new browser, their boss coincidentally discovered Tim Berners-Lee's creation.

Hardin was introduced to browsers by Dave Thompson, a programmer who was Bina's partner on the NCSA Collage project. One day, Hardin had stopped by Thompson's cluttered corner office, either to talk about the progress of the project, which was one of Hardin's top priorities, or maybe just to look wistfully out the window at Thompson's motorcycle, parked in the lot. It was no secret that Hardin lusted after Thompson's BMW R750. Thompson had gotten it at a steal a few months earlier. It was a light silver-gray model, and Hardin often stopped by to admire it. Anyway, on one such day, Hardin wandered by while Thompson was bashing around on the Web, running a simple http browser that he showed to his boss.

"What is this?" Hardin asked, fascinated.

Thompson explained that the browser could pull down text from documents stored all over the world and display it on the computer screen in front of them, that the Web had been created at the Swiss physics lab known as CERN, and that it already was considered a powerful research tool by physicists around the world.

"It looks like the kind of thing we could do with Collage," Hardin said. For Hardin, seeing the browser in action was one of those moments in his life that he described as an *ah-ha!* experience, the kind of situation in which some simple concept later turns out to have had life-changing consequences.

Hardin realized that developing a browser would be a perfect project for NCSA to undertake. He started asking himself questions: How easy would it be? How do we go about it? When can we do it? Who should I assign to the task?

Hardin heard that Andreessen also was interested in working on a browser project. So a week or two later, he called Thompson and Andreessen together to look at the Web and brainstorm. They were all interested in the same goal: the idea that if you could get this tool to a wide audience, perhaps you could create the kind of self-perpetuating loop that encourages people to put more information onto the Web, which in turn encourages more users to check it out.

Hardin had thought the best plan of attack was to create an X Windows version first, to run on Unix machines, and then move on to the Macintosh and Microsoft Windows environments. Maybe the programmers would have to settle for cramming in less functionality, but you'd reach the widest possible audience with that approach. It seemed like a reasonable trade-off. Plus, just by creating a browser capable of displaying graphic images on-screen in the same space where text was displayed, you'd vastly improve the functionality of the program.

The emphasis on incorporating graphics into text windows was an obvious choice because it played off one of the supercomputing center's natural strengths, which was building visualization tools that transformed data into images. The major projects under way in Hardin's division—such as PolyView and Collage—were, at their core, attempts to meld data and graphics in a meaningful way.

Both Andreessen and Thompson wanted to work on the project. Hardin told Thompson that he needed him to finish a portion of the NCSA Collage project first: "We needed to get the X Windows version stable," Hardin said. Hardin knew that Bina was interested in working on the browser project as well, and he believed that Andreessen and Bina would make a good team. So he decided to give Andreessen and Bina permission to put aside their other work and concentrate on the browser. Hardin was excited by the prospect; in fact, he told them he was excited by the possibility of mixing text and graphics together in a single on-screen window.

Possibility? No, when Bina heard about the new assignment, he figured it was impossible. He couldn't have been happier, as he reached for another Dew.

W-w-widgets

If you want to build a graphic browser, if you want to build an easy-to-use browser that allows people to navigate by clicking on images rather than plain text, there's only one place to start: a toolkit. Bina chose to use a toolkit called Motif.

Motif was software that helps Unix programmers design graphical user interfaces. Think of Motif as being like a box of Lego blocks; it comes with a collection of generic menu bars, pop-up windows, buttons, scroll bars, and text boxes—graphic elements known as widgets. Software designers mix and match those widgets to frame out how a program looks and, ultimately, works.

Now imagine that your Lego blocks are all wrong. You want to build a circle, and the blocks only allow you to create a square. The Motif widgets that enabled Andreessen to display text in a window weren't designed to do the kinds of specialized tasks he wanted. For instance, at the top of Andreessen's wish list was the ability to display text in different font styles and sizes. That way Web pages could look as appealing as, say, magazine pages. But the standard Motif widget only allowed one default-font style. Andreessen and Bina wanted other things, too. They wanted a widget that would display color text. And of course the browser would have to display text and images together, in the same window.

The first question was: How to fix this problem? Happily, Bina was skeptical about whether the Motif widget could even be customized to do the stuff Marc was suggesting. It was all very well that Andreessen wanted to mix text fonts in a single window, but, as Bina felt it necessary to point out, "You simply can't do that in Motif."

"Oh, so it would be impossible then?" Andreessen asked in an innocent tone.

"Well, not impossible, just really, really hard."

"Too hard for you to be able to do it?" Andreessen asked, calm as toast.

The only conceivable response to such a challenge was for Bina to camp out in his office and work continuously until his scalable, mixed-font widget was built. And until the widget would allow images and text to be handled together. He knew Andreessen was manipulating him. But it didn't matter. Bina coded straight through for seventy-two hours.

He started with a very simple widget called DrawingArea. DrawingArea displayed a simple empty space on the screen, a blank slate where he could create any kind of image—and, presumably, text. Everything was possible in that space.

Bina's mind works geometrically; he sees things in pictures. So the programming problem he faced seemed to him to be three-dimensional. All the pieces of the answer were floating around out there somewhere. All he had to do was to put them together to make the perfect geometric shape. In his mind, a solution would look elegant, a suddenly crystallized, beautifully complex shape that would stay with him until he finished writing code.

The flash of a solution could hit him at any time—whether he was actively thinking about the problem or not—but experience had taught him that the best way to jump-start his creativity was to drink lots and lots of Mountain Dew and then go jogging—preferably after not having slept for at least twenty-four hours.

He never remembered, afterward, exactly when and where the solution to the widget, now known as the HTML Layout Widget, occurred to him. (Is it any wonder?) And, afterward, he could never really describe the breakthrough in words; for him, it existed in his mind, as a beautiful geometric shape and as the string of code he created to translate his vision.

Bina's actual work—the lines of code he wrote—was, in the parlance of his peers, no more than "good programming." The real breakthrough was not the mere fact that he had figured out how to customize the widget. The real jaw-dropping achievement was that, after Bina had finished his work, the new widget worked *so incredibly well*.

And of course it would, because of Bina's particular gift: He always succeeded where other programmers fail. Lesser programmers might, in this instance, have gotten the same basic idea as Bina but then abandoned the task midway through, after it proved too difficult. Or they might have ended up creating something less robust in the end—without multiple fonts, say. Or if they clung to their vision, lesser programmers might have slogged away for weeks, months, years on the interminably complex task of achieving the early, lofty goal.

Bina was ready to move on to the next task.

By no means had he created a new browser—yet. It was just a frame, with places built into it where other code could be written and invoked. It needed a network interface so the browser client could communicate with servers. (The client sits downstream, on your PC; it communicates with the server, the upstream information bank.) It also needed a parser to turn the HTML into graphical objects to display in the glorious Layout Widget.

But the new widget was still a milestone; its creation convinced Andreessen that what he wanted to do was possible.

Now, if only he could convince Bina it wasn't!

Meanwhile, Back at the Network Library

While Bina was off working on the widget, Andreessen began to work on other components of the new browser. The browser in its finished state would consist of a user interface—all the menus and graphics and clickable buttons that a user sees on-screen—that contained a layout engine for viewing documents and a network library for retrieving them. Bina's widget would become the layout engine. Marc, in the meantine, struggled with the network library, a collection of code that would enable the browser to retrieve documents from many different kinds of servers.

Tim Berners-Lee had written a network library for the World Wide Web. Andreessen had to rewrite it to make it work with the new browser. He had to make sure the library's code would be able to communicate with all the different kinds of code on all the different computers around the world that house documents. The network library, for instance, would have to be able to connect as easily with machines that were configured to run as gopher servers as it would with Web servers. Not to mention WAIS servers, ftp servers, and all the other flavors.

Andreessen also wanted to make the network library work more smoothly than it had in the past. For instance, if you had been using one of the existing text-based browsers and you happened to request a document from a server that was not processing requests at the moment, your browser would stall. It would just hang there, waiting and waiting for the file, and there was no way you could break the connection. Another problem: If you requested a document from a server and it turned out to be an especially lengthy file, there was no way you could just change your mind and interrupt the download. You had to sit there—forever, it seemed.

So Andreessen came up with the idea of creating a STOP button that a user could click on to break the connection. It was a simple idea that made the browser much more functional. He also wrote the browser's user interface, following already published guidelines for graphical interface applications. His goal was to make the browser look familiar to users who were used to running applications like word processing programs. He decided on a minimalist user design. But even though he tried to keep it as simple as possible, Andreessen found himself coding around the clock. Whole days went by when he wouldn't leave his terminal, except to hold a conference with Bina, who was similarly camped out. His fuel of choice? Countless quarts of milk and endless bags of Pepperidge Farm Nantuckets.

Houck and Andreessen's other friends knew that Marc and Bina had been closeted for weeks working on the browser, obsessed with it. At first Andreessen had been secretive about the project, but by now it had a name; Andreessen had taken to calling it Mosaic. The name seemed like an obvious choice; after all, the different versions of the software would work on what Hardin thought of as a "mosaic of architectures," from Macs to PCs to Unix workstations.

The Guy from H-P Gets It

One December day in 1992, a few weeks after they began the project, Andreessen heard that Smarr was coming over to the Fishbowl to see a demonstration of the new browser.

Smarr brought a visitor, a vice president from Hewlett-Packard, one of the corporate partners who worked with NCSA from time to time. Hewlett-Packard had long been interested in advancing the state of high-performance computing and, in that capacity, had worked closely with NCSA on various projects over the years. From time to time, emissaries from H-P (or other corporate partners) would drift through the supercomputing center. When that happened, Smarr liked to give visiting dignitaries demonstrations of the work-in-progress, just to make sure they understood that NCSA was an interesting place.

A sophisticated new projector had just been installed in the Fishbowl, with three guns ready to shoot larger-than-life images of Mosaic onto an eight-foot-high screen at one end of the room. As the H-P guy, Smarr, Hardin, Bina, and Andreessen crowded around the computer, Hardin said to Marc, "Would you like to show the latest stuff?"

The casual question belied the fact that this would be the first time the NCSA team let the new project out of the group and showed an outsider what they were doing. This would be the first time Smarr saw Mosaic in action, too. He didn't know these kids from Adam at this point, and he thought of the browser as just one of ten or so development projects under way.

Andreessen was good at running demos. He was a natural marketer. He knew how to get people excited about a work-in-progress; his friends teased him that his polished sales and marketing techniques must have been something he learned at IBM.

So he loaded the browser, gave a quick pitch about the Web and what Mosaic was supposed to do, and then *click!* The browser lit up the darkened room as Marc moved back and forth among documents archived on the Web.

For Smarr, the moment was a revelation. As he watched Marc run the demo, Smarr realized that Mosaic was going to be a super winner for the center. Just to look at the thing, up there on the screen, you felt as if all human knowledge was linkable, as if the whole world had suddenly been brought into the room, baldly visible on an eight-foot-high screen. It was a completely different gestalt from a PC, which mastered the universe of its own hard drive. Instead, Smarr thought, the browser was like a windshield that looked onto the vast open reaches of cyberspace. This could change the world, he thought.

In later years, when Smarr recalled that demo session, he would remember the vision of Mosaic on-screen as one of the signal moments of his life. He realized the computing world would never be the same. The demonstration launched him on a highly visible cross-country crusade to drum up more funds so that Hardin and Mosaic could go all out.

And what of the Hewlett-Packard exec, who sat next to Smarr in the Fishbowl that day? At first, he was unmoved. Maybe the concept of the Web was too abstract. Andreessen would point and click to a document stored on a server at, say, some university halfway around the world and say something like, "Now we are looking at pictures stored on a computer thousands of miles from here," but somehow the demonstration wasn't arousing even a flutter of excitement.

Nothing. An emotional flat line.

Andreessen tried again. He clicked to a site where a trove of Unix manual pages, the venerable "man pages" that every Unix worker must consult from time to time, had been translated to HTML. Marc explained that while, yes, we're all familiar with the on-line manual that came with every Unix machine, this site took things one step farther. This site translated those same pages into hypertext, so all a reader had to do to read about related Unix commands was click on a link that would connect with the correct document. The whole mess was now a Web! It was cross-linked and interlinked and hyperlinked into one endless knot of information. It was fun! It was cool!

The H-P man stirred. It wasn't exactly the reaction everyone hoped for, but it was enough for Marc. He moved in for the kill.

"And here," he said, clicking again, "are your own pages on-line."

It was true. Hewlett-Packard had already hooked up some of its own corporate computers to the dull text-only world of the World Wide Web. But here in the University of Illinois Fishbowl, miles and miles from H-P headquarters in Silicon Valley, a small group of people could click around and read those H-P documents, stored on a dozen web servers, as easily as channel surfing with a TV remote control.

That did it. The mood in the Fishbowl changed from polite interest to real enthusiasm, with the executive from Hewlett-Packard saying things like *This is the next generation of networking and information.* Hardin and Smarr could tell he couldn't wait to get back home to find out more, from his own tech team, about the Web.

By the end of the demonstration, the visitor from Hewlett-Packard was hooked. He was excited. He promised a big gift to help NCSA develop the browser—H-P would send twenty, thirty, maybe even forty workstations to Illinois to speed the development.

More important than the promise of hardware was the lesson that the NCSA team learned from the first outsider to see the demo: He got it. Maybe, just maybe, there was hope for the rest of the world.

CHAPTER FOUR

Go, Team!

By the middle of winter, barely two months after they began, Andreessen and Bina had cobbled together a rough but workable piece of code and had created the Unix version of the Mosaic browser. They had written one hundred thousand lines of code—minuscule in size when compared to, say, an operating system like Windows 95, which would turn out to be eleven million lines long.

Best of all, they had achieved what Bina had once believed impossible: mixing text and pictures in a single on-screen window.

When Mosaic was ready for a test drive, Andreessen and Bina loaded a preliminary version of their code on one of NCSA's public servers, which was hooked up to the Internet. Then Andreessen sent out a birth announcement to an Internet discussion group.

From: Marc Andreessen (marca@ncsa.uiuc.edu)
Sat, 23 Jan 93 07:21:17 -0800

By the power vested in me by nobody in particular, alpha/ beta version 0.5 of NCSA's Motif-based networked information systems andWorldWide web browser, X Mosaic, is hereby released.

Cheers,
Marc

Anybody who wanted one could make a copy of Mosaic for free and use it. That method of distribution over the Internet was a time-honored tradition at NCSA, originating as far back as the debut of NCSA Telnet. Back in those days, the Net was strictly noncommercial, funded as it was by the federal government. The NCSA software developers put versions of Telnet onto a publicly accessible NCSA server, where anyone in the world could download a mirror image of the program.

Developers at MIT and Columbia University, among others, had used a similar distribution method in the past but never on such a large scale. And it had an amazing benefit to NCSA: Suddenly, the user was incorporated into the development process. People who downloaded and used the new software would inevitably find bugs or think of improvements. Grateful for the free program, they would send E-mail to the NCSA developers—who could then fix the problem.

Smarr called the process "rapid prototyping." It compressed the development cycle for software and saved money. In a sense, the users around the world became a volunteer quality assurance department.

Free distribution was a cheap and useful method of testing new software.

In addition, Marc and Eric also posted the original language in which they had written the browser—the source code—which would enable other programmers to see exactly how they had built the program. In a software program, the source code is what a programmer writes; before distribution, the code typically is translated into a format that a computer can understand and run. Revealing the source code is tantamount to unveiling a secret recipe. It was as if two young chefs who dreamed up a new kind of flaming dessert had published a list of their ingredients, measurements, and cooking time.

It was common in the Unix world for programmers to post source code publicly. For one thing, the Unix world was fragmented, with many different flavors of Unix—such as BSD Unix, created at the University of California at Berkeley, and Sun Microsystems' proprietary flavor of Unix, and Apple's version, and—well, the list goes on and on. Depending on what type of Unix your computer runs, you might have to tinker with the browser's code to get it to work for you.

Marc and Eric published the source code to make it possible for developers to tinker; in fact, they wanted Unix programmers to come up with good ideas for new features and solutions to fixing unknown bugs that might be in the program. That practice of collaborative programming, too, had long been a tradition on the Internet, a world inhabited primarily by academics and researchers more than willing to pool their knowledge in the service of improving software.

The university would still own Mosaic, and no one else could use the source code to make money. Along with the code, NCSA published a licensing agreement making it clear that no one was allowed to use the program for commercial purposes without permission.

Before they posted the program, no one really knew how great the interest might be. But the response was remarkable.

From his computer, Andreessen could monitor the NCSA logs to keep track of how many people were making copies of Mosaic. Within ten minutes after it was posted, someone downloaded it. Within thirty minutes, a hundred people had it. In less than an hour, he was already getting feedback via E-mail from excited users around the world.

For a programmer, it was the purest kind of high imaginable. He had an idea, he implemented it from nothing, and suddenly people all over the world were using it and telling him how wonderful it was! Soon he was getting hundreds of E-mail messages a day. He heard from people in Amsterdam and Asia and Ann Arbor. The circle of people who were using Mosaic and commenting on it were the elite: smart people who were using the Net years before it was to become a mass-market medium, programmers who understood the complexity and potential of the World Wide Web, students like him, engineers who had been writing software for decades. It felt like a celebrity cocktail party—and he was the guest of honor.

Andreessen's friends at NCSA (including Houck, graduate student Aleks Totic, and a couple of Windows programmers named Jon Mittelhauser and Chris Wilson) watched it happen. They would sometimes go out for drinks together on a Saturday night, and he would fill their heads with intoxicating visions of how Mosaic was going to change the world. Some of them started to believe him; after all, working on the Mosaic browser seemed like a more exciting task than their own assignments. (Of course, not Houck the antivisionary. He wasn't buying any of Marc's world-changing catastrophic revolutionary-paradigm-shifting talk. He wouldn't snort in derision, exactly, but he made it clear that he was withholding judgment.) Some of the others were eager recruits.

Take Aleks Totic, for example. He was a graduate student, a Mac programmer assigned at NCSA to work on Mesher, a graphical user interface tool for designing three-dimensional models used in supercomputer simulation. Aleks wasn't averse to the idea of working on a riskier project, and to him it sounded like Marc needed some help taking Mosaic to the next level.

Aleks belonged to the sailing club at the university. In the middle of flat farm country, thousands of miles from the ocean, finding a place to sail involved considerable ingenuity; Aleks and the other members would drive forty miles to a nearby nuclear power plant and sail on its cooling lake, blue dome in the background. It was kind of muddy, and some of them wondered if it was totally, uh, safe. To cover their doubts, they made a lot of jokes about three-eyed fish. Aleks thought it was fun.

Born in Belgrade and raised in Kuwait, Aleks was ostensibly working toward a doctorate in artificial intelligence, but he had been souring on the idea. The field of artificial intelligence was too theoretical for his taste; Mosaic, on the other hand, was something that would work *now,* as soon as somebody wrote code and posted it on the Net.

And the Web seemed like a big, limitless open space and you had a license to do whatever you wanted. You could discover gold.

That same sense of immediate satisfaction appealed to Jon Mittelhauser. Another graduate student, he was a serious coder who worked on PCs in the basement of the Oil Chemistry Building. For months he'd watched as Andreessen and Bina scurried around the place, busy little beavers at work building a new kind of dam. He had to admit that Mosaic looked like more fun than he was having. Mittelhauser was bored with his part-time job—it didn't seem to him as if his bosses expected him, as a student, to really *do* anything—that he probably would have latched on to the first interesting thing that came along. The fact that Mosaic was more than interesting, that it was something people around the world could use to surf the Web, something even his mom could use, convinced him to sign up, weeks before he officially got assigned to the project.

Mittelhauser particularly loved the creative feeling that came from hard-core coding. "I have no artistic ability," he liked to tell people. "I can't sing, can't dance, can't paint, can't play music. But when I code I'm creating something out of nothing. It's really bizarre to think of a computer nerd as an artist, but in a way you are. You're taking absolutely nothing—I mean electrons—and creating something that people are going to find useful."

Soon Andreessen told them that since the Unix code was in pretty good shape, it was time to start on the other versions and turn the browser into a truly populist program. It was time to write a version of Mosaic that would work on Macintosh computers and a version that would run on Windows machines.

Of course, whoever worked on those projects would have to catch up to the Unix version, which had a four-month head start.

Speed

From day one, they were chasing Bina.

He worked whenever he wasn't asleep—he later figured out it came out to about eighteen hours a day for weeks—no, months—until he had created a Mosaic version that would run on Windows machines. It helped that he was working with his friend Chris Wilson, who sat near him in a big open room in the basement of the Oil Chemistry Building.

Mittelhauser and Chris were writing the Windows version from scratch because the existing code that Andreessen and Bina already had written was not cross-platform. That meant Mittelhauser and Wilson couldn't just lift big chunks of the Unix version and graft them onto the Windows browser. The fact that they couldn't share code caused some problems; for instance, the different versions of the browser worked in different ways. Sometimes the Unix version would display a Web page on the screen in a manner that looked totally different from how the Windows version or the Mac version would display it. You wouldn't even know you were looking at the same layout.

But those weren't problems they needed to solve now. Now they just needed to keep working, faster, faster, faster, to catch up. Bina kept improving the Unix code, adding new features, fixing bugs, staying a few steps ahead of everyone else. On top of that, Mittelhauser and Chris also had to catch up to Aleks, who had been assigned by Hardin a month earlier to write a Macintosh version. They all had the sense that they were working on something that might turn out to be far more interesting than anything they had worked on in the past. Aleks thought of it as the interface of the future. He could imagine doing *anything* with Mosaic.

Aleks had looked at the HTML Text Widget created by Bina and decided to begin at the same point. He basically sat down and winged it: Here's the window on the screen; how do we get some HTML into it? He'd yell for help from time to time. "Marc, how do you guys do this?"

Aleks relied on the network library that Andreessen had reworked to give him ideas on how to modify the same code to run on Macintosh machines. When he had trouble and was grumbling, "I can't believe this code ever worked," he'd take a look at how Andreessen and Bina had solved the same problem in the Unix version.

Time meant nothing to them. Slaving away in the basement, surrounded by discarded pizza boxes, they were in it for the fun, because they were trying to solve problems, trying to add new features to the program. Besides, they were kids; they had nothing to compare the experience to. They had no idea their pace was frenetic, their output enormous, their browser emerging fast, fast, faster than it had any right to, given the small number of programmers who were writing the code.

There were no walls or even cubicles in the big open room where Mittelhauser and Chris worked, just a sea of desks spread out all over the place. Aleks was down the hall, in a tiny office of his own. Aleks liked the atmosphere—totally dark, no windows, soda machine nearby. It was the perfect work environment as far as he was concerned. It was his biosphere.

Andreessen moved downstairs too, to be with the team, and eventually everyone started calling the basement the Cave. They could have called it Cave II: The Sequel, if they'd thought of it. But nobody had time to think about anything except the work. It was too exciting, too all-consuming. They didn't like to leave the building, even for meals, if they could help it. After a couple of months the stacks of empty pizza boxes were ten feet high: white cardboard boxes, all from the same place, Grog's, where you could get two ten-inch pies for six bucks, delivered.

Staying at work overnight was part of the regular schedule; night was when everything interesting happened. During the day the programmers would go home to sleep or, rarely, to class.

Andreessen worked until he was ready to drop. Then he'd go crash for a few hours in his apartment, a small and squalid place a few blocks away. It was always a mess, with his clothes and classical music CDs spread across the floor. Somewhere in the deep recesses of his lair were hidden heavy-metal cassette tapes, vestiges of some stage he went through, but he never played them anymore.

If Andreessen didn't show up again at the Oil Chemistry Building after three or four hours, the rest of them would go over to try to wake him. They'd pound on the door: "Marc, get your ass out of bed!" They stood in the hall, banging and yelling. After a while, it was usually Aleks who figured out what to yell under the door to bring Marc back to consciousness. The right algorithm, according to Aleks, relied more on volume—"being really loud"—than on any particular word or phrase. Andreessen would stumble out, bleary-eyed, and back to work they would go.

Mittelhauser wanted more than anything to catch up to the Unix version. The competition was intense, but he liked it that way. Ever since he was ten years old, playing computer games against his dad at home in the suburban Chicago town of Naperville, Mittelhauser had wanted to win. They had a game called Lemonade, in which the players had to run lemonade stands—deciding how much lemonade to make, how much sugar to use, how much to charge per glass— each trying to make the most profit. Mittelhauser's dad won all the time, until one day Jon went into the source code for the game and changed the parameters to make it easier for himself. He told the game that if a player was named Jon, that player was supposed to win.

Now, everybody was keenly aware of each other's progress. They kept track of each other's milestones. Who could get their version of Mosaic to display an image first? Who could add the coolest functionality?

One time Mittelhauser took a night off. Big mistake. The next day when he came in, Aleks had a big grin on his face.

"Look what I did," Aleks said, gesturing toward his computer screen, where the nascent Mac browser was pulling down a beautiful image from the Web.

Oh, damn, why didn't I think of that? Mittelhauser wondered. Then he stayed at work himself until his eyes were blurry. By the time he finally went home, he had figured out how to duplicate Aleks's effort in the Windows version.

Mittelhauser thought if he just worked harder and faster he could catch up. But then, everybody else was working at the same pace. Bina was legendary for pulling three-day work shifts, coding away without a break for up to seventy-two hours, going home to sleep for about four hours—and then returning.

As often as possible, Mittelhauser would throw Bina and Marc curveballs, just to keep them guessing.

It was always little things. Once Mittelhauser woke up in the middle of the night with an idea. It made perfect sense: Change the cursor's appearance if it is positioned over a hypertext link. Mittelhauser decided to write the code to change the cursor into the shape of a hand. That symbolized how a user could grab hold of the information in the hyperlink just by clicking on it.

It was a simple idea, obvious in retrospect, and Mittelhauser got a devious chuckle out of it. He realized immediately that writing code to get the cursor to change would be an easy thing to do in Windows. He wrote the code in an hour.

Then he showed the new feature to Andreessen. "Isn't this a good idea?" he asked.

It was clearly a good idea; it was elegant. Without question, the feature should be incorporated into all versions of Mosaic. But Andreessen cursed about it all the same; it took *him* about four hours to write the same code for the Unix version.

Part of the reason they could move so fast was, frankly, they were writing for their own amusement. If the code was buggy, if 10 percent of the users out there couldn't operate the software because it crashed too much, then big deal. They weren't selling it, after all.

As soon as they got a working version of the code hammered together, they put it up on the Net for people to download and test. But they didn't spend too much time fixing the bugs that were reported. Fixing bugs was no fun. The fun was thinking up new features and putting them into the code.

The goal all along was to write a program that would excite people—and also to keep moving.

In the end, Andreessen even convinced Houck, the old anti-visionary, to help out. Andreessen needed someone to write two thou-

sand or so lines of code for X Windows Mosaic that would allow scientists who used the program to pull up a summary of a data file.
Houck wrote the code from scratch in about forty-eight hours.

The McCools

The client gets all the glory. The client is the program a computer
user loads onto a PC or a Mac and fires up to cruise across the Web.
But once the client reaches its destination, it relies on the server software to do the real work.

The Mosaic team was full of new ideas for improvements that
would make the browser more fun and useful: forms users could fill
in to interact with the Web page, check boxes, toggle buttons, new
ways to search. But for that they needed a better server program. So
far, Mosaic was just a client; it connected to any of the relatively generic servers that had been spawned by the CERN scientists. With
flashier server code, optimized for Mosaic, the browser could become
a genuine killer.

What the team needed, then, was someone to write the stuff.
Marc, naturally, had some ideas about where to go. When you're
looking for a programmer to write server software, you look for the
same kinds of qualities that the best servers themselves exhibit: steady,
dependable, low-key, patient. You look for somebody like, say, Rob
or Mike McCool.

Rob and Mike McCool did almost everything in tandem. The
best way to tell these identical twins apart was to have a conversation
with them. While Mike was a born storyteller, Rob was more reti-
cent. Ask Rob a direct question, and he'd always give a direct answer—in five words or less. Ask Mike, and you could be in for a
heart-to-heart chat.

Growing up in the suburban Chicago town of Westchester,
the brothers transferred after one year of public high school to the
Illinois Math and Science Academy, a boarding school in Aurora. The

school had an Internet connection, and the McCools quickly got on-line. E-mail became a way of life. They thought of themselves as total computer geeks.

The nights that the McCool brothers would sneak out of their dorm room at 1 or 2 A.M., they didn't go off to party or meet girls. Instead, they went to the computer lab, where they entertained themselves by running fractal programs for hours on a Macintosh. They remembered boarding school as being a lot of fun.

When it came time to apply to college, they both decided on the University of Illinois. Both were computer science majors. They roomed together. During summer breaks, they even went back home to the suburbs and worked together. One time they worked for the Cook County Public Works Department as sanitary sewer inspectors. Their job was to open every single manhole cover in the village of Westchester, stick a steel tape measure down to see how high the water was, and check to make sure the sewers weren't backed up.

They could see the water flowing by, about eight feet below, and if you were patient and kept looking, every once in a while something really kooky would float by, like a golf club or a remote-controlled car.

Some people might blow off a job like that, but the McCool brothers approached it with the same methodical patience that they applied to computer coding. After they finished their assignment, they actually started cleaning up some of the manholes. It made sense to them; they got full of dirt and gook and crud, after all. Somebody had to go down there and scoop it out every so often.

Not exactly glory work, but then, the McCools weren't working for glory. Not at that job, and not when they were programming, either.

The major difference in the McCools' college careers was that they had different jobs at first. Rob had been working at the super-computing center since his freshman year, as a systems administrator. Mike worked at the university's Computing and Communications

Services Office, where he thought of himself as "basically a front-end support grunt." Mike's job was to be a troubleshooter for anybody who called in with a problem. He handled really tough stuff, like the professor who called because he couldn't get his modem to work. It turned out that the professor had never plugged it into his phone. After Mike's office closed at 10 P.M., he used to wander over to the supercomputing center, where Rob was, and hang out there until 1 or 2 A.M. It was just like in high school, except that at NCSA there were always extra machines no one was using at that hour. The McCools would play around on them.

That's when the McCool brothers met Andreessen wandering around the halls late at night. He would call out, in a big booming voice that carried through the whole building, "Rob! Mike! How's it going?"

One day, Andreessen stopped by Rob's desk and said, "You know, I'm writing this Mosaic thing."

At first, Rob didn't see the appeal of the World Wide Web. It wasn't very exciting, mainly a bunch of text files that universities or scientific labs had published on-line; it was like, OK, we've got these blue things you can click on and get other documents, but big deal.

Of course, the McCool brothers, in general, weren't the kinds of people who got swept up and carried away by the excitement of an abstract idea. Their world was concrete. If you made a logical argument, that was one thing. If you told them to measure the depth of every manhole in the village of Westchester, they'd do it and finish the job a month early. But to keep telling them that you were going to change the world? Come on.

But Andreessen was persistent; he kept evangelizing.

One day, Andreessen asked Rob, "Do you want to write an http server for Mosaic?"

That night Rob went home to the apartment he shared with Mike. He told his brother, "It sounds kind of funny, but it would be a way to get out of systems administration, get more into programming, you know?"

Rob knew full well that the kind of programming he was good at was the back end. He had learned to live with the fact that his work didn't have a lot of glory associated with it. He'd just shrug and say, "Hey, the back end is like building bridges. You build ten thousand bridges. A million people drive across them every day, and nobody notices. One of them falls down? That's the one everyone's going to remember."

It would be fine with him if no one remembered that any of his software existed. It would just mean nothing had gone wrong.

CHAPTER FIVE

Web Wizards

By early summer of 1993, the buzz was that the Mosaic team in Illinois was hot. There were no more than a few dozen people in the whole world who were writing browsers or other programs to run on Tim Berners-Lee's World Wide Web, and Mosaic was getting worldwide attention for its ability to display images and text together in a single window. Andreessen was getting to be a minor celebrity on the Usenet newsgroups devoted to the Web, particularly on the www-talk newsgroup, where he posted vociferously. As more and more people around the world started to use the early versions of X Windows Mosaic, the NCSA programmers' reputation grew.

So it was no wonder that they were invited to go to Boston in July, where O'Reilly & Associates was sponsoring a World Wide Web Wizards Workshop. O'Reilly, which published a sophisticated blend of technical books known, among other things, for the fine line drawings of exotic animals on their covers, had sponsored the development of Pei Wei's Viola browser. O'Reilly understood that a new publishing platform—the Web—was being born and hoped the conference would speed the development of content on-line. (O'Reilly already had plans to launch the first commercial site on the Web, which would be called the Global Network Navigator.)

O'Reilly hoped to work more closely with developers to make sure that, while different browsers that displayed documents might come and go, all the documents—that is, all content—would be written in a universal format. This was trickier than it sounded. Was it possible, for instance, for the Web to support new graphical browsers like Mosaic while remaining compatible with text-based browsers?

The Wizards Workshop was a two-day conference, held in O'Reilly's Cambridge offices, a converted warehouse called the Brickyard. Just about everybody who was anybody in Web programming was there. That amounted to about thirty people, including the Mosaic team, led by Hardin. It was a major rush for the boys from Illinois—and not just because the hotel rooms were paid for and they got free food on the last night of the conference. The Mosaic team already felt like rock stars. As soon as beta versions of Mosaic for Mac and for Windows had been publicly released, NCSA's server had been overwhelmed by people who wanted to download copies. The response was as strong as it had been for X Windows Mosaic. The momentum was building.

The wizards convened in a kind of rec room where O'Reilly had a pool table. The developers of the Midas browser and the Cello browser were there. Pei Wei and two students came from Berkeley. Jay Weber of the software services company Enterprise Integration Technologies came. The pool table was pushed against the back wall to make room for folding chairs arranged in a semicircle to face the speaker, the man himself: Tim Berners-Lee.

Dale Dougherty, who organized the workshop for O'Reilly, had convinced Berners-Lee (who was planning a vacation to the United States at around the same time) to lead the discussion. With the creator of the World Wide Web standing up in front, the workshop felt like the center of the universe. Picture God standing in a conference room in front of you, describing why he had decided to create the world in seven days and justifying his decision to create light and darkness.

Now picture God as an Englishman in his late thirties, with kind eyes and hands that move constantly to illustrate the points he's trying to make. The universe that Berners-Lee created had grown out of some hypertext code he wrote back in 1980, called Enquire, to help him link documents to each other. That was during Berners-Lee's first stint working at the European physics lab known as CERN, where he was a consultant.

By 1989, the idea had blossomed and Berners-Lee, back at CERN, wanted to use the Internet to link CERN's vast reservoirs of data to other physics researchers around the world. He envisioned a network that enabled a physicist who worked at, say, Brookhaven Labs on Long Island to access information—text, charts, video—from CERN with the click of a mouse. That idea set Berners-Lee on a path to create the World Wide Web, a world he built by developing three standards: the HTML language, the http system for linking documents, and the URL address system.

Berners-Lee started the conference off by describing the architecture of the Web and answering technical questions about why he had done things in one way or another. The wizards wrote down every idea they came up with—everything from how to use the Net for collaboration to primitive scripting—on sheets of poster paper on a big easel. Then they pasted the sheets on the wall around the room, covering most of the available wall space. There was no limit to the ideas.

Impressed by Lou

One other thing of momentous importance to the Mosaic team occurred at the Wizards Workshop: That's where they met Lou Montulli for the first time.

When he arrived at the O'Reilly conference, Lou's first impression of Andreessen was: Well, *he's* pretty confident. Lou got that feeling when everyone was signing in. They were writing their names on name tags: *Joseph Hardin, Aleks Totic, Eric Bina*. And then Andreessen sailed in, and he just scrawled *Marc* across his tag and stuck it to his shirt. He didn't even write Marc A. He figured that by then everyone knew who Marc was—or should know. He had reached one-name celebrity, like Cher.

Lou, on the other hand, wrote *Lou Montulli* in big letters on his name tag. He wasn't sure that people would know who he was—an undergraduate at the University of Kansas in Lawrence. He also happened to be the creator of Lynx, which was quickly emerging as the gold standard of text-based browsers. After all, while Mosaic was cool—who wouldn't want to use an image browser?—lots of people were stuck on slow 2400-baud connections to the Web and didn't have the bandwidth to run it. Lynx was the browser of choice for the Volkswagen crowd.

Along with his boss from the university's computing center, Lou had come to the workshop to make sure that Mosaic didn't leave Lynx behind in the dust.

The Mosaic team already was known to Lou by reputation, and for months he had been corresponding via E-mail with Andreessen. In the fall and winter of 1992, Lou had been an avid member of an online group that discussed campus-wide information systems. The group posted to the cwis-l listserve, a computer that automatically played postmaster to all the users on its mailing list. Lou first heard about the Mosaic program from a message Andreessen posted to the listserve. The program intrigued him. But then, so would any really creative manifestation of software engineering.

Lou's dad, a former engineer in the air force, had been design director of the MX missile and special assistant to the Secretary of Defense. So Lou was the kind of kid who grew up around military bases, without being a typical army brat. He saw things from a slightly different perspective. When his dad retired from the military, the family moved to Kansas, where Lou's dad became vice president of engineering for Boeing.

For a while, Lou had been ambivalent about even going to college. He considered enlisting in the military. It sounded cool: spy stuff, learn a second language. It didn't look as if you had to work that hard on a day-to-day basis to have a cool job. Instead, he enrolled in the University of Kansas.

As an undergraduate, Lou got a job at the University of Kansas computing center. His first assignment was reminiscent of a scene from an old science fiction movie where the "computer lab" consists of a big room with blinking lights and big old reel tapes. The university actually had tapes like those in operation; in fact, they were the primary storage mechanism, and Lou's job was to load them. He soon graduated to consulting and support work. When his boss at the computing center assigned him to work on developing a campus-wide information system—an idea that had been floating around for some time before they decided to implement it—Lou was thrilled.

In his junior year, Lou started writing a software program called Lynx, which was destined to become almost as popular in its own way as Mosaic. Lynx was conceived as a program that would access a campus-wide information system at the University of Kansas. An easier, more elegant way to obtain information on-line than using gopher and WAIS, the current available tools, Lynx enabled users to call up documents stored in the university's computer system and to select hyperlinks to move from document to document.

Coincidentally, around the time Lou started to read on-line about the development of Mosaic, he had been about to embark on writing versions of Lynx that would run on Unix, Windows, and Macintosh machines.

Lou downloaded Mosaic and was impressed; he thought it was a slick program that basically accomplished the same thing as Lynx. But instead of merely mining a campus-wide information system, Mosaic could obtain information from all over the world.

Why not make it possible for Lynx to run as a web browser as well? It occurred to Lou that if he simply wrote a gateway from the Lynx data format to the Mosaic format, he wouldn't have to write a separate X Windows version of Lynx. Instead, he could simply piggyback onto the X Windows version of Mosaic.

Boom, he saved himself a lot of work. Lou transformed the native Lynx data format to HTML, the Mosaic data format. It was basically just sort of a translator. Suddenly, Mosaic could read the same files that Lynx could read.

Lynx had already been a publicly released product in use in a variety of places—like universities—but then it suddenly became a text web browser. Its popularity soared. Lou thought of it as being out of control. Previously, Lynx had thousands of users. Suddenly, Lynx had hundreds of thousands of users.

It soon became clear to Lou that the Web was going to steamroll over the universe, so he decided to purge the old Lynx data formats and write conversion programs. That's how Lynx became a purely HTML program.

From time to time, Lou had E-mailed Andreessen, offering ideas about how to fix bugs or enhance the Mosaic browser. Lou sent him an enhancement for Mosaic's gopher functionality, just some code, nothing major to Lou, but Andreessen had been impressed.

Near-Death Experience

At the Wizards Workshop, it quickly became clear that the entire landscape of the World Wide Web was about to shift, courtesy of Mosaic. The NCSA team showed demos of their early Mac and PC versions, which would make the browser instantly accessible to anyone using a home computer. It was wild. For Dale Dougherty of O'Reilly this was the best news possible; he thought this meant the Web would grow quickly beyond its early base of academic and scientific users. But the widespread accessibility of Mosaic raised a fundamental question: Who was going to control the future direction of the Web?

Two camps were emerging at the workshop. On one hand, the Web was Tim Berners-Lee's creation, and Berners-Lee argued fervently that the developers should agree on standard approaches to writing software. Berners-Lee didn't want the Web to evolve into, say, sixteen different Webs, each accessible only with a single browser.

HTML had been developed as a kind of generic language that an author would use to convey text. But HTML didn't dictate any graphical parameters for how a document would be presented on-screen. That was fine with Berners-Lee; in fact, it was almost a mantra. He kept making the point that he wanted users with text-only monitors to have the same equal experience on the Web as users who had fancier computers with graphical capabilities.

Berners-Lee said he thought the basic idea behind the markup language was the *content* it conveyed. Let each individual user decide how to display it, rather than creating a browser that dictated how content should be displayed.

It was a purist's view, an idealist's view, and the Mosaic team saw it was holding back the Web. They understood Berners-Lee, certainly, but they were on the other side of the argument. He wanted to do the pure thing; they wanted to create a browser that did fun and cool things.

There was no easy way to reconcile the two points of view. For instance, Berners-Lee advocated moderate change on the Web and suggested that developers agree ahead of time on how to approach new developments so they could be implemented equally.

Moderate? That didn't sound like Andreessen, not one bit. The word wasn't in his vocabulary. It was clear, from the tenor of the workshop and the growing importance of Mosaic, that Andreessen would assume a position of leadership in determining the future of Web development. And his attitude toward change was anything but moderate. If he thought of a new feature for his browser, he simply sat down and banged it out. He didn't call for a committee vote.

While the Mosaic browser obviously could never have existed without Berners-Lee's innovations, once Andreessen and Bina had gotten under way, the momentum passed to them.

The situation caused some visible tension at the workshop. While Berners-Lee was obviously leading the discussion, Andreessen grumbled off in the corner. He and the Mosaic team were impatient with some of the people at the workshop: the kind of people who would dream up things to say but then couldn't take the essential next step of going back to their computers and coding. The Mosaic guys were results-oriented. Think of an idea today, create it tomorrow, release it to the public a week later.

Everyone in the room respected the power of Mosaic. But Dougherty sensed that some in the room worried that Andreessen and Bina's creation would take off on its own, leaving the rest of the Web behind.

One of the developers at the workshop was suffering from carpal tunnel syndrome and, to protect his wrist, wore a hard plastic wrap held in place by strips of Velcro. From time to time he would loosen the Velcro and then tighten it. Maybe it was a nervous habit, but by the end of the day the sound of the Velcro pulling away from the wrap every few minutes was getting under everyone's skin.

Whatever the level of tension, with that many highly creative people sitting in one room for two days, some historically significant ideas were bound to emerge: for instance, the <br> tag, which enabled programmers to make line breaks in a Web page. Formatting on the Web was very primitive at that time. On a typewriter, when you want a line break, you just hit the RETURN key. But on the Web, a line of text could wind on into infinity, with nothing to rein it in. So the Web Wizards invented the idea of embedding <br> into the text of a document as a kind of on-line RETURN key.

Lou Montulli brought up the point that all the images that were suddenly cropping up on the Web—thanks largely to the efforts of the Mosaic team—were giving his poor old text browser a hard time.

Back when Lou had started to write Lynx, he hadn't even been aware that Berners-Lee was creating a World Wide Web. So how could he have known that web browsers that displayed images would become ubiquitous? Lynx couldn't display images.

Wouldn't it be great if we had some way of substituting text for images? Lou wanted to know. That suggestion prompted the Web Wizards to come up with the idea of the ALT= tag, which enabled a programmer to specify a text label to be displayed in place of an image if a browser did not support graphics.

One thing the Mosaic team agreed on: They liked Lou Montulli. He was one of them. Aleks Totic went out with Lou to buy Rollerblades. They had a good time, and since Lou thought everybody on the NCSA team was pretty smart as well, they started to hang out together.

Aleks had access to a car. It turned out his parents lived about five minutes away from the workshop; he borrowed his sister's Jetta, crammed a half dozen people into it, and off they went to a Tower Records store in downtown Boston.

As an undergraduate at Boston College, Aleks had learned to drive while he lived in the city. He'd developed some weird and random road maneuvers while working in the field of pizza delivery. But the darting and feinting was off-putting to some of the rest of the guys, particularly Lou, who had never been exposed to this particular flavor of reckless driving before. The passengers were crammed in—both Andreessen and Mittelhauser were well over six feet tall—and Lou was hunched on the middle console between the seats. Blithely, Aleks ignored stop signs, red lights, yellow lines in the middle of the road, whatever.

With its peculiar narrow streets and notorious hairpin curves that double back on themselves, downtown Boston was a particularly challenging environment for Aleks's driving skills. Here he was, revving up and whipping around on streets that had evolved from cow paths three hundred years earlier, paved surfaces that had been dirt paths during the American Revolution. Now Aleks was barreling down them like George Washington leading a charge.

On the way back from Tower Records, there was a moment

as they exited Storrow Drive that Aleks later came to think of as "my chance to change history."

He came to an intersection at the crest of a hill. Three streets converged, and Aleks was too far over to the left side of the road. Traffic was coming toward them, and suddenly a huge semi was barreling up to the top of the hill, headed dead on for the car full of Web Wizards.

Some of them definitely thought they were going to die; others just held their breath. There seemed no way out, nowhere to go but straight, head-on into the truck's grillwork like a pathetic moth— until, at the last minute, Aleks swerved out of the way. He thought it was kind of fun.

They all joked about it later, how they had been a split second away from death, which definitely would have changed history; the world could have held a simultaneous funeral for Mosaic as well.

The Adults' Crusade

At the Wizards Workshop, it was clear that the young team of Mosaic programmers saw themselves as low-paid and overworked; they seemed to view NCSA as a bureaucratic government organization rather than a place of opportunity and ideas. The impression left with the rest of the group at the workshop was that the Mosaic team believed they were doing all the work but NCSA was getting all the credit.

To Dougherty, who believed Smarr and Hardin deserved a lot of credit for championing the Mosaic project in the first place and securing federal funds to aid its development, that attitude seemed a little unfair. But maybe the resentment was understandable, if you considered the fact that this team was working under intense conditions in an early developing market—conditions that almost perfectly mimicked the atmosphere of a Silicon Valley high-tech start-up, come to think of it—but was forced to follow the rules of academia. How could you avoid friction?

On the other hand, how could the team avoid feeling superior? Working on the Mosaic team was like being a rock star. Fans and critics deluged the programmers with E-mail every time a new beta version of Mosaic went on-line. Andreessen had emerged as a cult personality on the Net. Everyone knew who he was; he was outspoken on-line, posting to newsgroups, trading E-mail with Mosaic users, reaching out to new converts. He was invited to conferences and meetings all over the country, flying off to meet more people. He was getting to be a face.

Even Aleks was getting six hundred E-mail messages a day about the Mac version, and he tried to respond to all of them. He could keep going around the clock, alternating between programming and responding to E-mail, because when the Mosaic users in the United States were going to sleep at night, Europe would wake up.

Aleks was riding high, fueled by constant feedback from people who cared about Mosaic, who understood its potential. He had long E-mail discussions with people in Sweden and Australia, not just about bugs in Mac Mosaic but about the future of the Web. Big ideas.

It would keep him going forever. He never had to leave his cube, never had to step outside. He'd exchange ten E-mail messages an hour with one person when a conversation was really stimulating. The experience was intense.

Then, one day, management called a meeting about the Mosaic project. This had been happening more frequently, to the programmers' dismay—meetings where midlevel managers and administrative types and people who didn't do any of the actual coding would throw in their two cents about what Mosaic should be and where the program should go next. It was starting to rankle the team.

For instance, Hardin wanted to meld his social science interests with Mosaic. He wanted to gather information about the Web by tracking the surfing habits of Mosaic users and having the results tabulated on NCSA's servers. The Mosaic team thought that was a dumb idea. Why waste time on a social sciences research project when you could be thinking up new features to incorporate into the code?

At this particular meeting, management made an announcement. From now on, no E-mail messages and feedback regarding Mosaic were to be directed to the programmers. Instead, NCSA had set up a generic E-mail address for feedback. Someone from the department would be assigned to respond to it.

Aleks said, "That's cool. As long as I can read it, no problem." He said he got a lot of good ideas from feedback. Most of the people sending E-mail were smart; they'd thought a lot about Mosaic, and he liked to incorporate their ideas into his own thinking.

Well, no, he was told, he *couldn't* read it. The managers had decided it was a waste of the programmers' time to be dealing with stuff like this. It would be better to hand it off to some other grunts. Indeed, all the Mosaic programmers' access to E-mail would be blocked. It was more productive that way.

From management's point of view, the move would protect the programmers. Downloads of Mosaic were increasing at an exponential rate. So was E-mail. If Aleks was getting six hundred a day today, in two more months he might be getting eighteen hundred. How could one person handle that? The traffic generated by Mosaic was overwhelming. The NCSA website had become the world's busiest. To handle the traffic, the center had to disassemble a Hewlett-Packard supercomputer and put it back together in a new incarnation, as the world's first scalable web server. No way could the kids handle that kind of a deluge by themselves.

But the way Aleks saw it, management just didn't want the programmers talking to people, didn't want the kids on the team to *be* Net stars, didn't want them to get credit for the Mosaic project. He protested strongly. He said everybody on the team thought this idea was complete bullshit.

Management wouldn't back down.

Now, that may seem like a little thing. But it was the turning point as far as Aleks and some of the other programmers were concerned: the moment they lost the Mosaic project. Up until then, they had been a band of hotshot computer jocks in control of their destiny. But the new message was undeniable: You're the hired help. Get in there and code—and we'll take care of the rest.

Of course, the programmers knew all the guys who ran the NCSA computer system, so it was impossible to keep them from reading feedback if they wanted to. Aleks just went to someone he knew and said, "How do I get access to this stuff?" The answer was: Simple. Aleks kept reading the feedback about Mac Mosaic. But whereas in the past he was the point man for Mac feedback, now he had to sneak around. And it pissed him off.

Throughout the summer and early fall, it became clear in many small ways that the days of the Wild Wild Web were over.

The porn scare was another example. Andreessen had created a Web page on NCSA's website called "What's New," because people were always telling him about interesting and unusual websites that were popping up—a page that displayed some interesting weather photos or an interactive game of Hangman, for example. He updated the "What's New" page every day, and according to NCSA's logs it was a popular destination with Web surfers all around the world.

Then the daughter of one of NCSA's employees came into the office one day and began messing around on one of the computers. She clicked on a hyperlink on the "What's New" page—and was suddenly transported to a website that displayed a nude figure. It caused a huge stink, although the irony was that the figure wasn't pornographic at all; it was a perfectly respectable site that displayed fine art. Everybody knows that some fine art consists of nudes (remember the Venus de Milo?), but the incident still created an uproar.

The porn scare illustrated the huge gulf between management and the programmers. Afterward, Andreessen was assigned to devise a kind of page-rating feature. He came up with a pretty sarcastic solution, what was later referred to as the "protect-me-from-myself" flag. Every time a user would click on a hyperlink, a dialog box would appear on the screen. In the box was bold black text that would warn the user that dangerous ideas might lurk on the other side of the link—

dirty pictures, even! The flag would ask the user: ARE YOU SURE YOU WANT TO TAKE THIS CRAZY STEP AND KEEP SURFING? The user would click *yes,* of course.

The Mosaic programmers loved it. But some people were not amused.

Out of the Midwest at Last

By the time Marc was ready to graduate from college, in December of 1993, relations between most of the Mosaic programmers and management had become seriously strained. Unsure what he wanted to do after he graduated, Marc asked his bosses for a full-time job managing the growth of the Mosaic project. They made him an offer that was financially generous by NCSA's standards, an annual salary in the range of $50,000. But there was one serious drawback to the offer: Marc would not be assigned to manage the Mosaic team.

Marc decided to leave instead. Frustrated that the university wasn't moving fast enough to license Mosaic or privatize the software, as had been done with earlier generations of NCSA creations such as Image and Telnet, he knew his destiny was in the private sector. Naturally, he had plenty of job offers to choose among. He'd been doing the conference and workshop circuit for months and seemed to have met everyone worth meeting. He was a certified Net personality, written about everywhere, up to and including *The New York Times.*

He took a job working as a programmer at a company called Enterprise Integration Technologies (EIT), writing Internet security code. He accepted that offer because the company was interested in writing software for the Internet—he had in fact met his future boss, Jay Weber, at O'Reilly's Web Wizards conference a few months earlier—and because the job enabled him to move to the center of his universe, Silicon Valley.

Marc had read plenty of books extolling the birthplace of the computer revolution and knew as much about it as anybody. The Valley had been the inevitable birthplace of a silicon economy in the 1970s. All the ingredients had been there: a postwar indigenous pool of talented and underemployed aerospace engineers and a ready supply of brilliant students from Stanford University.

One of the Valley's earliest anchors was Intel, the company that invented the microprocessor in the early 1970s, making it possible to embed on a single chip all the information to drive a computer. Xerox's Palo Alto Research Center, birthplace of the mouse, provided a steady stream of technological ideas that spurred the growth of its neighbors, including, notably, Apple Computer. The Valley had become a magnet for the high-tech industry, and everyone from Hewlett-Packard to Sun Microsystems maintained office parks along Route 101, which resembled nothing so much as sprawling designer shopping malls.

But despite the innovation, the Valley experienced the same recession that hit the rest of the country in the early 1990s. By the time Andreessen arrived, Japan was challenging the Valley's hardware primacy with its ever-cheaper, high-quality consumer electronics industry (much as Detroit had faced stiff competition from auto imports Honda and Toyota). In 1993, the Valley's economy felt stalled, if only temporarily.

Few people knew it yet, but because of the Internet, the Valley was about to spawn a new generation of grand ideas for another industry—software. Virtually overnight, the Internet would create a fantastic new platform for any kind of application you could imagine—software that would enable you to make phone calls, watch videos, hear voice clips through the speakers of your computer. Ideas already were percolating; in Palo Alto, for instance, Sun Microsystems had set up an office for a team of engineers who were hacking away on a new kind of programming language that might one day take advantage of the Internet to supersede the need for a desktop operating system.

No one knew it yet, least of all Andreessen—although his idea of a browser that would enable any PC user to navigate the on-line world would soon form the foundation for the whole wild, teeming mass of engineering creativity that would rise up to embrace the new platform of the Net.

Andreessen had made it out of the Midwest at last. In short order, he found an apartment and a girlfriend. He sent E-mail back to Illinois to update his friends on all the things he was doing—and all the people he was meeting.

PART TWO

Start-up

CHAPTER SIX

Professor Clark Gets Antsy

Dr. James Clark, founder of Silicon Graphics Inc., was looking for the next big thing during the winter of 1993–94. Despite being a multi-millionaire ex-Stanford professor who had created one of the hottest companies in Silicon Valley, he was ready for a new challenge.

Silicon Graphics barely resembled the tiny start-up he had launched with a world-shaking idea a decade earlier. The company he had founded with six graduate students back when he was an associate professor at Stanford University had grown into a $2 billion corporation that employed thousands of people and manufactured some of the world's most powerful workstations—computers whose ability to render three-dimensional graphics had become indispensable tools to scientists, artists, and Hollywood filmmakers.

In the early days, Clark had relied on venture capitalists for cash to expand the business. In retrospect, he often said he believed that had been a mistake born of naïveté. By the time Silicon Graphics went public in the mid 1980s, Clark owned only a minority share worth $16 million. And as the company grew, Clark's influence on its day-to-day operations had become diluted. He no longer was calling enough of the shots at Silicon Graphics. He was frustrated by a slow-moving bureaucracy that made it impossible to quickly turn his company in a new direction. And he was bored. It was time to start the next chapter of his life.

Breathing the supercharged air in Silicon Valley could turn nearly anyone into an entrepreneur. How many places exist on earth where a person with a good idea today can turn it into a commercial venture tomorrow, backed by what seems to be a limitless supply of venture capital? No wonder the atmosphere infected Clark, who had marshaled a good idea into a successful business once already. In an environment where the vast majority of new companies got bought up by older, established companies or else went out of business, the solid growth of Silicon Graphics was a rare accomplishment. Consider: Hundreds, maybe thousands, of bright engineers with new ideas form business ventures around the promise of a single technological marvel; very few of those ventures grow into well-managed, stable companies that produce trusted products, service long-term customers, and turn a profit quarter after quarter, fiscal year after fiscal year. Clark's company had achieved the status of being one of the major established players in the Valley, alongside companies like Sun and Cisco and Hewlett-Packard.

Clark was in a good position to try a second time. Getting a new company up and running would be no problem for him. A wealthy man in his own right, Clark was also well respected in the Valley as a visionary whose high-flying ideas translated into tangible markets and profits. He was well-known to the Valley's top venture capitalists, among them John Doerr of Kleiner, Perkins, Caufield and Byers. Doerr, a man who will surely go down in history as the Johnny Appleseed of high tech, had made it clear he would be only too happy to help Clark launch a new business. All Clark really needed was one great idea. In the meantime, he was ready to tender his resignation.

The fact that Clark was walking away from Silicon Graphics would be a big story to the business world. It was the kind of news that could affect the company's stock price, or even that of its competitors, the kind of story that Clark and his staff didn't want to leak out before the official announcement. To help manage the news, a trusted member of the corporate relations staff named Rosanne Siino was called to the office of the company president. When she arrived, she found some of the company's top managers—including Clark— in deep discussion about how best to announce that SGI's founder was about to sever all ties with the company. Siino was asked to join a small team, working under tight security, to come up with a plan to announce Clark's resignation. The goal was to make it clear that Clark was leaving of his own free will, that he harbored no ill feelings toward SGI, and that the company and its course were entirely stable.

Siino wasn't shocked by the news that Clark was leaving; it was common knowledge around the office that he wanted to focus on new ventures. But the time frame she had to work within was a surprise. The executives had decided to announce Clark's resignation publicly within a week of when he broached it to the company's board of directors.

> MOUNTAIN VIEW, California (January 27, 1994)—Silicon Graphics, Inc. (NYSE: SGI) announced today that its chairman and founder Dr. James H. Clark has stated his intention to resign his position with the company effective February 28. Dr. Clark, who founded Silicon Graphics in 1982, made the decision in order to pursue applications software opportunities in the emerging interactive broadband network and television market.

The press release was deliberately vague. Because although Jim Clark had attained true visionary status in Silicon Valley, in truth, he didn't know what he was going to do next.

The professorial Dr. Clark, known for his propensity to expound and his ability to convince almost anyone in the world of the value of any idea he backed, was vague as well. "I am leaving at this time because I believe there are major entrepreneurial opportunities in applications software for interactive television, and I want to explore those opportunities," he told reporters.

Clark belonged to a certain breed of adventurous entrepreneurs who had found their way to Silicon Valley—and thrived. He had taken a circuitous route to his success. Raised in Plainview, Texas, with little money but an avid curiosity about the world, Clark had dropped out of high school to join the navy at age seventeen. After the service and another, successful attempt at securing an undergraduate degree, he earned a doctorate in physics at the University of Utah in 1974 and took his first teaching job, at the University of Santa Cruz, where he stayed until 1978. Following a brief stint as a consultant, he became an associate professor at Stanford University in 1979.

Clark had landed in the epicenter of the furious creativity and rampant capitalism that form a unique backdrop to the high-tech economy of Silicon Valley. Stanford's brain trust—the best and the brightest engineers, students, researchers—fuel the businesses in the Valley; in return, even the most successful entrepreneurs return to campus to teach or deliver guest lectures.

On campus, Clark found himself steeped in the same culture of ambitious ideas that had launched the careers of countless entrepreneurs over the years. It was a tradition that stretched back before World War II, when two young engineering students named William Hewlett and David Packard set out on the path to transform a graduate thesis into one of the world's most powerful companies. Ever since those days, Stanford had fed a steady stream of innovative ideas into the surrounding area's high-tech ventures.

It was the perfect home for Clark, who years later reminisced, "I've been told I went to Stanford with the express purpose of starting a company. I guess that's true."

When Clark arrived on campus and began work on a project on the second floor of Margaret Jacks Hall, which housed the university's computer science department, the air was heavy with the best kind of ideas, the kind that turn into commercially successful businesses. Two floors above him, graduate student Andy Bechtolsheim was building a new kind of computer, called the SUN, for the university. Soon, the workstation would launch Sun Microsystems. In the basement, research on how to connect campus networks to one another spawned Cisco Systems.

For his part, Clark spent years doing research that formed the basis for his breakthrough technology: a geometry engine that enables

a computer to display realistic three-dimensional graphics. He pat-
ented it in 1981.

Soon after, Clark founded Silicon Graphics to commercialize
his idea of creating inexpensive high-quality graphics on the desktop.
The time was ripe for innovation. It was just a few months after Bill
Gates had incorporated Microsoft, and MS-DOS had been introduced
on the IBM personal computer.

Clark's technology, enabling computers to draw pictures inter-
actively and in real time, was adopted by Hollywood and incorporated
into the big-budget animation-heavy films of the late 1980s. As SGI's
chief technical officer, Clark pushed the company to develop affordable
workstations—affordable, at least, compared to the Crays and Thinking Machines that Andreessen would rebel against. The Iris and the Indigo are the legacies of that vision, workhorses that can be found in
every design shop from New York to Hollywood, among other places.

By 1986, Clark decided to take the company public to raise
money to fund expansion. He spent months traveling around the
world, preaching to potential investors about the new technology.
His mission was twofold. Not only did Clark have to explain the
validity of the new technology; he also had to convince investors
that there was a market out there, an untapped segment of the industry poised to flourish. The market for workstations was growing, as the mainframe model started to crumble.

In New York and London and Paris, he explained that the chips
in his machines needed to run at billions and billions of operations per
second; speedy benchmarks previously thought impossible were being
smashed with seasonal regularity. Clark sketched in the big picture
and told investors about how the technology had the potential to change
the world, to revolutionize digital graphics endeavors, to create a new
future for visual industries.

The company's initial public stock offering was a financial success by Wall Street standards—but at what cost? In later years Clark
made it clear that he felt he had relinquished too much control over
SGI's direction to outside investors.

Clark had a nearly unlimited amount of new ideas about how to change the world, but he knew he wasn't a businessman. Early on, he ceded the day-to-day management of the company to Ed McCracken, whom he had persuaded to be CEO.

In 1988, SGI introduced its first affordable workstation, and the company went stratospheric. Its revenues more than quintupled, from $40 million in 1986 to $2.2 billion eight years later.

Clark "had to get out of the box," he later said. Out of the box, he was free to sort through independent projects he wanted to pursue. He had been instrumental in steering SGI into the consumer electronics field, striking a deal with Nintendo Corporation the year before to provide graphics for its next-generation video game system. It was an idea that still held his interest. He had worked closely with Time Warner Cable in the creation of its experimental Full Service Network in Orlando, Florida, which promised fully interactive programming to subscribers who could call up video on demand—an à la carte offering of movies and TV shows. But that experiment was turning out to be very expensive; would subscribers be willing to pay for the technology? The question hung in the air without an answer. Clark had observed Silicon Valley's high-flying creative culture long enough to understand how a technical dream that outruns reality can end up as a sobering failure.

Clark was meanwhile emerging as one of the spokesmen for the coming information highway. Technology would remake the world. The transformation was inevitable, he said. The only variable of the equation left to be filled in was, What form would it take? Who would build the road? Would the big telephone companies foot the bill to run fiber-optic cable to our homes, giving us the ability to conduct the daily business of our lives in front of the TV? Or would we rely on the the cable companies' hybrid networks of coaxial and fiber-optic cable to bring the information highway to our doorsteps? What about direct broadcast satellite? Or microcellular? Who could afford to make the multi-billion-dollar investment and hook us up fastest?

His hunch was that the direction would come from cable companies and interactive TV, that a future generation of set-top boxes would enable consumers to push information back out into the world as well as to pull it into their homes. The possibilities were endless. Click on the remote control and order a pizza. Consult your physician over the TV. Play high-speed, fully interactive, and immersive games from your living room. Plenty of big players in the industry were investing enormous sums of money trying to make that technological dream a reality.

Clark told people who were close to him that he knew he wanted to create another software company; he was very interested in how the kind of high-end graphics technology he had pioneered could make the leap to interactive TV. His recent foray into the consumer electronics market of computer games led him to muse on the feasibility of creating a kind of interactive on-line video-game service.

Clark repeatedly had voiced his frustration about his inability to move Silicon Graphics in that direction and had decided that it was time to start clean. He wanted to push the envelope of the consumer market, to see if he could leverage the new technology into a widespread mass market.

Dr. Clark, I Presume?

Clark spent his last days at the company saying good-bye to people he had worked with for years. An eclectic group was invited to his office—engineers whose work he respected, marketing people, employees he liked to chat with in the company cafeteria. Siino was struck by the fact that he surrounded himself with people he liked rather than with an elite cadre of top managers. Clark was talking not necessarily to the movers and shakers of the corporate structure but to the people who had ideas. And he was listening, figuring that sooner or later he'd get a lead on the next big thing.

On one of his last days at SGI, he asked an engineer named Bill Foss to steer him toward other high-tech visionaries, other people with ideas.

Foss came up with a single suggestion: Talk to this twenty-two-year-old kid named Marc Andreessen.

Clark had never heard of either Marc or Mosaic, although the program had been in use at Silicon Graphics since the previous fall. The company had been using Mosaic in its customer demo center; the software was a perfect vehicle to showcase the graphics capabilities of SGI's products. Silicon Graphics employees often ran Mosaic when they were conducting a demonstration of the Indigo workstation.

Foss called up Mosaic on his computer screen and showed it to Clark. Then he called up Andreessen's home page and pointed out the kid's E-mail address. Mosaic had given Clark an idea. He sat at a keyboard and piped a message off to Andreessen:

> *You may not know me, but I'm the founder of Silicon Graphics.*
> *I've resigned and intend to form a new company. Would you*
> *be interested in getting together to talk?*

Clark and Andreessen met at seven in the morning at a trendy coffee shop in downtown Palo Alto, called Caffe Verona, and stood in line behind a couple of graduate students in backpacks who had popped in to pick up double cappuccinos and muffins to eat on the walk to their early class.

Then they sat down at one of the little cafe tables near the big plate-glass window in front. For Clark, early morning was the perfect time for a meeting; he was wide awake and full of ideas. Andreessen was pretty much asleep.

But he woke up quickly. He liked Clark immediately, and he was seduced by the professor's talk about the future of interactive TV. They talked about the Time Warner cable venture, and Andreessen thought, Jesus, these people are putting money into this. It must be the next big thing. It must be the future.

Despite his enthusiasm, Clark had plenty of unanswered questions about that venture. Where was the market? Where was the bandwidth? How soon could interactive TV start to make money? And
what was the business model?

They also talked about Mosaic, and how it had become so popular so fast. They talked about selling an on-line service to Nintendo,
and Andreessen said he had some ideas about that. He told Clark he'd
write a memo. They agreed to meet again.

For Clark, informal meetings like these were part of the process. All over town, he was picking the brains of some of the brightest
people he knew: engineers from SGI, colleagues he'd worked with
before, young kids fresh from the Midwest. He was trying to hone in
on his vision, trying to shape the germ of an idea into a viable company that could make money.

Sometimes he invited people over to his house to talk; sometimes he held get-togethers on his boat. There were plenty of people
to talk to. Clark had even been approached by a handful of people at
Silicon Graphics who were restless, people who had heard that he was
about to launch a new start-up, adventurous mavericks who wanted
to climb on board.

"Tell Me When to Quit"

Michael Toy was one of the first. Toy was a tall, hcavyset bulldog of a
man with a slicked-back ponytail. He was a demon programmer; since
childhood his idea of heaven had been to spend about twenty hours a
day trying to solve really hard technological problems.

Toy liked toys, of course. He had an arsenal of Super-Soakers
and was obsessed with golf. But he had decided long ago that he couldn't
earn a living playing golf.

As an engineer at SGI for more than six years, Toy had earned
a reputation for getting the impossible done. As the primary programmer assigned in the late '80s to a problematic project to meld
the company's Graphics Layer technology with a streamlined Win-

dows interface, Toy had helped ensure the success of the new Indigo workstation.

Toy thought of himself as an itinerant bright person, assigned to whatever project intrigued him, currently working on interactive TV projects that didn't seem to be moving ahead very quickly. Toy was burned out. The atmosphere of SGI had changed radically since he had started there in 1987. It had become, at some point, a big company, and that's when the job stopped being fun. He no longer thought of his work at SGI as the meaning of life—which for Toy meant he would have to search elsewhere.

When Toy heard that Clark, a major booster of the kinds of interactive TV technology Toy was working on, was leaving SGI, his first thought was, He's given up.

Toy's second thought was, Maybe he'll take me with him. Toy figured it was time to try the start-up thing. It probably would fail because most start-ups do, but it was worth a shot.

He E-mailed Clark, saying, "I don't know where you're going, but wherever it is I'd really like to go with you."

He heard Clark was checking his sources, asking, "Who is this Michael Toy? Is he good? Do I want him?"

Clark called Toy. He asked him if he was serious about wanting to leave SGI.

Toy said, "OK, I don't want to be stupid, because I have a family to feed. Just tell me when to quit, and I will."

Maybe it sounds flippant, but Toy was deadly serious; he had decided to trust Clark implicitly. Partly it was because he respected the integrity of Clark's vision at SGI, where the company's founder had always known what he wanted to do; partly it was because Clark had a reputation for having a strong ethic of taking care of the people who helped him turn his visions into reality. You didn't feel Clark was out to exploit you. You felt he was out to do interesting stuff. And Clark had an impressive track record in the category of interesting stuff.

Clark started to invite Toy to the meetings on his boat and at his house. That's where Toy first met Marc Andreessen. Tom Paquin, another respected engineer at SGI, was often present. Bill Foss, who had introduced Clark to Marc and Mosaic, was part of the inner circle. But Clark's taste was eclectic. He also invited students, like Greg Sands, who was finishing his business degree at Stanford, to attend some sessions. For the invitees, it seemed like a wonderful opportunity to talk about ideas, technologies, strategies, where the world was headed. For Clark, it was the first step toward building a team of talented like-minded people who could populate his new company.

The ideas they discussed were all over the map. One day, talk would focus on creating a company that would sell an on-line service to Nintendo. The next time, Clark and Andreessen would be leading a discussion about the failed promise of interactive TV, arguing that the technology was a sideshow, not likely to transform itself into the one true information superhighway. Eventually, Andreessen and Clark became convinced that the superhighway already existed, in an entirely different form, and that it had a name: the Internet. That theory turned out to be one big step in their efforts to create a new company.

But first, they had to convince the rest of the group that the Internet had the power and the potential to emerge as the single worldwide network for conveying information. This was a radical point of view, nothing short of a paradigm shift in the universe, tantamount to telling everyone aboard Clark's boat that the earth was flat. That's because in those days, the Internet was—well, it still hadn't quite made the leap from academia to mass-market medium, especially to the commercial world, where the money was. Few people besides academics were plugged into the Net. Bandwidth was so limited that travel on the Net was achingly slow; video, at least of the kind imagined on the Full Service Network, wasn't even a possibility. No, for most people—indeed, from the White House on down—the Internet was one of the things that would ride on the information superhigh-way. The conventional wisdom was that *after* people became com-fortable with interactive TVs and speedy cable modems, then they would start to get onto the Internet.

But that's where Clark saw his opportunity. The fact that others had underestimated the vast commercial potential of the network could play to his new company's advantage. So Clark came right out and said it: The Internet *is* the information superhighway.

The next logical step, then, was to form a company to create software to transport people along that highway. And what could be more perfect than a business venture that would pair Clark with Andreessen to create a commercial browser based on the same prin-ciples as Mosaic?

Clark was convincing, of course but some of his advisers had doubts. The day Clark and Andreessen told the others they wanted to build a new and commercial version of the Mosaic browser—a *killer* Mosaic program so fast, so rich, so stable, so cool it would wipe out the memory of the original NCSA software—Toy was skeptical.

He sat listening to Clark talk on and on about how the new company's stock would be worth hundreds of millions of dollars and everyone in the room would be rich. Toy did a back-of-the-envelope calculation, doodling on a napkin, dividing everything Clark said by ten, thinking, Yeah, right.

Like the others, Toy had used Mosaic, but he wasn't a true believer in the potential of the Internet to become a mass market. The problem with building a web browser was that it just wasn't techno-logically challenging, not in the way interactive TV was. Toy thought, It's just an application. Take this thing off the shelf, that thing off the shelf, put them together there.

But he also second-guessed himself. "I'm not a visionary. I mean, I didn't have the idea to create SGI either, but that seemed to do pretty well. I'll let Clark do what he's good at, and then I'll do what I'm good at. I'll make his ideas go."

In the Shadow of the Giant

As soon as Clark settled on the idea of a new Mosaic browser, he formed his company and its business plan at breathtaking speed. He had to; he needed to capitalize on his slim head start in realizing the vast potential of a commercial browser. Persuaded of the Internet's importance, Clark was also aware that the rest of the world would catch on pretty quickly to the idea, as well.

In the spring of 1994, at the time that Clark and Andreessen became cofounders of Mosaic Communications, Inc., their idea was so relatively esoteric that the new company's strongest short-term competition came from NCSA, a federally funded supercomputing center at a midwestern state university. But Clark was experienced enough to know that his head start wouldn't last. He knew, even before he had created a solid business plan for his new venture, that if Mosaic Communications turned out to be successful, the biggest long-term threat would be from better-established software companies. He worried about one company in particular that had the vast resources to create competitive products, a mammoth market-gobbling company with a huge hunger for new opportunities, a company with a long-standing reputation for its take-no-prisoners business strategies—Microsoft.

Year after year, Microsoft made all the right moves, confounding critics who dismissed its software and unabashedly expanding its business beyond all expectations. Microsoft was ruled by a ruthless and endlessly fascinating genius whose mere appearance on the cover of any national magazine guaranteed a spike in newsstand sales. Employing fourteen thousand of the best and the brightest, all pulling in the same direction, Microsoft had a forever lock on the future. A darling of Wall Street, its stock had increased in value an average of 60 percent a year since going public in 1986, and the value of the company had overtaken IBM—once the biggest software company in the world, among other things—in January 1993.

Beneath the surface lurked a more disturbing beast. No one likes a winner but, increasingly, the stories people were telling about

Microsoft, if true, depicted a company whose activities were troubling. The federal government had been investigating Microsoft's
business tactics since 1990, in fact. *Extend and embrace* was the official
Microsoft mantra, chanted throughout the great Redmond empire.
Bill Gates, who knew how quickly the tables could turn in a world
whose pace was dictated by the exponentially improving microchip,
wanted to inculcate in his managers the need to be ever vigilant for
the next new thing. The seeds of our destruction are being sown right
now, unless we get there first. So, extend and embrace: *Extend* the
functionality of the operating system and *embrace* new ideas and new
technologies.

But to lots of people outside of Microsoft, the message was
crasser: Extend, embrace, and *smother* the competition was more like
it. The company's tactics were legendary in Silicon Valley, where
many developers believed that doing business with Microsoft was worse
than striking a pact with the devil. You either played by Microsoft's
rules, or you didn't play.

Microsoft had a monopoly over the market for desktop operating systems, but that wasn't enough for company founder and CEO
Bill Gates. The advent of any new technology represented a threat to
his hegemony. If, as Clark and Andreessen believed, the core of information technology was moving away from the personal computer and
onto the Internet as quickly as it had moved from the mainframe to
the personal computer a mere decade earlier, Microsoft would have
to move as well. The new battle for control over the software industry would be fought on the Net, not on the desktop.

To protect its core business, Microsoft routinely expanded into
any new software market that seemed promising. If Clark and Andreessen
had latched onto a truly great idea, they could be sure Microsoft would
jump into the field as well. There was no way that a tiny Silicon Valley
start-up could compete head-to-head with the mightiest software company in the world, especially since Microsoft could be expected to
leverage its advantage over the operating-system market. The only question was, When would Microsoft catch on to the Internet?

Clark and Andreessen hoped to exploit the factors that had created a window of opportunity. For one thing, geography gave them a minor advantage. Headquartered in Redmond, Washington, Microsoft was cut off from many of the intellectual currents of Silicon Valley. For another, Bill Gates was preoccupied with other problems. Since 1990, Microsoft had been the target of a painful and grueling federal antitrust investigation that seemed to be hurtling toward some sort of conclusion in early 1994. Also, Microsoft's top engineering priority was to get the long-awaited new versions of the Windows operating system to market as soon as possible.

But the threat of Microsoft was real, omnipresent, a constant ache that accompanied the founding of Mosaic Communications. The new company would have to move fast, or else Microsoft could destroy it.

Keeping that in mind, Clark and Andreessen formulated the genesis of the company's business plan. Even in those early days, when no one knew how to make money off the Internet, Clark understood that sales of a mere stand-alone browser would not be enough to sustain a long-term business. Who were the customers? Currently, the core group of Mosaic users consisted primarily of individual users—students, academics, researchers, computer programmers, and some savvy Net surfers who thought Mosaic was "cool"—who could not be expected to shell out large sums of money for the program. Furthermore, the early adopters were by and large people who were used to the Internet ethos of sharing software, of freeware and shareware that you really didn't need to pay for. So it was clear to Clark and Andreessen that a new browser would have to be the first step in a broader plan to sell Internet software to businesses, large companies with deep pockets.

But corporate America would not be persuaded to embrace the Internet without a clear idea of what you could sell on-line. So Clark and Andreessen tried to create a business plan that would call for companies to buy and sell something on-line. But what would they buy and sell? Information? Products? Ideas? Was the Internet a natural venue for certain kinds of retailers to sell product to customers? Was it a network that a huge corporation could take advantage of for its own internal purposes, to move data around from one division to another via modem? Was the Internet, as a communications medium, a natural next step for certain industries such as publishers or newspapers?

The first business plan that Clark and Andreessen settled on defined Mosaic Communications in broad terms as a consultant, to provide assistance to companies that were eager to learn how to use the Internet—and the soon-to-be-written new Mosaic browser. The idea was that as a consultant, Mosaic Communications would teach its customers how to do business more efficiently via the Internet. Clark and Andreessen also discussed the possibility of creating a "cyberspace mall" on their new company's computers, a virtual shopping space where retailers and other companies could "lease space" and sell their wares.

But the most important component of the business plan was to develop and license a commercial-grade version of the Mosaic browser—a new generation that would be stable, bug-free, and chockful of new and useful features.

Clark of course continued to ponder theoretical questions about the information superhighway and its potential as a new medium. He was preparing for another kind of job as well—he was about to become an evangelist for what he believed was its true incarnation, the Internet.

I Only Made a Million Dollars

Clark moved quickly. On April 4, 1994, he incorporated the company. He moved forward on a number of fronts: He identified key people he had worked with at Silicon Graphics whom he wanted to bring to his new company, invested more than $4 million of his own money to seed the venture, leased office space on the top floor of a nondescript office buiding on Castro Street in Mountain View, and hired a core group of engineers to write code.

When it came to putting together a knowledgeable engineering team fast, Clark chose the most efficient solution. He decided to hire most of the programmers who had worked on the original Mosaic browser at the University of Illinois. He had no time to spare; he bought a round-trip plane ticket to Champaign-Urbana.

So one day in the early spring of 1994, Marc Andreessen's friends back at NCSA all got similar E-mail. The message said, simply: *Something's going down. Be ready to move.* The details may have been a mystery, but the tone was welcome. The Mosaic programmers had become even more disillusioned about the future of the project after Marc graduated and left town. If they didn't quite know what they were being summoned for, they knew it sounded tantalizing. When Marc was involved, things happened. It was always interesting to be along for the ride.

Marc sent similar E-mail to Kansas to Lou Montulli, the creator of Lynx. But Montulli, who also happened to be a pretty good racquetball player, went to Arizona in April for the Collegiate World Championship and missed Jim Clark's follow-up call. When Lou got back, he drove from the airport to his office at the campus computing center. A blinking light indicated voice mail. It could have been almost anyone, of course, but when he played the tape, he realized his life was about to change.

The voice on the machine was that of Jim Clark's personal secretary. Her message was succinct: *"Go to Illinois. Right away."*

Those instructions seemed pretty clear. Lou got into his car and drove back to the airport, using a credit card to buy a ticket. Then it hit him: I don't have any money. This ticket costs about $200. How do I even know Jim Clark is going to pay for it?

Lou phoned Clark's secretary. "Jim's going to pay for this, right?"

Reassured, he boarded the plane. Then he started to wonder exactly why he was being summoned to Illinois. He'd had a couple of hazy, mysterious conversations with Marc about some exciting new venture. And there had been the E-mail. That was about it. Lou had no idea that Clark and Marc already had boarded another plane, in California, and were headed for the same destination. All Lou knew, at that point, was what he wanted to do: Write a web client. None of the jobs he'd been offered or companies where he'd interviewed were doing that. He also knew he didn't want to work for a big company. He didn't want to start at the bottom of a structured environment and plod his way up toward the top of the heap. He wanted to work for a start-up.

He'd had that epiphany earlier in the spring, when he was interviewing for a job at a tiny company based in Kansas. After the interview, he and another applicant who had chatted together in the lobby had been invited out to have a beer with the company's founders. Lou never remembered the name of the other man, but he remembered riding in the passenger seat of his Lexus on the way to the bar. And the other applicant, whom Lou later thought of as the Start-up Guy, had said some things that shaped Lou's point of view forever.

"At my last start-up, I only made a million dollars," the Start-up Guy complained, gunning his Lexus. "Get in on the ground floor and ask for equity in the company."

So Lou got off the plane in Illinois with more than an open mind. He got off excited.

Following the instructions Clark's secretary had given him, he drove to the University Inn and checked in. Then he went down to the lobby to see what would happen next.

There, he saw Jon Mittelhauser and Aleks Totic hanging out too. Soon the other programmers who had worked on the Mosaic team started filtering in. There wasn't much to do in the lobby, but the air was charged with excitement. Something big was about to go down. They were trying to be casual. But they couldn't hide the fact that they were getting positively giddy.

They figured out that, altogether, six programmers had gotten the call: Houck, Mittelhauser, Totic, Rob McCool, Montulli, and, of course, Bina.

Then I Woke Up and It Was
Even Better Than the Dream!

It didn't feel like a job interview.

In fact, by the time Clark called the programmers up to his University Inn room, one by one, the next afternoon, they felt as if they were interviewing *him*.

Clark's plane had been delayed for several hours the previous night because of an unusually strong April snowstorm; by the time he and Marc got to town, it was too late to see anyone. If anything, the delay made him more impatient than ever to get moving on his new project. He'd convinced himself that he needed to hire these six kids to get his company started. He'd flown across the country to do it—and he wasn't about to take no for an answer.

While the rest of the group waited downstairs in the bar, Mittelhauser was the first to go upstairs. To his surprise, Clark didn't ask anything about his qualifications or experience; he just tried to convince him to come along on a wild ride.

Clark's approach was direct: The Internet is the future. We're starting a new company. We can own the future if we get there first. Chance of a lifetime. Stock options. Plus a week's vacation on my sailing yacht (Clark loved that boat) in Tahiti.

Clark was running at high speed, talking in his most charming, professorial tone. He already knew everything he needed to know about these kids. In addition to the backgrounds provided by Marc, he'd just taken them all to lunch at Joe's Microbrewery in town and observed how well they interacted. They would make a good team.

Who could resist one of the most persuasive businessmen in America? For that matter, who could resist the lure of a week in Tahiti on a yacht?

Of course, the risks of failure were great—Mittelhauser kept repeating to himself, over and over, "Ninety-nine out of a hundred start-ups fail, ninety-nine out of a hundred"—but he and the team had never wanted to work as programmers solely for the money. They worked on Mosaic because it was fun.

Mittelhauser was graduating anyway. He was in the process of lashing together a thesis based on his work on the Mosaic program— it was one of those theses that gets written in about ten days, does anyone notice?—and figured, What do I have to lose if I went out to Silicon Valley and flopped? Big deal. In the meantime, work could be fun again.

Clark said he was going to offer each of the programmers an identical financial package, including stock options worth roughly 1 percent of the new company.

Stock options: the two sweetest words in the English language, if you happened to be a Silicon Valley software entrepreneur or just a really hot programmer. Stock options were a way of life in the high-rolling start-up culture. Forget salary. There was nothing exciting about a safe, steady weekly paycheck. Stock options were much more glamorous. You could sit around for hours, playing the What If game with your stock options. It was a favorite pastime in the Valley, scribbling various calculations on little bits of paper, dreaming about how rich you might one day be. What if we go public and my options are worth a hundred times the option price? What if my options are worth $10 million in five years and I can retire?

The way stock options worked was this: An employee would be given the option to buy a certain number of shares—say one hundred—at a certain price—say $1. If the stock price rose to $10 before the employee cashed in, the employee could buy the shares for $100 and sell them for $1,000. Multiply that scenario by a factor of thousands and thousands of options, and you can forget the lottery; in the Valley the heroes of the best rags-to-riches stories were the lucky employees (secretaries and janitors, even, with portfolios worth six figures!) who had the sense to be among the earliest employees at risky start-ups that made good.

Thank Microsoft for popularizing the concept of "options millionaires." Bill Gates was legendary for offering employees generous

amounts of stock options; people were more than willing to take salary *cuts* to go work for him because his options packages were so
attractive. In the early 1990s, a Wall Street analyst estimated that
twenty-two hundred Microsoft employees each held options worth at
least $1 million.

Giving employees generous stock options is also good for business. It looks good on the balance sheet, for one thing, because a book-
keeper doesn't have to deduct unexercised employee options as an
expense against profits on a company's income statement (but you do
have to deduct the amount of those employees' salaries). Also, the
IRS allows a company to deduct the amount employees realize on
options as an *expense* on the tax form.

So of course the first thing Clark was going to start offering
the young programmers was a bucketful of options. It worked out in
everyone's best interests. The options he was offering could be worth
millions someday, or they could be worth nothing if the company
went belly up. He didn't mention that possibility, however. Jim had
figured out all the numbers, and he was spouting huge multi-million-
dollar figures, assuring them they'd be rich within five years.

"Fine," Mittelhauser said. They shook hands on it.

Clark didn't have to work too hard to convince Aleks Totic to
sign on, either. The programmers had daydreamed for months about
having a company of their own. Much of their frustration stemmed
from the fact that although they had created the Mosaic browser, they
had no ownership rights. The code belonged to the university. But
what if they could start over again, write a new version of Mosaic that
they owned and controlled? Maybe things would be different. It would
be really cool if they worked on a boat with a big satellite link, Aleks
thought. We could all work on the boat. The company would be a
pure commercial venture—no government funding allowed—so we
would call it com.com.com.

In the back of his mind, Aleks had been waiting for this very
opportunity. From the day Marc left town, Aleks had had faith that he
would return with a plan. "I didn't know Jim Clark, he was just some

company guy, but Marc said, 'He's got a really nice house and we had a nice dinner and talked about really interesting stuff.' I trusted Marc, so I was ready to sign on. I was sold on the idea," Aleks said.

As for Lou Montulli, he still had the words of the Start-up Guy ringing in his ears. It was almost a mantra: Ask for equity. Ask for equity.

When Clark told him the deal included salary plus stock options, Lou thought, I'm from Kansas, where anything more than $30,000 a year seems like a lot. Clark offered him more than Intel had offered him, 20 percent more than EIT had. More than enough to pay for that plane ticket. Not that it would have made much difference. Montulli was twenty-three years old, for God's sake, and this was the most exciting proposition he had ever heard. If there was any perfect situation in the world for Lou, this was it. Here was this great idea, writing a web client. And suddenly the idea was being ratified by none other than a legendary figure from Silicon Valley. Jim Clark was about to step out and say, "I will guide you."

Rob McCool was more taciturn. "It was an interesting offer, hard to pass up," McCool remembered. He still had to complete one more year of school to earn his undergraduate degree, but he accepted Clark's offer anyway. He figured he could move to California for the summer, then move back to Illinois in the fall. If the business failed by then, nothing lost. If Mosaic was still in business, he could telecommute, couldn't he?

Houck and Bina were a little tougher to convince. They were more pragmatic. They both had full-time jobs at NCSA, where they had benefits—Bina kept asking Clark if the new company was going to offer health insurance coverage—and Houck owned a house. He wasn't thrilled about the idea of selling it.

Before meeting with Clark, Houck had convened an ad hoc meeting of his own. With Marc, Aleks, and Jon, he had sat on the living room floor in his house (he didn't own any chairs), discussed the whole thing from as many points of view as he could think of, and reached a conclusion. "Even if we did fail, it would be a hell of a ride, and a lot of fun." Houck was in. It was probably a big mistake, but he was in.

Bina, however, had more serious reservations. He had recently become engaged; his fiancée was a professor at the University of Illinois, and he didn't want to move to California. He was determined to stay in Illinois.

Eric Bina was essential to the success of the new venture— his was the coding brain behind the whole original Mosaic browser! He probably could have gotten Clark to agree to give him a helicopter chauffeured by the world's only trained chimpanzee pilot if he had asked. But Bina was modest. He accepted the offer after Clark assured him he could telecommute. And have health insurance coverage.

To Celebrate, They Got Wasted

After the six programmers had accepted his offers, Clark sat in his room and wrote up a single letter detailing the terms of their employment. It was a bare-bones document that basically said, We're going to start a company, and here's the salary and here's the stock, and we'll figure out something in terms of benefits (hello, health insurance!). Then he faxed it six times down to the front desk, where Marc picked up the copies.

The others were waiting for him at Gully's bar. Andreessen handed the letters to each of them, and Mittelhauser folded his and slipped it into his pocket without even reading it. He'd already said yes, they'd all said yes, so there wasn't much to do beyond that.

To celebrate, they got wasted. They started out drinking pitchers of beer. On top of that, the Jaegerettes were in the bar—they're the equivalent of the Bud girls, but they represent the alcoholic beverage Jaegermeister—and they were walking around in short black skirts, selling test-tube shots of Jaeger. The programmers lost count of how many they bought.

The next morning, the Mosaic programmers went in to work just like usual—and quit. What none of them knew at the time was that NCSA was in serious negotiations with Spyglass—the start-up founded by former NCSA programmer Tim Krauskopf—to license the Mosaic code. Nor did Krauskopf, who happened to be visiting the Oil Chemistry Building for a meeting the day after Clark sealed the deal with the six programmers, know the group was planning a mass exodus to compete with Mosaic.

In fact, Krauskopf was sitting in the meeting when the buzz started in the hallway. People stopped in the doorway to discuss the uproar. A bunch of programmers just resigned all at once! They're off to California to launch a new company! And they won't talk about what they're going to do, it's a secret! It was an amazing day at NCSA.

The only details the programmers were willing to reveal were that the new company would be headquartered in Silicon Valley, they were being hired en masse to create software, and they needed to get out there right away. Some of them were already clearing their desks and packing personal belongings.

At one point, Eric Bina wandered up to Krauskopf and started asking him about the logistics of leasing 56-kilobit lines, and that's how Krauskopf learned Bina was planning to telecommute. The whole time they were talking, Krauskopf had no idea he was helping a potential competitor, and Bina had no idea that Spyglass had that very day made an offer to license the Mosaic code from NCSA.

Krauskopf had kept in close touch with Hardin even after he left his job at NCSA in 1990. Spyglass's flagship product, Spyglass Transform, was a package of scientific visualization software that used the core code of NCSA Image. After becoming profitable in 1993, Spyglass was starting to look for opportunities to broaden its product line.

Over lunch one day the previous fall, Hardin told Krauskopf about the Mosaic code. Hardin said he was very excited about the commercial possibilities of Mosaic; the supercomputing center had been fielding inquiries about the software. Intrigued, Krauskopf attended a Mosaic demo in the Fishbowl that December. He thought the browser was fantastic, but he wasn't convinced the product was right for Spyglass. It wasn't even in the same category of business as the visualization software Spyglass was selling. But a few weeks before the Mosaic programmers resigned, Krauskopf had changed his mind. It was clear to him that the Web was a wide-open field of opportunity, the Mosaic program was unique, and others in his company thought the risk was worth taking.

If Krauskopf had known, on that day in April, that the bulk of the Mosaic team was defecting for the sole purpose of creating a Mosaic killer, would he still have licensed the software from NCSA?

Probably. Back then, Spyglass was merely testing the waters. NCSA licensed the code to Spyglass for nonexclusive use. The company was the ninth or tenth to get a license; Quarterdeck, Spry, and SCO all were licensing Mosaic as well. Nor was the deal expensive. Such a license typically would require the licensee to pay NCSA a small nonrefundable amount of, say, $10,000, and promise the supercomputing center a percentage of each copy sold.

By the end of the summer, however, Spyglass and the university would be on a collision course with Clark's company. And by the end of the year, Mosaic Communications would be running out of money and Spyglass would be helping Microsoft to cobble together its own browser.

CHAPTER SEVEN

In the Valley of the Doomed

Within a matter of days after he returned from Illinois, Jim Clark officially opened his new company's offices at 650 Castro Street. He had rented space on the top floor of a nondescript five-story office building in downtown Mountain View. There was a Mexican restaurant on the building's ground floor where Clark could conduct informal job interviews over lunch. Upstairs, a visitor stepped off the elevator into a hallway with commercial carpet and bland lighting. To one side was a door with a small black plaque that read, simply, MOSAIC COMMUNICATIONS. No logo, no explanation. As generic as a CIA front.

Accompanied by his wife, his secretary, Marc Andreessen, and a few others, who had followed him from Silicon Graphics, Clark cut the ribbon and proffered a bottle of champagne on that first day. It was a low-key affair. Most of the members of the original Mosaic crew were still in Illinois, wrapping up their lives and getting ready to parachute into Silicon Valley. Within a few weeks, the empty desks and cubicles would be populated by engineers working around the clock, racing against time, racing against themselves.

By now, Clark and Andreessen had a clear idea of how they wanted to develop their business. First, trounce the immediate enemy, NCSA Mosaic. Next, keep an eye on Microsoft, and if it came after them, force the giant company to fight on the unfamiliar turf of the Internet, turf that Mosaic Communications would define and control. But first things first. NCSA Mosaic must die. The Castro Street company would win by building a *better* browser—and *faster*, before people got too comfortable with the NCSA model.

Mosaic Communications would populate the world with copies of its new client. But the company's real revenues would come from selling copies of its soon-to-be-created web server software. The concept was simple: Distribute the razor and then sell the razor blades.

To make the new software attractive to businesses, Mosaic Communications would build in a layer of security—something no one else had yet included on clients or servers—that would make it feasible to conduct private on-line transactions that no evil hacker-cracker could intercept. The Mosaic team would develop a layer of security to embed in its browser called the Secure Sockets Layer, which would use 40-bit digital keys to encrypt on-line communications. Clark and Andreessen believed that businesses would be willing to spend $1,500 per server if the code were hacker-proof enough to allow customers to buy and sell products on-line.

It made more sense than trying to survive by selling the client browser to single private customers. What would someone pay for a copy of the program? Maybe $49 in a consumer channel, where the customer could then turn around and pass it on for free to any number of pals. The business market was where the money was.

The browser and the server code would be the tongue-and-groove of the great bridge that was being built, connecting everyone securely to everyone else. And to everything else. (What appliance won't have a microchip in it one day? Your toaster, microwave, stereo, thermostat, and car already do. Easy enough to mesh them into the Net.)

Mosaic Communications Wants You

One of Andreessen's first duties was to augment the core team of engineers. He needed to hire more bodies—fast. For one thing, he needed to hire a Unix programmer who would, in effect, replace himself. Andreessen's new job as cofounder of the company would re-

quire him to play a far different role from that which created the original Mosaic program: he would no longer write code. Instead,
Andreessen's job would be to build an engineering department that
SGI transplant Tom Paquin would manage on a day-to-day basis.
Andreessen would be looking over everyone's shoulder, of course,
but mostly he needed to concentrate on the big-picture stuff. He had
to refine, with Clark, how to build a business out of a browser. He
would travel with Clark to drum up excitement for the product among
potential customers. And he would continue to get the word out via
the Net.

That's how, in fact, Andreessen found a replacement for himself. He posted a corporate backgrounder on one of the Usenet newsgroups he frequented, a newsgroup called comp.infosystems.www.
Many of the people who read the postings were likely candidates to
fill the engineering ranks at Mosaic Communications.

Mosaic Communications Corporation Corporate Synopsis

*Mosaic Communications Corporation, based in Mountain
View, California, is a new technology company that intends
to provide software and services to companies and consumers for commercial activities on the Internet.*

The company's cofounders are:

- *Dr. James Clark, founder and former chairman of Silicon
  Graphics.*
- *Marc Andreessen, originator of Mosaic.*

Mosaic Communications core technical staff consists of:

- *Virtually the entire core Mosaic technology development
  team from the National Center for Supercomputing Applications (NCSA)—Eric Bina, Chris Houck, Rob McCool, Jon
  Mittelhauser, and Aleks Totic—as well as Lou Montulli,
  author of Lynx.*
- *A number of top-notch engineers from Silicon Graphics.*

Mosaic is a state-of-the-art Internet-based hypermedia information system that has recently taken the computer world by storm. In the year since its release, it has acquired a global user base of about 2 million people and has been widely hailed as the "killer application" of the Internet and of data networks in general. Mosaic was developed at NCSA by the core staff of Mosaic Communications Corp. and has until now only been available in unsupported, noncommercial-grade form.

Mosaic Communications Corp. intends to do the following:

- *Provide consulting and support to companies that want to use the Internet and Mosaic to serve information, interact with customers, or improve efficiency and productivity.*
- *Provide support to companies currently using Mosaic as a tool for accessing information, communicating with customers, or tying together workgroups.*
- *Run an Internet information server complex—a "cyberspace mall"—to support hypermedia information distribution and interactive transactions on behalf of companies and organizations that lease space on the server.*
- *Develop, deploy, and widely license a next-generation, commercial-grade Mosaic client, server, and authoring suite.*

Mosaic Communications Corp. believes that the Internet is in a fundamental transformation into the broadband consumer-oriented information superhighway of the future. We intend to support companies and consumers throughout this transition and to grow into a significant force in network-based information and entertainment by the end of the decade.

One of the people who read the posting was a young programmer named Jamie Zawinski, who worked at Lucid in Menlo Park and happened to be trolling for a new job. Coincidentally, he had

already corresponded with Marc Andreessen, back in the days when
Andreessen was still a grunt at the University of Illinois. Back then,
one morning around 2 A.M., Andreessen had sent E-mail to Zawinski
reporting a bug he had found in Lucid's Emacs program. The two
didn't know each other; Andreessen didn't even know that Zawinski
was then on-line. A half hour later, though, Zawinski had sent back
a fix. As Andreessen later told people, that definitely made an
impression.

Now, as Zawinski prepared to leave Lucid, he sent out a salvo
of E-mail, asking various people if they knew of any good jobs.

> Date: Tue, 10 May 94 05:21:54 PDT
> From: Jamie Zawinski <jwz@lucid.com>
> Subject: outta here
>
> Hi,
> I think the end is really quite near for Lucid. It's not common
> knowledge, and I might be wrong, but I don't think so. Any-
> way, I'm not the one who told you; please don't forward this
> message.
>
> So, let the job hunt begin. This is the part where I send mail
> to just about everyone I know and ask them for employ-
> ment suggestions. Feel free to spread the word that I'm
> looking to anyone you think might be interested . . . But of
> course it would be best if this not get back to anyone at
> Lucid yet.
>
> It would be nice if I could find a way to continue hacking on
> Emacs; I enjoy that a lot. But I don't think that's a particu-
> larly likely possibility, so I'm not holding out for it. However,
> one idea I've toyed with is trying to make a living just doing
> Emacs consulting work. If you know of anyone who might be
> willing to pay for specific emacs improvements, I'd like to
> hear about it.

Failing that, I'm interested in just about anything interesting . . . As long as I'm involved in producing something cool, I'm not picky.

I definitely want to stay in the Bay area, so I'm hoping for something either within an hour of Berkeley or tele-commutable.

Do any of you know anyone at Industrial Light and Magic? I've wanted to work there since I was twelve. What about Berkeley Systems? I don't know Macs or PCs yet, but getting paid to hack screensavers would be a good gig.

Anyway, here's my resume, in both text and uuencoded compressed PostScript. If folded properly it makes a fine hat!

—Jamie

The next day, Jamie got a message from Andreessen.

Date: Wed, 11 May 1994 01:43:19 -0700

From: marca@netcom.com (Marc Andreessen)
To: Jamie Zawinski <jwz@lucid.com>
Subject: outta here
Hi Jamie,

What a fortuitous note. Have you read the Mosaic Communications Corp. overview I posted to comp.infosystems.www on Monday?

Anyhow, we should definitely talk—how soon are you looking to have a new job?

Cheers, Marc

—Marc Andreessen

It certainly sounded pretty interesting, whatever it was, Zawinski thought. A few days later, he replied:

Date: Mon, 16 May 94 01:25:55 -0700
From: Jamie Zawinski <jwz@lucid.com>
To: Marc Andreessen <marca@netcom.com>
Subject: so let's schmooze

I'm ready to hop on the multimedia bandwagon :-)

You know, you're making me feel like an old man. I'm 25, my whiz kid days are over now!

—Jamie

Date: Mon, 16 May 1994 01:39:58 -0700
From: marca@netcom.com (Marc Andreessen)
To: Jamie Zawinski <jwz@lucid.com>
Subject: so let's schmooze

Too cool! Want to stop by tomorrow afternoon? Anytime after 2 or so should be OK . . . I'll confirm tomorrow.

You know, you're making me feel like an old man. I'm 25, my whiz kid days are over now!

Hmmm, wondered how old you are. Where'd you get Lisp Machine experience? Don't worry, though, we have a few people in the company already who are over 25—like Jim, who's exactly twice your age :-).

Talk to you soon,

Marc

A few minutes later, Andressen fired off another message that would prove to be especially prescient:

Date: Mon, 16 May 1994 01:56:47 -0700
From: marca@netcom.com (Marc Andreessen)
To: Jamie Zawinski <jwz@lucid.com>
Subject: Re: so let's schmooze

... In other news, Microsoft apparently has announced that they're doing a Mosaic clone for either 3.1 or Chicago (or both). Not happy news. But it will keep us running scared ...

Later,

Marc

Jamie wrote back:

Resistance is futile, you will be assimilated! So what is your immediate game plan, anyway? The description you sent out was pretty wide-ranging. Someone told me that they had read something about you guys being involved with set-top boxes too? And what's up with that semi-veiled-threat message from NCSA?

Marc replied:

Description we sent out was intentionally fluff; no set-top boxes nowhere nohow; NCSA is irrelevant (really—we have all the good people). We are going to focus very tightly on a specific piece of technology and a set of particularly suitable applications in a way that we don't think anyone else will be able to match—and have a lot of fun in the process. We gotta move goddamn fast, though.

An Impact as Big as Apple

When Jamie Zawinski arrived at the Mosaic offices for his interview, he wasn't exactly sure what he was interviewing for or even what the company did. He'd read about Mosaic; he'd even used various web browsers; he'd heard that Clark and Andreessen had hired away the team of engineers who had written the original Mosaic program at the University of Illinois. But the software was free, so where was the business model?

He told the receptionist he wanted to see Andreessen, and of course she picked up the phone and dialed his extension and there was no answer. "Marc!" she yelled, "Marrrc!" and when the big guy stood up at a cubicle a few feet away, the five-foot seven-inch Zawinski was startled at the size of him. It's always a shock to see someone you know only through E-mail.

They chatted for a bit. Zawinski waited for Andreessen to clue him in to the big picture, but instead Marc handed him off to Michael Toy, who Zawinski learned was a refugee from Silicon Graphics who was segueing from coding to management. Toy was queued and barrel-chested as a sumo wrestler, gruff and lovable as a stuffed animal. (One day the other engineers staged a Michael Toy Appreciation Day in which they all dressed like him, in shorts and sneakers, their hair pulled back in ponytails.)

The two talked generic shop, smart hackers communing in Code World, Toy gently probing for Zawinski's idea of "what would be cool to work on," not for a moment telling him what the company planned to do. "Well, what do you *want* to do?" Toy asked.

Oh, this will be an easy interview, thought Zawinski, who figured the job was his—if only he knew what job it was. Of course, he did not know he was to be Andreessen's stand-in, picking up all the Unix programming that Marc used to do.

Toy suggested that Zawinski meet Jon Mittelhauser and took him next door, to an apartment building where Mittelhauser lived. General genialities were exchanged. The mystery deepened; it was like being passed from one secret society member to another.

Zawinski's first impression of Mittelhauser, another clean-cut, shorts-wearing Andreessen-sized kid, was "Frat boy!" Zawinski hated frat boys; a nest of them lived in the apartment above him and caused him no end of grief, accidentally disconnecting his phone one day, zotzing the electricity the next, making unpleasant late-night frat-boy noises, emitting beer-inspired frat-boy smells.

His first impression of Mittelhauser was 180 degrees from the truth, as it turned out. Mittelhauser was an avid sci-fi reader, sensitive and mountainously mellow. Still, at this point Zawinski was uncomfortable, in the dark. Everyone was quoting Andreessen as if he were Chairman Mao, but so far Zawinski had yet to hear anyone explain how, exactly, Mosaic Communications would survive.

They were sitting in the apartment that Mittelhauser had just moved into, an apartment he found in a single day, whose chief virtue was that it was so close to the office he could use his home's cordless phone in his office cubicle. His bed was still leaning against the wall. Then the door opened and Andreessen came in.

Just like that, out spilled the design—razors and razor blades, secure transactions, the Microsoft threat—using his most persuasive delivery, in a tone of voice suitable for delivering a luncheon speech at the Elks Club. The message that Zawinski heard from Andreessen was: We are unbeatable, we are great, we are going to make a difference. We are going to change the world.

Zawinski was fairly vibrating that night when he hopped into his car and headed north to Berkeley. These guys are going to be so fucking rich it's not funny, he thought. There's no question that they're going to succeed. But he still had reservations about joining them.

On a personal note, it's not healthy working yourself to death, and he was already exhausted and ready for a long vacation. He wanted a job he could leave at the office; Silicon Graphics was attempting to woo him with that kind of stable, mature-business, nine-to-five gig.

Still, Zawinski loved writing software that people found useful or entertaining. He liked to feel, at the end of the day, that he had created something of value. Mosaic Communications wanted to create products that were intellectually cool. The company already was generating enough media interest to create a buzz. A number of magazines and newspapers already had published stories about Jim Clark's new adventure. The hype promised an almost guaranteed channel to the audience, he figured. So here was a company with potentially cool products *and* a mass market. It's rare to get both at once.

He also believed that the company, by virtue of being in the right place at the right time, would change the world. "Or, maybe more accurately, be the locus for a change that was going to happen," he told people later. Mosaic might "have an impact as big as Apple, and it's hard to pass up the chance to be a part of that. The money makes it even harder to pass up." Apple was the quintessential Silicon Valley archetype: It made cool technology that was humanistic, that empowered people and changed the planet. It expanded their horizons and even their consciousness. Here was an opportunity to do it again and go farther.

The Web-as-mass-market phenomenon was going to happen whether the company existed or not, that was clear, just as, a decade earlier, the personal computer was going to happen regardless of Apple. "Maybe it wouldn't have happened just when it did, but it was coming; it was an inevitable result of what had come before," Zawinski figured. "This seems to happen a lot: the telephone, the airplane. The time for a state change comes; a few different people 'invent' it independently and simultaneously. And one of them tends to get remembered and the others forgotten, not necessarily for good or fair reasons."

Zawinski was still young enough to be a dreamer, to have ideals that had nothing to do with money. Though he was roughly the same age as most of the NCSA gang, he'd been around a lot longer. At the ossified old age of twenty-five, Zawinski had already put in seven and a half years at two failed software-related enterprises.

Portrait of the Artist as a Young Zawinski

An only child raised by a mom who taught learning-disabled kids in Pittsburgh, Zawinski sneaked into computer labs at Carnegie Mellon University and taught himself programming when he was fourteen.

At sixteen, he scored a computer lab job, working for Scott Fahlman, a professor at CMU and one of the world's experts in artificial intelligence and neural networks. (Fahlman also was the inventor of the computer smiley.) Under Fahlman's direction, a group of students were trying to standardize the many dialects of Lisp, a programming language that was the precursor to artificial intelligence. (Lisp is the second oldest of the high-level programming languages, after Fortran.) Zawinski learned so-called Common Lisp here, at the feet of the master, just as the language was enjoying a popularity fostered by the Defense Department.

He managed to finish high school. He detested it, though; the environment was just too structured for him. Part of a semester at CMU confirmed that loathing. But with his newfound expertise, the teenager got a job at his first start-up. Expert Technologies, a local company, used Lisp to develop software that automated the human decision-making process of pasting up the Yellow Pages. He worked there for three and a half years, hung around with smart hackers, and sharpened his programming skills.

In the summer of 1989, he followed a girlfriend out to Berkeley and found a Lisp-related job on campus before moving on to Lucid, in Menlo Park, which sold Lisp compilers. But a few months after he got there, Zawinski was forced to dumb down and peddle himself as a C++ programmer: Lisp, archaic and beautiful as ancient Greek, was dying as a language. It broke his heart. "Leaving Lisp to go work on C was like going to work for the Peace Corps." Mediocrity, he was coming to learn, has a better chance for survival than perfection. (A footnote to history: A lot of Lisp, as it turns out, lives on in the programming pidgin language known as Java.)

Zawinski grudgingly honed his Unix skills at Lucid, working on a flavor of Emacs. What is Emacs? Considered by many to be the ultimate coder's tool, it's a Swiss army knife kind of thing, a program that contains many other applications, though its most important function is to allow one to edit other programs and text. (It also contains a number of E-mail and news readers, databases, calendars, games, and even a spreadsheet. And an entire Lisp system, which naturally made Zawinski happy.)

Another critical thing about Emacs is this: Almost as old as the Unix operating system itself, it was one of the first cross-platform programs. That means an application written to run inside of Emacs will work on any platform on which Emacs runs, including all Unix flavors, Windows NT, and Macintosh. The idea of cross-platform compatibility is sexy to anyone writing code for obvious reasons: There's a much broader market for an application that can run on many different kinds of computers.

But now Jamie thought Lucid wasn't going to make it, and Andreessen's job offer sounded pretty good. He accepted on June 15. Andreessen was thrilled. "Did I mention that I think this is fucking fantastic yet?" he asked Zawinski.

Later, Andreessen asked how soon Zawinski could start. Monday would be perfect.

"But I have a job. It would be wrong not to give two weeks' notice," Zawinski pointed out, who also wanted to take a few weeks off to unwind.

"Therein lies a problem," said Andreessen. "That's almost halfway through our initial coding cycle. And there's another reason to get you in ASAP. We'll be closing a second financing round sometime in the next few weeks, and if we get you in before that happens, we can probably give you more stock to start with (while we still have total control).

"Let's put it this way: It would work out very well for everyone involved if you could start really really soon. Next Monday would be fine with me, or as soon thereafter as possible. Besides, the Windows guys have working code already. The X platform has to catch up; you must help us recapture our honor. (OK, OK, so a patriotic appeal probably won't cut it.)"

Zawinski, nonplussed, returned to Lucid. But a few days later his boss called him in and they chatted, and it turned into one of those conversations in which either Zawinski got laid off or he quit, depending on the point of view. (Zawinski said he was laid off; the company said he quit.) It all turned out for the best, and he went to work for Mosaic.

One day shortly after he arrived, he complained to Andreessen about the rush-rush strong-arm tactics. "Why were you acting like that?"

Think of it, said Andreessen, as a kind of personality test. "I want to see if people are willing to grab opportunity at a moment's notice," he said.

"But," Zawinski said, "it can really screw people over."

The Next Bill Gates

Soon after Andreessen began building his team, Rosanne Siino started to build an image for the new company.

Siino had a good relationship with Clark from their time together at Silicon Graphics, where she had worked for four years. She came to Mosaic Communications in the late spring, after Clark convinced her over lunch that the opportunity was "a PR person's dream."

"I started putting it together, and I thought, OK, let's see, I've got the Internet, which is hot; I know I can make a big deal out of that. I've got Jim Clark, who is hot; it was no mystery to me that this guy I could make a star, no matter what. And then I've got this twenty-two-year-old wonder kid. No matter what, it's going to get a lot of coverage."

Clark offered her a raise and stock options in the start-up, but it wasn't the money that persuaded Siino to leave Silicon Graphics. He also asked her to take over early corporate communications responsibilities—helping to define the company's image—in addition to dealing with the media.

"I was at a point where I was pretty stuck at SGI because the people above me weren't going anywhere, and I thought, I'm of an age, I don't have any debt, I don't own a house . . . and how many times in your life is Jim Clark going to ask you to start a company with him?"

When Siino showed up for her first day of work in late June, Clark gave her an office the size of a conference room. "I started calling folks I knew at some of the magazines, because my initial mission was to let people know that I was here and that this little company existed," she remembered.

From day one, she had a clear idea of what facts she wanted to share with the world and what she wanted to guard. But on the surface her personality was easygoing, friendly, cooperative. Before a reporter would show up for a tour of the office, Siino might brief the engineers (since the engineers were colorful, there was no way she could keep the press totally away from them) on what they could or couldn't say about the developing products. If someone later blurted something unfortunate during the interview, Siino remained calm; the reporter had no idea that a faux pas had been committed.

Unlike most people in corporate communications, Siino had the benefit of being one of the company's decision makers. So whenever she answered a journalist's question, her voice had the ring of authority; she knew what she was talking about. From her previous job, she had plenty of media names in her Rolodex. Soon she had people coming through the door every day, journalists from around the world who wanted the increasingly famous Marc Andreessen to take them on a personal tour of the Web.

She started to create the company's earliest marketing infrastructure: writing a new background paper about the company, working with Clark on a mission statement, shaping how the world would perceive Mosaic Communications. She assisted Clark as he worked with a firm in San Francisco to create a company logo, a little M surrounded by mosaic tiles. She decided that the right time to announce the company's product line would be at two popular industry conferences in September. To prepare, she took Andreessen and Clark to meetings to ask industry analysts for advice on what Mosaic should charge, how the company should position their products, what message sounded best.

Siino quickly realized that getting coverage would never be the problem. Shaping coverage would be the challenge. She wanted to pique journalist interest without giving away too much information about the young company's strategy or upcoming products.

"My other real challenge was to build up Marc as a persona, make sure people really understood what his role was. He would get tired of the interviews, but he generally took my advice," she remembered. "He'd be like, 'I don't want to do this interview,' or, 'I don't want to take this picture,' but I'd be like, 'Look, we really need to do this.' And he's savvy in that way. He caught on."

Journalists loved the Andreessen story. They loved the fact that he seemed to be a hacker wunderkind who was nourished on a diet of junk food and cheeseburgers, that he kept empty pizza boxes on the backseat of his car, that he had seemingly been catapulted from the middle of nowhere to the epicenter of the Internet revolution. *Fortune* dubbed him "the hayseed with the know-how." But that was just the beginning. Andreessen would appear barefoot on the cover of *Time* magazine, and eventually the venerable cyber sage George Gilder would declare Andreessen to be "the next Bill Gates."

Demo Days

Clark and Andreessen realized that an obvious source of customers would be publishers. With the Internet emerging as a new communications medium, it seemed only a matter of time until the on-line world offered obvious business opportunities to companies already in the business of communicating information.

Clark began traveling around the country, extolling to various publishers what he believed were the growing opportunities offered by the Web. He visited editors at NBC, ABC, Hearst, Time Inc., *The Wall*

Street Journal, and other media powerhouses. His goal was to convince them that the Net was a potentially profitable publishing medium.

Mid-1994 was a confusing time for publishers who were trying to navigate the landscape of emerging technologies. Many of them already had invested heavily in the hard-distribution model of CD-ROMs; now they struggled to understand the possibilities of the future. Many already had partnered with on-line services like America Online, CompuServe, and Prodigy to create electronic sites in a closed proprietary environment. Clark's mission was to convince them to abandon that model in favor of the open free-for-all environment of the Web. To bolster his argument on frequent trips to publishers in New York, Clark took along what the Mosaic Communications team called demoware.

One time, he took along a program that depicted a fictional Rolling Stone website, that Mosaic's Jeff Treuhaft had created. The demo took all the information Rolling Stone printed in its paper magazine and transferred it to the more flexible medium of a Web page. As the editors watched, Clark clicked on video clips, audio clips, links that brought up Top 10 charts. He clicked on a link labeled TICKETS to show how the program could sell actual concert tickets. With one click, the demo linked to a picture of a stadium. A second click took the user inside, to select the mezzanine, orchestra, or balcony section. Another click, and the program would tell the user which seats were available. Then Clark showed how a user could actually key in a credit card number to place an order.

It was a dramatic illustration of how the Web—working in tandem with the Mosaic browser, of course—could deliver enormous amounts of information to audiences. But Clark and Andreessen were still wrestling with the value proposition, Treuhaft remembered. That is, they knew how Mosaic Communications would make money if every publisher in the world licensed the software to create interactive websites. That part was obvious. What they still weren't sure of was how the *publishers* would make money.

Kill Your Darling

And so it began, the race to build a better browser: a browser that would leapfrog NCSA Mosaic, a browser that would own the marketplace. On one side was market leader NCSA Mosaic and its assorted licensees, most notably Spyglass. On the other were a bunch of refugees from SGI and the key people who built the thing in the first place.

At first, the NCSA programmers were suspicious of the SGI veterans, if for no other reason than the older, more experienced programmers represented management. Most of the team from Illinois resented the way the original Mosaic project had been managed—it had, in their minds, been appropriated by managment—and so were inclined to distrust anyone in a supervisory position. They felt pride of ownership not only over their code but over the very concept of the Mosaic browser. How could anyone not involved from the beginning dare tell them what to do or how to do it?

Part of that difficult task fell to Tom Paquin, in his thirties one of the few adults in the shop. He was the multitasker, the fellow who made the trains run on time. Paquin, who could move at all deliberate speed in three directions at once, always under total control, directed the factionalized engineering team (composed of six former college kids, who were suspicious of adults and managers on one side; and four SGI guys, people with children and responsibilities on the other). Paquin did everything that needed doing. Say a new employee showed up. That meant connecting another computer to the Net, right? Paquin got out his punchdown tool and went into the box with a trillion wires and—*kachunk, kachunk*—new connection. The programmers needed to be fed, too, and if Paquin didn't do it, who would? So he drove the office van on daily runs to the computer store for gear and Costco for junk food, including marshmallows for marshmallow battles. Over time, he won over the younger programmers.

In some respects, building a web browser was like building a stock car or a dragster. A few of the components were off-the-shelf (windows and menu bars and sliders and such). A lot of it, though, had to be built from scratch.

The browser they were building had to do everything that the NCSA browser did but be smarter and, above all, faster. Smarter meant cross-platform—it would run in Unix and Macintosh as well as in Microsoft's Windows. It meant the program would perform better whether you were on a modem or a T-3 connection and would be stable, meaning it wouldn't crash your computer, at least not too much. And it would be secure. Andreessen was adamant about the importance of handling secure transactions, so that businesses could use it to serve customers.

Everyone agreed that the Unix version of the NCSA browser that Andreessen and Bina had built in Illinois was the best version and the one to beat. So they sat down to figure out how.

One easy way to win on speed would be to design the browser so that Web pages were displayed in pieces. The NCSA browser waited for all the information to download before drawing a Web page on the screen; the user was stuck staring at a blank screen. A better solution would be to create an asynchronous connection: Text could come in immediately while images were loading. It wasn't really faster—you didn't get the whole document more quickly—but at least you could start interacting with it sooner.

Other huge improvements would be made as well. NCSA Mosaic used separate code bases for its Unix, Windows, and Macintosh browsers. That led to some platforms being better built and more stable than others. It was also inefficient, because so much work was duplicated from platform to platform. As much as possible, they wanted to create a single base of code to run in native mode on each platform, meaning that the Mac flavor would look and behave like a Mac program, Windows would feel like Windows, and Unix would be Unixy. In the end, 80 percent of the code would be shared (compared to 5 percent in the original NCSA

Mosaic). That meant bug fixes would be easier and future development even faster.

The Castro Street office soon filled with the litter of their haste—stacks of cardboard computer boxes, ripped open and cast aside; crates and cubes; ethernet cables snaking along the floor. A homey odor of unwashed bodies and junk food settled over the eleven-thousand-square-foot office. At times, their goal seemed impossible to achieve. Some of the programmers began to greet each other by saying, "We're doomed!" Not long after, it became the sign-off at their meetings, the spoken and unspoken message of the day. They were engineers; they knew that everything finally ends in entropy and disarray. Like Kierkegaard, they were comforted to know that, in the end, nothing mattered but hard work. It was organized religion: We're all doomed together, so let's get to work—faster.

The former student programmers and pony-tailed Super-Soaker refugees from Silicon Graphics quickly became stressed out, overworked, and nearly delusional. They were cranking 120 hours a week, going three days without bathing, crashing on futons (Clark's secretary regularly changed the sheets) in the office when they couldn't keep their eyes open for one minute more.

From the day he arrived, Zawinski hunkered down and never looked up. He tended to work most closely with Bina, who had remained behind, in Illinois.

Bina was working on the layout engine. Meanwhile, Zawinski decided to build a front end, or user interface. The front end is the structure of a program that you actually see on a screen. In a browser, it's the menu bar and the window frame and the various buttons and sliders you use to dictate the flow of information. Since the look and feel of the program would change, Zawinski didn't see the point in killing too much time on it—it was like worrying about a car's paint job instead of the motor—so he simply cloned NCSA Mosaic's front end. Now at least you could see how Bina's work on the layout engine was progressing. You couldn't actually browse the Web yet; all you could do was display a page of text. Still, it was something.

It was a bit troubling to the other engineers at first. Hey, some-one said, you made it look exactly like NCSA Mosaic. "Do you have a better idea?" Zawinski asked.

Working hard, insane hours is a tradition among Silicon Val-ley start-ups. Well before Steve Wozniak met Steve Jobs and built the first Apple in a garage, hackers had abandoned the nine-to-five routine, opting for something closer to their own unnatural circa-dian rhythms. Zawinski preferred two days of straight work, fol-lowed by four hours of sleep, for instance. Others' mileage varied. (Bina could go four days straight, according to legend.) One day a market survey drone called Lou Montulli at home, after a typical thirty-six hours at the office, and asked him how many hours he worked a week. "Uh, one hundred and ten to one hundred and twenty," Montulli replied. The surveyor's computer wouldn't al-low him to enter a figure that high.

Even by the draconian Gulag-like standards of the Valley, though, the Castro Street team worked harder, longer, and faster than the norm. At first, Andreessen functioned as coxswain and team leader, cracking the whip. He liked what he saw, but still wanted to go faster.

One day during early summer, Andreessen and some other folks were standing around in Rosanne Siino's office, talking about how cool it would be to get something to market by an unrealisti-cally optimistic deadline, say, December. And he said, Let's do it. Why not? Later, after Andreessen wandered down to Engineering and repeated his query, the veterans from SGI (the adults) raised their eyebrows. A full-blown commercial product seven months from start-up to market? It was crazy, really. But they *were* hammering out code at a hellishly snappy clip. Why not, indeed? Andreessen and Clark talked, and Clark assembled everyone and sweetened the pot: He said that if the team made the deadline, everyone would get more stock.

More stock in what? The company wasn't public yet. But of course it would be. That was what fueled an enterprise like this, that was one of the main incentives for working triple-overtime hours—

the idea that you were working for yourself and those dynamic option offers on legal paper that (supposedly) are redeemable (someday) as cash. Because on that glorious day when the Company meets the Street, suddenly those Monopoly money shares and options you hold have value. And maybe, just maybe, if you work harder and faster, you'll make even more.

That was the idea, anyway. Lots of Silicon Valley prospectors have become wealthy at the game. Of course, many more have pursued the dream, only to see it vanish in poor public offerings or, worse, aborted public offerings. Zawinski, for instance, had spent nearly all of the previous four years of his life working for a place that never got there. Forget an IPO; when Zawinski left, the company was barely even in business. So that was almost four years down the old dream hole.

And yet Zawinski and lot of other people would say that much more than money was at stake at Mosaic Communications. The median age in the place may have been about twenty-four, but the great American competitive spirit was certainly in attendance. Since it was too late to get there first, they wanted to win by being first to market with the *best* product. Hacking good code is an end in itself, but the goal now was doing it good *and fast*. If they could deliver by the end of 1994, MCI Communications was considering a deal to distribute the browser on a new Internet service that the telecommunications company wanted to launch.

A bunch of them tried to hatch a name for the new baby. The name Mosaic would have to belong to the past; it represented their old browser, the thing the programmers were trying to kill. Zawinski remembered listening to the marketing folks' litany of cliché names: Cyber-this and Net-that and Power-blah and Foo-ware. It inspired headaches. It hardly boded well for the industry if they couldn't come up with something snappier than that. Then someone gave voice to the programmers' greatest hope for redemption: that the browser they were all hacking away on would *crush NCSA Mosaic like a dry bug.*

"Mozilla!" Zawinski yelled one day, as they were walking to lunch. As in, Mosaic meets Godzilla. As in, Fear us, for we shall rule the Net. Mozilla. Everyone say it aloud, together. And by this name the new browser came to be (unofficially) known.

Time was running out. Market leader NCSA Mosaic already had an estimated three million users and was gobbling newbies at the astounding rate of six hundred thousand a month. You could launch the most remarkable browser in the world in January, but who'd be left to use it?

To drive that point home, to goad his comrades on, to impress upon them the need for speed, the notoriously nonathletic, junk-food-inhaling Andreessen made a pledge: If the team got the commercial version of the new browser to market by December 1994, he'd do any of three things:

1. Wear Rollerblades.
2. Wear spandex.
3. Eat (gag) *health food*. Publicly.

Desperate times call for desperate measures.

The engineers were giddy and excited as they hacked away on Mozilla. They had a huge ace in the hole: Having built Mosaic, they knew all the flaws of the NCSA browser.

But the kids from the University of Illinois felt they had something else to prove as well. They weren't simply at the right place at the right time, fungible programmers who got lucky by being assigned to a meaty project. They were great programmers who built something brilliant and enduring.

Hierarchically, the Mosaic Communications engineering team was flat; it functioned without a clear leader. Short fifteen-minute meetings would occur spontaneously, everyone standing up, someone saying, "Here's the problem. Now, how do you think I should fix it?" The preferred method of reaching consensus was that whoever yelled the loudest usually won. Then everyone went back to work.

The trick, from the engineering standpoint, was to divvy up the work efficiently among the team members and get everyone to work together like parallel processors in a supercomputer. Tasks were distributed among the programmers who hacked away at them, sometimes in tandem, usually alone. As chunks of code got written, they were shared, incorporated into a whole, and assembled.

There were never enough programmers to get all the work done, at least not fast enough. As soon as Marc plugged one hole in the dike (such as hiring Zawinski), another started spurting. The biggest problem, of course, was no time to conduct formal interviews, no time to go looking for people. Marc was pulled in five hundred different directions, with a job title that included about ten different jobs. He barely had time to phone someone to make a formal job offer, let alone institute a formal recruiting process. He relied on the people he knew.

That's how he ended up hiring Rob McCool's twin brother, Mike, who was attending summer school back at the University of Illinois. One day Andreessen sent E-mail to Mike, who now worked at NCSA.

Hi, Mike,

Your brother said he needed some help in doing some work on the server, and he also mentioned you were looking for something to do. You know, we'd love to have you come and help us out here.

The E-mail went on, describing the salary and the working conditions—Mike could stay in Illinois to finish school—and how Andreessen would expect the two brothers to work very closely together since they'd be living together in the same apartment (Rob was going back to the University of Illinois in the fall as well, to telecommute while he was finishing his degree).

Mike read it all, of course, but the only thing that really mattered to him was in the first paragraph: *You know, we'd love to have you come and help us out here.*

It was an answer to a prayer. Ever since Rob had left town a few months earlier, Mike had been knocking around their three-bedroom apartment, going to classes and working at NCSA, thinking about taking a job with a friend of his who was starting a video game business. But it had turned out that the friend's business was in trouble, and Mike realistically didn't have enough money to pay his school bills, and he was trying to get a raise at NCSA, but you know how that goes. He didn't want to take out another loan on top of it all, just to pay for the upcoming academic year.

Mike E-mailed Marc a response right away: *Yeah, that sounds great.*

Out the Door in '94

The programmers cranked code all day and hard into the night. They cranked code in the gray interstices in between. Nothing existed outside of the office; it was pointless to leave. So they stayed, endlessly. Everything that mattered was bounded by a keyboard, a workstation, and a code-crunching brain.

Out the door in '94: That was the goal. But how? There was no easy way to make it happen. "If I don't sleep, and if I write bug-free code—which is a joke, there's no such thing—then maybe I can make it," Zawinski told himself. He refused to waste time sleeping in the futon room, preferring instead to nap at his desk. He draped a blanket over his head and snapped headphones on to drown out the occasional Doom matches being fought around him. Aleks Totic insisted he saw Jamie wake up with keyboard imprints on his face.

Zawinski was putting in 120 hours a week, driving to work, doing thirty-five hours straight, then sleeping for two hours while his stuff compiled. Then back to work for twelve hours and home for a real sleep—say, five hours. The alarm rang and Zawinski awakened, his heart fibrillating like a bolt in a bucket. Back he flopped, into his

Miata and the bright slide down Route 101 to the office. People who love coding have a hard time stopping. There's always one more thing to finish. Which was why Zawinski went to the drugstore, bought a pair of Ace bandages, and wrapped them around his wrists. He needed to work through the pain.

He worked until his eyes unfocused. Zawinski's headphone-capped mass under a blanket became a common sight. One day, when Zawinski was out of the office, Aleks Totic constructed a life-sized mass out of Coke cans in Jamie's chair and wrapped the blanket around it, clamping the scarecrow with the headphones. The cube mates agreed it was a passable likeness.

Presently, Mittelhauser walked by. "Hi, Jamie," he said, never once batting an eye.

Andreessen had asked Zawinski to finish his Unix client within two months. The goal was to finish it in time to coincide with the release of a new Silicon Graphics operating system release, Irix 5.3. If the Mozilla code passed muster, SGI would bundle it with its new Indigo machines. Zawinski didn't even know if this was remotely possible, since he had so little of the code written. Sections of it were done, but they'd yet to be assembled. *I don't want to miss,* he wrote in his diary. *The stakes are too high this time, too many people watching us for us to be able to screw up at all.*

A few of the coders knew that sometimes the best way to keep from screwing up is to screw off. Bill Foss found a decent pump-action Ping Pong–ball shotgun on the Internet and ordered a case of them—a notable achievement, since it was the first time anyone in the office purchased something on the Net. The shotguns allowed for a periodic Elliot Ness–style ambush. Aleks played Doom, reveling in the thunderous sounds of nail-gun combat.

Even if you don't sleep, you have to eat. Often the programmers traveled in a pack to a nearby all-night restaurant to grab a quick meal of bacon and eggs. But other times they needed a humanity check, just to reassure themselves that an outside world existed. On those nights, they would arrive, en masse, on the doorstep of one of the fancier restaurants in tony Palo Alto, smelly, unshaven, grungy from long hours of coding. They could see the panic in the eyes of the maître d' as he surveyed their unkempt group, trying to decide what to do with these loud guys. Invariably, they were whisked off to the worst table in the place, near the kitchen, near the bathroom, or sometimes in an otherwise empty room that had been opened up just to uh—accommodate them.

Lou Montulli and Rob McCool discovered a hobby shop where they could buy parts to build radio-controlled cars. One day, they spent hours putting the models together and racing them on the floor. Zawinski, who was frantically doing the Unix build, wandered over to Houck's cube at around 4 A.M.

"Is this car thing annoying you?" he asked.

Houck stretched out his arms bigger than a bread box. "Only about this much," he said, making a sour face. Zawinski shuffled back to his own desk.

Ten minutes later, Houck came over to Zawinski's cubicle. "So does it annoy you too, or were you just wondering whether it annoyed me because I'm so easily annoyed?" he asked.

"It annoys me too," said the spleenful Zawinski. "But probably a bit less than it annoys you."

CHAPTER EIGHT

The Gold Standard

Clark made no secret of the fact that he did not care to run the company on a day-to-day basis. He wanted to be free to think about the big picture—where should the company be headed?—and to travel widely to spread the word of the Internet. As soon as possible, Clark wanted to hire a chief executive officer who could take care of the business operations and manage the company's growth, freeing him to fill the role of technovisionary.

Venture capitalist John Doerr agreed to help Clark put together a team of top managers—and to help him, in particular, with the chore of finding the right CEO. For years Doerr had been saying he wanted to work with Clark on a business deal. (But because Doerr had invested heavily in SGI's competitor, Sun Microsystems, the two men had no opportunity to work as partners until Clark left Silicon Graphics.)

Clark had been leery of working with venture capitalists after his experience at SGI in the 1980s, when his influence over the company's direction was diluted even before the company's IPO. By the time the company went public, outside investors had whittled away so many pieces of equity that Clark only held 5 percent of the stock.

But Clark realized he needed an injection of cash to keep Mosaic Communications afloat during its critical early days. Doerr offered up to $5 million.

Doerr was excited about investing in Clark's new venture. He had recently been given a demonstration of the original Mosaic browser by Sun cofounder Bill Joy in the editorial offices of the *San Francisco Chronicle,* while publisher Will Hearst looked on. Doerr was already bullish on the whole on-line scene after taking America Online public. People were getting connected. And with every new connection, the Network itself became exponentially more valuable.

"I shamelessly appropriated the idea from Bill Joy, even though at the time it was not clear to me that it was as big as it turned out to be," Doerr remembered. "It wasn't that I realized the Web changes everything, it was that this was moving so fast the only thing to do was to dive in. Remember, there had been two million copies of Mosaic adopted by the marketplace within five months."

Doerr was used to diving in. Ever since he started at Kleiner, Perkins in 1980, he had been looking for—and often successfully identifying—the next big thing in technology. The son of a mechanical engineer, Doerr became an engineer himself before going to Harvard Business School to earn an M.B.A. At the time he landed at Kleiner, Perkins, Clark already was at Stanford, fomenting his idea of a three-dimensional geometry engine. Hanging around at Stanford, Doerr met Clark. In the early 1980s, he also became acquainted with the founders of Lotus, Sun, and Compaq. Those three companies created hardware and software products that moved the world away from mainframe computers and onto the desktop. At Doerr's urging, Kleiner, Perkins had invested heavily in all three.

Of course, Doerr sponsored his share of failures, as well. The list included GO, a pioneer in "pen-based" computing, and Dynabook Technologies, whose goal was to make featherweight laptop computers.

But the venture capitalist's instincts led the company in the right direction more often than not; by the late 1990s, Kleiner, Perkins would be invested in a group of technology companies with a combined worth of $125 billion.

By the beginning of the summer of 1994, Clark and Doerr had spent two months interviewing two dozen potential CEO candidates. Clark had hired a headhunter to help find the right candidate. One day in July, the headhunter called Clark with a name: Jim Barksdale.

As the president of McCaw Cellular Communications in Seattle, Barksdale was in the throes of steering McCaw's $2.2 billion nationwide cellular network toward an acquisition by AT&T. It would be a historic deal that would sanctify the communications revolution— and free up Barksdale for other work.

Barksdale knew next to nothing about Silicon Valley, having spent the better part of his career working for IBM and Federal Express before accepting the job at McCaw in 1991. He had never run a software start-up, had never even seen Mosaic's main product, the browser. He wasn't exactly sure, frankly, what the thing was or what it did. Barksdale hadn't even experienced the Internet yet. He had never been on the Net, didn't know a gopher site from a rat bite, couldn't ftp a .txt file to save his life.

But in the cowboy atmosphere of Silicon Valley, where a Pepsi-Cola executive (John Sculley) ran Apple Computer during its gravy days, where a Hungarian immigrant (Andy Grove) made Intel the biggest computer chip maker in the galaxy, and where a poor kid from the South Side of Chicago (Larry Ellison) built the world's second-largest software company, Oracle, and became one of the Valley's best-known billionaires, either you had it or you didn't. And some of the smartest string-pullers in the Valley devoutly believed that Jim Barksdale had it.

Doerr, who was so excited by Mosaic Communications that he had briefly considered himself for CEO, had concluded that you couldn't do better than Barksdale. "Every fast-growing start-up looks for a Jim Barksdale," Doerr once observed. "He's the gold standard."

Clark and Doerr agreed that Barksdale's accomplishments were stellar. His track record was unparalleled. And, with his company about to be bought out by megacorporation AT&T, he might just be available.

The two booked a flight up to Seattle to find out.

A Third Bite of the Apple

Clark and Doerr met Barksdale for dinner at the Red Lion Hotel, hard by the airport. Anyone who knew Barksdale well would have known that the very fact that he agreed to the meeting was evidence that he was intrigued. He didn't like to go out at night and turned down most invitations.

As president of McCaw, Barksdale had experienced one of the biggest business success stories of the early nineties. He arrived at the company during a particularly suspenseful juncture: Craig McCaw, the company's maverick founder, had borrowed a bankload of debt—$4.9 billion—to finance a national cellular network. From his vantage at McCaw, Barksdale surveyed the entire landscape of the developing wireless communications industry—cell phones, pagers, fax machines, notebook computers that could send E-mail without using a phone jack—and saw how the vast network would create untold new business opportunities as it expanded. If all went well, Craig McCaw would be hailed as the man who had the foresight to buy up lucrative cellular franchises across the United States and build an enormous wireless network that changed the meaning of the phrase "local phone call." But many analysts were predicting that McCaw had gambled too much money too early in the game and the company would go under well before the year 2002, when the mobile communications revolution was expected to grow to a $43 billion industry with ninety million users.

Instead, AT&T bought the company for a delirious $11.5 billion. With his share worth $20 million, Barksdale could now retire—not that AT&T wanted him to; the company offered him a two-year "stay bonus" of several million dollars if he agreed to remain. While Barksdale said he'd help during the transition process, he declined a longer-term commitment.

But after that? He had told his wife, Sally, he wasn't looking for another high-stress job. He'd worked for enough big companies. Maybe it was time to take life easy, invest in other people's businesses.

Still, there was one goal left for Barksdale to attain. After years of toiling for other entrepreneurs, building their businesses into lucrative empires, he still had an urge to run his own company. He'd had what he called "two bites of the apple" at FedEx and McCaw. But in each of those instances, much of the game plan had been chalked out before he signed on. He'd seen how Craig McCaw had fomented a wireless revolution, building an empire that had its roots in a minuscule four-thousand-subscriber cable TV system McCaw had inherited from his father in 1969. McCaw had gotten in early on the cable game; less than two decades later he had sold the company for $755 million, and only then envisioned a nationwide cellular network. At FedEx, Barksdale had been right-hand man to the company's founder, Frederick Smith, and helped carve out a new segment in the duopolistic mail delivery industry.

Besides, his career had prepared him well to lead the kind of venture that Clark and Andreessen had embarked upon. From his days as a salesman at IBM, to Federal Express, to McCaw, Barksdale had done more than master the art of operations; he had learned to thrive in a business world where someone else had seemingly cornered the market. He had learned that sometimes the best place to build a business is where other competitors are scared off by a monopoly. If Mosaic Communications was to survive, it would have to carve out a niche in a software industry unquestionably dominated by the monopoly power of Microsoft.

Coincidentally, Barksdale had learned of the existence of Mosaic Communications just a few weeks earlier. Sitting in the den of his Seattle home, Barksdale came across an article in *Fortune* magazine touting Cool New Companies. One of them was Mosaic Communications. "Listen to this, Sally," he said, uncharacteristically interrupting their silent-reading time, "this is a clever idea these guys have got."

He read that the new company, which had a scant eighteen employees, planned to sell software for commerce on the Internet.

> You're Jim Clark, 50, Silicon Valley legend [the *Fortune* article began]. You've just left Silicon Graphics, the company that brought 3-D computer graphics to workstations and to Hollywood. You're walking away with about $37 million in stock, not to mention any other money you've made in the dozen years since you founded the company. What to do?
>
> You think the real action lies on the Internet, which links 20 million people around the world and is growing, by some estimates, at a rate of 20% a month.

The article went on to describe Clark's new partner, the twenty-two-year-old programmer, Marc Andreessen, as "the hayseed with the know-how." The article noted that the original Mosaic browser was now "the hottest software on the Internet," with employees at places like General Electric and J. P. Morgan using it. It sounded pretty intriguing; and exciting, too, Barksdale thought.

That might have been the end of it had Barksdale not been working late one evening a few days later. Sitting in his office after his secretary had gone home, Barksdale answered his own phone. On the line was the corporate headhunter Clark had hired to find a CEO— who had heard that Barksdale might be in the market for another job after the AT&T acquisition of McCaw was complete.

The headhunter first asked Barksdale about another job he was helping to fill: the number-four job at Microsoft. It could mean a lot of money, of course, since Microsoft was known to be exceedingly generous with stock options, and the shares of the company had been appreciating like a nonrenewable natural resource. But Barksdale wasn't particularly interested in the money angle. "I don't think so," he told the headhunter. "There's no way I can leave my mark on Microsoft, and I don't care to be part of an executive team where I'm fourth man out."

Well, said the headhunter, there is this other opportunity. Perhaps Barksdale had heard of Jim Clark? Would Barksdale consider a leadership role in a Silicon Valley start-up called Mosaic Communications?

At dinner at the Red Lion, the three men played a cautious game. Clark and Doerr wanted to interest Barksdale in the job without revealing long-term strategies and secrets about the company; they knew Microsoft was trying to recruit him too. And Barksdale was trying to learn as much as he could about Mosaic without expressing any excitement one way or the other. It was hard to stay neutral, though. "Jim Clark tells a good story," Barksdale later said. "He's a very persuasive guy. And Doerr is equally persuasive."

Doerr, who later said he did most of the talking, wanted to assure Barksdale that if he took the job he would have free rein. The company would be his to run; Clark wasn't interested in day-to-day management.

Doerr launched into his stem-winder, the speech he usually gave as a power-point presentation. "Connectivity will be more important than compatibility. PCs not on the Net will be worthless." The idea, he readily admitted, came from cyberpundit Esther Dyson, publisher of the *Release 1.0* newsletter. "If you're not on the Net, you're out of it. Every business is involved, from banking to publishing." Doerr rattled off the companies that Kleiner, Perkins had helped take public, including Sun and AOL, companies that were number one or two in their markets. "Mosaic could be as big as any of those—if not bigger."

Something's about to get going here, and it will be huge, Barksdale believed. He got swept up in the excitement. He was in the right place at the right time. This was his chance to get in early on the next information revolution: the Internet. Here was his chance to make his mark in an emerging industry that had yet to produce either product or business strategy. Here was his chance at "a third bite of the apple."

Doerr and Clark said they'd even move the operation up to Seattle, if Barksdale was wedded to the area. "No, there isn't enough time," Barksdale said. "Why don't I come down and look at your place?"

Portrait of a Businessman

One day in August 1994, a cab with a flat tire pulled up to 650 Castro Street and out stepped Jim Barksdale, in a suit and tie. He paid the fare and stared up at an office building that looked like a commercial cliff dwelling. Technically, he was supposed to be on vacation. With McCaw becoming the property of AT&T in another month, he had taken time off to go to Memphis, where his wife was in the final throes of planning their daughter's wedding, scheduled for that week. But today's daylong reconnaissance trip was not off to a relaxing start. The cab had had a flat tire on the ride from the airport, right on Route 101, the eight-lane artery connecting the most vital place on the planet—Silicon Valley— to its cosmopolitan, commuter suburb, San Francisco. As traffic whizzed by, the cabdriver ignored Barksdale's imprecations and pleas to pull over and fix the damn thing, and drove along on the rim—*thump, thump, thump*—at twenty miles per hour.

That flat tire was an inauspicious beginning, Barksdale thought. But then, he was here to take a look at a four-month-old company that had yet to produce anything. It had no revenues and didn't expect to break even until some murky, to-be-determined date. When (and if) it finally would turn a profit was anybody's guess. Its talent pool consisted primarily of a bunch of twenty-ish hackers who yelled and screamed and threw things at each other (and who worked all night). Some of them slept under their desks. To hear the company line was to experience the hubris of young Icarus himself; its goal was nothing less than to tame the untameable and burgeoning Internet. Barksdale's goal was to assess whether Mosaic Communications could conquer the worldwide network—and whether he wanted to navigate this new territory.

For their part, Clark and Doerr already had decided that Barksdale was their best choice for CEO. What was it about Barksdale that convinced them he would be the best candidate? Quite simply, Barksdale had spent his life learning about networks. Federal Express had demonstrated to Barksdale the power of the network made flesh; computers could simplify the process of coordinating tens of thousands of people around the globe to deliver parcels. McCaw extended his education to the wired and wireless realm of telecommunications and impressed on him how we're still at the earliest stages of a bottoms-up communications revolution. Now the worldwide Internet was changing everything, redistributing power once again. While Jim Barksdale might not yet have known the specific mechanics of this particular network, he understood, more than most people, the underlying, intertwining, pullulating connections—both wired and human— that made the Internet grow.

The first network Barksdale learned to navigate, naturally enough, was the family. His was an unexpectedly big one. First to be born was Jack, and then came Tommy. Shortly after baby Tommy's arrival, Mary Bryan Barksdale contracted a virulent case of pneumonia. Her doctor said that was the end of her childbearing years. Six years later Jim was born, followed in eighteen months by Rees. And then came Bryan. "Mary Bryan," the doctor said, "you can stop calling my bluff." She had one more baby for good measure, Claiborne. The final count was six strapping Barksdale boys.

Barksdale's father, John Woodson Barksdale, Jr., was an officer at the Deposit Guaranty Bank and Trust, the largest bank in Mississippi. Despite his position, the family lived modestly. Barksdale remembers it as a comfortable middle-class Jackson life, in a house filled with books that Mary Bryan, who loved literature, collected.

So many brothers made for frequent competition. "When you have six boys and only one car, and everybody's got a date, five guys get to learn the meaning of the word no," Barksdale recalled. "Whoever had the best sales pitch got the car." Jim did a lot of driving.

The boys used their wiles to get their share of parental attention as well. But Mary Bryan, a homemaker who was often a substitute schoolteacher, had the rare ability to make them all feel loved. "Some-

how, she convinced all six boys—I don't know how you do this—
that she loved each one the most," Barksdale would later say, in his
best dipped-in-Mississippi voice. Pause for two beats. "Now, the fact
is, she did love *me* the most."

That line actually belonged to older brother Tommy, but a
good salesman knows when he needs to borrow material to make
his case. And Barksdale was always a good salesman, right from the
tenth grade, when he got a job at his neighbor Ed Helms's clothing
store. Helms was a pretty shrewd guy and figured the young
Barksdale would have an inside track selling dress clothes to his class-
mates. "Shoes," the redheaded, freckled youth would tell his pals.
"Suits. Full-service young men's store. You want a blue suit? Turn
on the blue light."

He also held the usual summer grunt jobs, such as working for
a power-line contractor in Texas, "a hundred-plus degrees out there
in the desert, digging holes to put telephone poles in. Climbing up
these creosote poles." Barksdale had the same epiphany that strikes
many high school kids who toil away at backbreaking summer jobs. "I
said to myself, You know, I have to get an education, because I don't
want to be doing this all my life."

The rigors of shoulder-to-shoulder competition with five
brothers taught Barksdale to go for what he wanted, with little shy-
ness or fuss. As a freshman at the University of Mississippi in the early
1960s, he attended an autumn dance—called a swap—where he caught
sight of a handsome young woman wearing a green wool sweater and
matching skirt. He didn't get a chance to speak to her, but he learned
that her name was Sally and that although she too was a freshman, she
dated mainly upperclassmen. Her list of suitors already included about
a dozen members of Barksdale's own fraternity.

Barksdale knew enough to wait for the right opportunity. One
day he saw Sally walking along a campus path outside the imposing
red-brick Graduate Building. Weeks had passed, but the Sigma Chi
pledge with the shaved head had been biding his time, steeling his

courage. Approaching Sally was the most nerve-racking moment of his life. ("You know, this is making me nervous *now,* talking about it," he remarked, thirty-five years and three children later.)

In front of the building, they talked about their plans for the upcoming Christmas break—Sally was going home to Hazelhurst, a small town south of Jackson where her father was a country doctor—and about the classes they had together. "I tried everything I could think of."

That moment of pure energy, the high-stakes and go-for-broke desperation of a young man hopelessly in love, stuck with him. "Let me tell you, if you could bottle the intensity of young people in love, how focused they are in their actions, and apply it to business, you'd never lose a sale," he said.

On their first date, he told Sally he was going to marry her. She laughed then, but in the end she married him, of course. Who could resist the force of that unbottled emotion? The lesson Barksdale learned so many decades ago, in front of the Graduate Building, was one that served him well in the corporate world. He learned to bide his time and to watch, hoping for a quick glimpse of the same rare intensity in the workplace. He learned to look for people who display that all-consuming excitement: the salesman who ignores sleep deprivation to close a deal, the engineer who doesn't realize he's hungry as he works around the clock to create a software program. (Barksdale later recognized that intensity in venture capitalist John Doerr.)

By the time he graduated from the University of Mississippi in 1965 with a degree in business administration, Barksdale found something else he wanted: a job at IBM. That's what he told the company's recruiter when he went to Memphis for a job interview with the district manager, Jim Mills. Barksdale's oldest brother and role model, Jack, already worked there, had in fact risen to the job of branch manager in Little Rock. That was both a plus and a minus for the job applicant.

"I don't know if I can have two Barksdales working for me," Mills confessed.

"Well, then, fire Jack," said Barksdale.

Acceptable Business Conduct

What better place to cut one's teeth? Back in the late 1960s, when mainframe computers ruled the world, IBM ruled the world of mainframes, with a more than 70 percent share of the computer industry. In those days, no one could have predicted the looming revolution of the personal computer; the first rudimentary PC wouldn't even be introduced until the Altair 8800 debuted as a hobbyist's fetish on the cover of *Popular Electronics* in January 1975. In the meantime, IBM seemed to have a solid lock on the serious machines that companies procured to do data processing. IBM's business was exploding; in fact, the year Barksdale signed on it hired more college grads than the next six companies combined, something like eight thousand new employees. By the late 1960s, IBM's preeminence in the mainframe market alarmed the federal government enough to trigger a federal antitrust investigation into the company's business practices. The way IBM worked was this: First, hook the customer with one of those machines. Then move in to sell a whole line of add-ons and accoutrements, software also manufactured by IBM. If Big Blue's tactics made the government suspect monopolization, they also provided a young salesman with an education he would never forget in how to leverage your strength.

There was a flip side as well: No one understood customer service better than IBM in the 1960s. The whole place was a monument not only to its mainframe technology but to the service that sold, maintained, and nurtured those international business machines. Some alumni of the sales training program called it brainwashing, but Barksdale thought that the program was unparalleled. The first time he laid eyes on California was when IBM sent him to a training facility in San Jose. First level of sales training, second level of sales training—it was like going for your black belt in judo. He learned what the company considered to be "acceptable business conduct." He learned about ethics and how to treat customers with respect. He learned to wear a dark suit, a white shirt, and dark shoes to work—an IBM tradition that dated back to the early days when Tom Watson, Sr., ruled the company and decreed that a suit impresses potential customers. Barksdale got on with the job, learning the sales route in Memphis, keeping his clients happy while figuring out who was who in the sales divisions of the sprawling company.

"I can remember the colors and the smell, the whole ambience of those new computers, those blue machines. It was like nothing I'd ever seen. It was marvelous. The computer was as big as this conference table." He could still rattle off from memory the IBM product line, circa 1965, more than two decades after leaving the company. ("The 1401, 1410, 1440, 1460, 360 model 20, 30, 40, 44, 50, 60, 65, and all the IBM tab equipment. I was first selling tab machines. You remember the punch-card machines? I mean, the 402 tabulator printer, 514 reproducer, 026, 602, 602A calculator. Computers then were expensive.")

He sold to banks and insurance companies and learned how to sell the idea that these things would solve real business problems. "You don't get to feed your family if you can't convince this guy he can do demand-deposit accounting on these things." And it wasn't enough just to make the sale, either. Sometimes Barksdale would have to set up as well. Night after night, going down to the Bank of Mississippi, to set up the new system. If he hadn't done it, the sale would have collapsed. Exercises like that teach you a lot about systems engineering.

It was worth learning the ins and outs of the machines, too, because IBM had a sticky sales plan: If, after using it for a while, a bank decided that it didn't like its mainframe, the salesman had to return his commission. "The worst was you'd pick up an account from another guy who had loaded them up with all this equipment, and then they'd get rid of some of it and you'd have to eat what the other guy had gotten paid for. That never seemed fair."

In 1972, both Barksdale's father and his oldest brother, Jack, died. By then, Barksdale had been promoted to a staff position in IBM's finance industry market, in Princeton, New Jersey. From there he could study the broad landscape of the mammoth company, which had grown from its humble beginnings at the turn of the century, as merely a division known as Computing-Tabulating-Recording in an odd conglomerate that also made cheese slicers and time clocks. Barksdale's own specialty at IBM, selling machines to the banking industry to automate data transactions, actually dated back to the days when the company had sold a data card sorter to the U.S. Census Department to tabulate statistics.

Barksdale was ready to listen that year when three of his friends came up from Memphis to persuade him that a great business opportunity existed in buying, selling, and leasing used IBM computers. The market was just emerging: smaller businesses who wanted to get into automation but didn't have the resources to go the top-drawer route. Barksdale returned to Memphis to help start the company, which was called Econocom, for "economic computers."

The new firm did well at first, but it was a tough business. The vagaries of depreciation every time IBM announced new models made it difficult to sell used computers. Over time, Cook Industries, a sprawling conglomerate with headquarters in Memphis, took over Econocom. Cook was into everything and seemed like yet another good opportunity for Barksdale. It had started out as a cotton company and diversified from agriculture into other areas, including insurance, real estate, chemicals, commodities, hardwood floors, and the termite-control business Terminix. Barksdale handled the data processing for the whole operation.

Then, in the late 1970s, Cook's fortunes fell after a major loss in the soybean futures market, and Cook had to sell off a number of its divisions. Barksdale's data-processing unit was hit hard; on a single Friday afternoon Barksdale had to lay off half of his 110 employees. It was awful; he began to search for a way to salvage what was left of the department.

One Sunday in church, he collared an old pal, Pete Willmott, who was then chief financial officer of a fledgling Memphis firm called Federal Express. The company's data-processing operation was in turmoil, attempting to convert from Burroughs machines to IBMs and trying to figure out how to automate the transportation unit so that computers could more efficiently handle routing. "Pete," Barksdale said, "you ought to buy our group." The idea was a natural: Barksdale's division was already outfitted with state-of-the-art IBM equipment and had the staff to run it. FedEx could buy the entire setup and sell data-processing services back to Cook. Better yet, the service fees could actually offset the cost of acquiring of the unit.

"That sounds great," Willmott said. "Why don't you get me and Fred a little proposal?" So Barksdale returned to his office and banged out a memo for Fred Smith, founder and chief executive of Federal Express, which he delivered later that afternoon. Smith immediately went for the deal, which was completed in a few days.

Ned Cook, the principal shareholder of Cook Industries, agreed to the sale, with one reservation. I don't want you to leave, he told Barksdale. Cook wanted him to stay and run the conglomerate's insurance business. That put the young man in a bit of a bind, since Federal Express had offered him the number-two job in systems. (It was a step down, but it came with a pile of stock options.)

Although Barksdale didn't know much about insurance, he decided to stay with Cook. He got his insurance license and took over the supervision of a series of agency brokerage underwriting operations in fifteen states.

Six months later, Willmott came back and repeated his request that Barksdale come aboard to run FedEx's data-processing operation. "You offered me that before, the number-two spot—"

FedEx would sweeten the deal. The job offer was now for the number-one guy, the MIS manager, a senior vice president. The company was prepared to throw in even more stock options. The offer was too good to refuse.

The entrepreneurial company turned out to be just right for the entrepreneurial Barksdale, who quickly rose through the ranks, eventually being promoted to chief operating officer of a company that employed ninety thousand people. With Barksdale playing coach, a smart young team of engineers built the largest single-image IBM Information Management System database in the world. "It was a huge, marvelous system of systems," Barksdale said. It did everything, from track airplanes, trucks, and vans to the parcels themselves. "I mean, some people could argue that FedEx is a systems company that happens to be in the transportation business."

Barksdale's team devised much of the computerized tracking and delivery system that enabled customers to call up, anytime, and find out where a package was and when it was scheduled to arrive. He helped the company get into private radio networks and all-digital dispatch systems that replaced voice dispatch. He was there when the first in-van computers were installed. When he took over as chief operating officer, sales were strong at about $1 billion; under his tenure they rocketed to a sensational $7.7 billion. Barksdale got a reputation for being an effective manager, able to cut through the layers of bureaucracy that can smother a company and ask the bottom-line question: Where's the money? Some of it, of course, was in his pocket. By the time he left FedEx, he was earning $531,576 a year and owned stock worth about $4 million.

It was obvious that Barksdale would never run Federal Express. It was strictly Fred Smith's company. So, when a headhunter called in 1991 about a job as chief operating officer of McCaw, up in Seattle—with a huge amount of equity that came with the job—he decided to move on again.

The Gorgeous Mosaic of Mosaic

Buccaneers—that was the first impression Barksdale had of the crew milling around the Mosaic offices. He thought they looked like a bunch of pirates going nine hundred miles an hour. He had *children* older than the gang that ran this four-month-old enterprise.

Inside the office was a sort of reception area and, from there, three choices—straight to Communication Director Rosanne Siino's spin-control room, the biggest room in the place, naturally; left to the business offices, where the only other guys with ties sat; or right to the area where the software engineers were in residence.

Engineering was a vast open space with a thirty-foot-square area partitioned off where the hackers themselves sat. It was where Chris Houck, the king of cool and high priest of the doomed, was likely to be padding around barefoot, carrying a huge mug full of water and looking dour, scowling the part of the antivisionary he claimed to be. Here a core group of a dozen scraggly kids in shorts might be playing armchair football (quarterbacking, receiving, and "running" without ever leaving their rolling office chairs) or racing their little homemade remote-controlled cars. More likely they'd be in their cubes, as if on a flagpole-sitting marathon, red eyes fixed on their computer screens, hammering away at code, feeling the pressure of tomorrow's deadlines.

Kuh-shunta! Kuh-shunta! Bizarre-sounding big sneezes erupted with the predictability of Ol' Faithful from a reedy kid in wire rims. That was Aleks Totic. Sometimes he telephoned his parents and talked to them in their native tongue. (The family was from Belgrade.) When Aleks was talking to the folks, Houck liked to lean over Jamie Zawinski's cubicle wall and say, sotto voce, "He's calling the mother ship again." Aleks was wacky enough to be from outer space. *Kuh-shunta!* You could hear his sneezes throughout the office. People worshiped him like he was Kramer on *Seinfeld*.

On a typical day in the early afternoon, emerging from under his cube, wrapped in a quilt and rubbing sleep from his eyes, would be Zawinski. He preferred to catnap under his desk rather than risk falling asleep on the hour-long drive home to Berkeley. He was so hardworking that once, after a thirty-nine-hour coding binge, he turned on MTV, and it was moving too fast for him to understand it. He was so hardworking he was blowing out his wrists with repetitive strain injury. Once, he covered his entire cubicle in duct tape. To keep his braids from unraveling, he wrapped the ends in multicolored telephone wire. Some people thought he looked like Mario Van Peebles in *Highlander III*.

Catty-corner from Zawinski sat Lou Montulli, banging on the networking component of the current browser. Everyone depended on his work, which made him a bit of a friction spot. An important Montulli development: He had just kissed the boss's daughter, Kathy Clark, for the first (but not the last) time. Although he and Zawinski were pretty tight, they bickered like brothers on an interminable car ride.

Off in a corner by himself, in stark contrast to the colorful eccentricity that permeated the rest of the room, sat brown-haired, neatly dressed, even-tempered Rob McCool. Since his twin brother Mike telecommuted from back home in Illinois, the two of them didn't get to sit next to each other to talk over the various bits of code they were tweaking. That might have been a drawback for another pair whose work was so closely intertwined, but as Marc once observed, with the McCools it didn't seem to matter. They communicated in a secret language of their own, composed not so much of words as of habit.

There was an empty cubicle, too, where Eric Bina sat when he came to the office every month or so. The rest of the time he telecommuted from Illinois. Bina was hard at work designing the software's layout engine, which took the hypertext markup language (HTML) of the Web and turned it into something that displayed on the screen. He was trying to make the layout engine cross-platform a task everyone else thought was impossible—which, naturally, was why Bina was doing it.

They're pirates! Barksdale thought again. They reminded him of wild adventurers out on the high seas—or, at least, in a sea of cubicles—careening around, shrill with excitement, climbing the walls, knives clenched in their teeth.

Andreessen appeared, figured out who Barksdale was, and stuck out his paw. He offered to show Barksdale a demo of Mozilla. Barksdale had seen him in photos before and remembered a shot from *Fortune* that showed the Mosaic team, with him jumping around in the picture. In person, Andreessen looked even better: affable, engaged, quick-witted. Clark bounded over, greeted Barksdale, pumped his hand. And they talked, these three, about strategy and plans, and opportunities and markets, and what Barksdale's role might be.

After Andreessen showed him the demo video and they talked some more, and he toured the place again and asked still more questions, the buccaneers took him out for supper. Something felt very right about the enterprise, but a part of him remained unconvinced. What did he need this for?

When Barksdale got back on the plane, he still wasn't sure whether he wanted the job. His first impression of the company— *Listen to this, Sally, this is a clever idea*—was dead-on accurate. But he needed to know more.

CHAPTER NINE

Dancing with Mozilla

On Castro Street, line after line of code started to flow, like minor tributaries in search of a river. By August, the programmers had strung together big sections of the new browser. From what they could tell, the thing appeared to work—at least, in the relatively stable, homogeneous environment of the office.

But the Net is anything but homogeneous. The recent spontaneous combustion of growth on the Internet will forever serve as a monument to the rightness of plug and play open standards. All you need to cruise the infobahn is a computer (any computer) and a modem, and that's the lowest common denominator. At the upper reaches, the same Net accommodates big business mainframes and academic supercomputers. If you want to create software that's truly useful for the Internet, then, you must be able to anticipate every conceivable permutation of hardware, software, and even connection speed.

Which is to say: you have to test for bugs.

Will Mozilla work on a Quadra 800 running system 6.0 with 5 megs of RAM on a T1? What about an IBM running 3.1 with eight megs on a 14.4 modem? Or an Indigo running Irix 5.3?

It was one thing to know that it worked fine when they tried it at their own desks; it was quite another to be sure the code would work reliably, time after time, after it was loaded onto a million idiosyncratic computers around the world. Back when they had created the original Mosaic browser at NCSA, no one had worried about quality assurance. After all, they had been distributing it for free over the Net as an experiment. All that had changed.

In a big corporation, there would be a quality assurance department, staffed by expert testers who knew how to sniff around inside programs to find bugs and white-knuckle glitches. But Mosaic Communications didn't employ a single QA specialist.

It hadn't been a problem during its first few months of existence. Why bother to hire people to test product before you've even *got* a product? But now there was suddenly—well, if not a product, exactly, at least some big preliminary chunks of one.

And beyond the arcane system-centric questions, they had bigger fears. Did their stuff really *work*? If they passed a URL string into Lou Montulli's network library, would it interpret the information correctly? Would Aleks's Macintosh version deliver the same response to a command as Mittelhauser's Windows version, but in a way that would make sense to a Mac user? Would Bina's layout engine work across platforms?

Testers would give the programmers something they had needed ever since the project began: peace of mind. If the testers didn't find problems, or if they found only eensy problems that could be solved quickly, the team would get a huge morale boost just when it needed it most. Perhaps what they were hacking on wasn't doomed to fail. It might even work.

Their fear was understandable. Too many Silicon Valley startups had crashed and burned because the emperor was wearing no clothes. It was a Valley of Death for all those who toiled long and hard to create something that didn't work—or, at least, not well enough for prime time. In the start-up segment of the high-tech business, among companies trying to create entirely new products and even industries, you get only one shot. The public is unforgiving, even hostile toward buggy first releases. Anyone remember the Newton, which was supposed to be Apple's next big thing? The handwriting-recognition fiasco alone was Doonesbury fodder, enough to torpedo years of smart people's hard work. Or its competitor, the Eo? Or General Magic and its revolutionary operating system? Or Slate? Or—on and on and on, enough good ideas that didn't catch on to fill a Wal-Mart from hell.

Sometimes Chris Houck would stand at the window in the early morning, after almost everyone else had gone home, watching the sun rise over the hills of the East Bay, and wonder just what he was doing. Management kept telling him the new browser was going to be a wipe-out success, but he never knew if they were saying that because they believed it or just so everyone wouldn't give up and walk away. Testers would help provide some kind of baseline, outside the distortion field appraisal.

The Monkey Testers

Hiring testers suddenly became another one of those problems for Paquin to solve. All Mosaic needed was a product line that *worked*. He needed some testers, fast.

Since he didn't have the money to go off and hire an entire QA group from the ground up, he printed up a little flyer: MAKE $$$ SURFING THE WEB! The job paid $10 an hour. Then he got in the van and drove around to all the local junior colleges, and to Stanford, and he tacked the flyer up on bulletin boards. A lot of students responded. Where else could you make money by having fun? Surfing the Web sounded like a much easier way to make a buck than, say, donating a pint of blood.

All the students had to do to be Mosaic testers was know enough about how computers worked to be able to run the new version of the Mosaic program on a machine for a few hours a day, keeping track of what caused it to crash and which features weren't working the way they should. All they needed to do the job was curiosity about what was out there on the Web, and a computer—

Oh, computers.

Paquin phoned a couple of hardware manufacturers and told them he needed some machines, quick, so please send him seven computers, fast, really fast—and by the way, make each one totally different from the others. He wanted each configured in an idiosyncratic way—with different graphics cards, different ethernet cards, different processors—so his—uh, his *QA department* could test Mosaic on the widest possible spectrum of equipment.

The manufacturers said, Sure, we can do that, and within days Paquin had a bunch of big cardboard boxes sitting in the office. Inside the boxes were two new Macs (flavor A and flavor B) and a bunch of different Windows machines, 486es and 386es, no two with the same components. So then all Paquin had to do was to set the machines up in the QA lab—

Oh, a lab.

There was a room where all the empty equipment boxes were kept—you never knew when you were going to have to pack up and send back a faulty monitor—so Paquin said, *get those cardboard boxes out of here fast*. He never even knew where they went, he was so focused on setting up a couple of those long tables with the fold-up legs along the walls. Then he got in the van and went out to buy some power strips and lightbulbs and a network hub. He put the new computers on the tables. Then he hooked up the ethernet cable to the hub and farmed it out to the new computers.

Suddenly, Mosaic had a QA lab, full of new equipment, staffed by students and other part-timers. One of them was Paul Davis, a freelance consultant whose background included Macintosh development and training for a number of small businesses. He had worked, previously, at the Whole Earth Catalog, where his expertise had been in massaging and crunching databases.

Being a Whole Earth guy, whenever Davis came into the QA lab he tried to grab one of the Mac machines. The basic idea was to do "monkey testing." Typically, there would be four or five testers crammed into the six-by-ten room. Davis and the others didn't follow any real, structured test methodology. They didn't have time to build test cases to apply systematically to the code. Instead, they tried to figure out weird ways—combinations of commands and keystrokes—to cause their boxes to crash.

Of course, testers always had to leave bread crumbs behind, so if something did go wrong, if they did find a bug, they could document it. That way they could call in the programmer who had written that piece of code to demonstrate how a problem was manifesting itself.

Occasionally the word would get passed along that the testers should concentrate on a particular new feature, but the rest of the time everybody sort of just monkey-tested the code, banging on it insistently, with the general goal of covering as much of the product as possible.

The more methodical testers would first make sure all the menu items worked and then browse the Web for a while: just read newsgroups or point-and-click from URL to URL. The testers would find sites that might strain the capacity of the browser. For instance, to test how well the browser could handle large graphic files, the testers would click to a site that some beer fan had created with a couple of hundred graphic images of beer labels on one page. And then hit RE-LOAD. And again.

They would zero in on cool sites that offered new and unusual ways of interacting with data. A Web page called "Blue Dog Can Count" was the place to go to test how well the browser was handling interactive sites with "forms" for users to fill in. The page had a simple HTML form, where you would type in a number and click. Say you clicked "4." The page would disappear for a bit, then return, and—voilà!—the blue dog would bark out the number. "Woof! Woof! Woof! Woof!"

A few insanely difficult hardware-dependent bugs surfaced. For some reason, the browser crashed on some Sun operating system 4.1.3 systems, but not others. It didn't crash Zawinski's, for instance. Another evil genie caused scrolling text to fail on the OpenWindows X server.

Davis ran across problems like images that wouldn't draw. But for the most part, the code was suprisingly usable. Davis was amazed that the browser worked as well as it did.

One day after the QA lab was up and running, Zawinski noticed a headline in the newspaper: A MONKEY CAN DO TEN TIMES THE WORK OF A HUMAN. Pleased, he enlarged it on the photocopier and hung it outside the lab. That kind of annoyed one of the QA leads, who was known as the "chimp wrangler."

The testers developed strategies for testing the code. Over time, they put all the strategies into a kind of uniform set of instructions that QA monkey testers could follow forever and always. They called the little monkey-testing manual "Dancing with Mozilla."

Paying Customers

One day in August, Zawinski actually left the office at about 8 A.M. to take a much-needed shower and grab a nap at his home in Berkeley. He planned to be back by midafternoon. Mosaic Communications (All Praise the Company! as the doomed had taken to saying) could live without him for seven hours. How much could happen while he was gone?

A lot, actually, because Zawinski was living in the parallel universe of Silicon Valley start-ups. Maybe the buildings that lined the streets looked normal enough from the outside, all glass and new fake stucco and shiny company nameplates reflecting the sun from the windshields of the new I-got-a-real-paying-job Miatas in the parking lots. But step inside the door of one of those buildings, say the building at 650 Castro, and face a surreal world where . . . a company with no product was about to land its first paying customer on the strength of vaporware!

By the time he got back, everyone was assembling for a major announcement at a company-wide meeting. Usually, these were the kinds of sessions where Marc or Jim Clark would be *on,* laying out the company line and trying to whip up enthusiasm and morale. At such times, invariably, Zawinski or someone else would duly and dully quote the hypnotized storm trooper in *Star Wars:* "These are not the 'droids we're looking for." But this was the real shit. Today, management announced that Digital Equipment Corporation wanted to license six hundred thousand copies of Mozilla! They planned to load the browser onto its new line of Unix servers. The sales and marketing people laid out the deal. They actually sounded like they knew what they were doing, which was a new one for Zawinski.

Marc Matoza was Mosaic's point man. At forty-six, a self-described "old dog" of a salesman and ex-engineer, Matoza was a veteran of three other start-ups when he signed on as the company's very first salesman.

Matoza explained to the kids why the DEC deal would be such an important milestone. The venerable company was one of the big guys in the computer world, an "original equipment manufacturer," or OEM, in trade-journal parlance. In the high-tech game, the best way for a start-up to inch its way into a crowded market was to close an OEM deal. Convince one major computer manufacturer to endorse your technology, and pretty soon you'd create a snowball effect in the Valley. Of course, no hardware guy really cares about selling *your* puny software program, he just wants to move his iron. Computer makers are always looking for little software add-ons to differentiate their machine from the competition.

A deal like this could pay off big for a teensy player like Mosaic, which had its own sales and marketing force of—oh, about three people, counting Matoza. But if the deal went through, Mosaic could leverage the power of Digital's massive worldwide sales and marketing effort, thousands of experienced salespeople suddenly out on the street touting Mozilla as a part of their server package.

Matoza had recently met with the DEC folks at an Internet networking show in Atlanta, where he got the impression they wanted to make the deal happen fast. The Unix machine vendors had suddenly gotten religion and decided the Internet was real. Competitors

Sun Microsystems and SGI were about to introduce a new generation of servers as well, and everyone wanted to ship with web-server software. Sun and SGI were starting to sniff around Mozilla too. Divining which way the parade was headed, the DEC people jumped to lead it. They told Matoza they figured if they could be out first, they'd garner a bigger market share for Internet servers than Sun or SGI.

Of course, Matoza's immediate problem was that he had nothing but expectations to sell. He couldn't tell DEC for sure what the product was, much less what the price was. Other than that, "It was a great sale, easy sale," he joked.

Any deal was good news; it was no secret that Mosaic was burning cash at an astonishing rate. On the other hand, it was bad news because there was no, no, no way they'd ever finish the product, ever fix the bugs the monkey team had outed, ever get it out the door. They all knew this in their souls, utterly and totally, and it sickened them.

Doomed, they went back to work with renewed vigor.

Meanwhile, Matoza was working another, totally different kind of deal at the same time. Media giant Knight-Ridder, which owned one of the more important national newspapers in America, had become convinced that the Internet represented the future of publishing—and, better yet, that Mosaic represented the future of the Net.

Knight-Ridder was on board, ready to develop an on-line version of its *San Jose Mercury-News* for publication on the Web. After a number of meetings, Matoza and Knight-Ridder came to an agreement: Knight-Ridder would buy a license, for a grand total of $50,000, that would entitle the media company to one copy of everything Mosaic would make in the next year.

Knight-Ridder would end up publishing the *Mercury-News* online, using a beta version of the Mozilla server software. Knight-Ridder also agreed to pay thirty-five cents a copy for each version of the Mozilla client. Matoza shook hands and sealed the deal. By the end of August,

Mosaic had a paying customer. It wasn't much, but you could tack the check up over the server as a symbol: They were really in business.

Business Is Personal

Faster, faster. Time was running out!

The engineers had cobbled together enough pieces of code to run rough demos of their new browser. It was time to see how well it did against the market leader, Brand X: Mosaic Classic.

Mittelhauser brought a stopwatch to work. He lined up two PCs, side by side, and configured one to run the challenger: his latest version of Mozilla for Windows. On the other machine was the reigning heavyweight champion of the browser world, the Windows version of Mosaic, a program he had coauthored as a student, a program the University of Illinois still owned and had licensed to nearly a dozen software companies. While others might have argued that the NCSA Bina-Andreessen Unix version was the land-speed champion, Mittelhauser believed in his own Windows hack. He had once sweated blood over it. Now he wanted more than anything in life to kill the sucker, to blow its doors off on the infobahn.

"Press LOAD," Mittelhauser said, clicking the START button on his stopwatch. The two PCs faced off, simultaneously loading the browsers, racing to see which iteration could call up a Web page first.

Mittelhauser watched in amazement and glee as one of the computer screens quickly began to fill with the unmistakable outline of a Web page, the comforting blue type of a hyperlink—and, in the corner, a little M with tiles around it, the proud logo of Mosaic Communications.

Mozilla ruled! He glanced at his stopwatch. Mozilla was running ten times faster.

"We killed them on the faster issue," Mittelhauser announced to anyone who was within earshot. "We killed them."

The others wandered over to inspect the evidence, briefly and uncharacteristically hopeful as they squinted at the two computer screens. By now both browsers had displayed Web pages. Oh, look how ugly it looks in Mosaic, no rich text formatting—and how pretty in Mozilla! We're going to be a lot more powerful, too!

In truth they were killing their firstborn—and it was just business. It was survival of the fittest. They felt they had the right. After all, hadn't the original Mosaic code burst forth from their minds during a frenzied season of mind-bending creativity in the gloomy basement of the university's Oil Chemistry Building all those months ago?

If Mozilla failed to supplant Mosaic in the marketplace, then they would be out of work. They would be failures. It was just business.

Except that Don Corleone had it right: All business is personal.

Not so secretly, the NCSA expatriates still nursed grudges against their former employers. They muscled me aside! They thought we were just a bunch of interchangeable student programmers! They acted like they weren't even going to offer me a job when I graduated!

What they didn't realize, during those first months on Castro Street, was that NCSA felt just as betrayed by the kids it had nurtured. It became pretty clear, though, by the end of the summer. The University of Illinois began to fight back. Business is personal: In 1994, the university licensed the original Mosaic code and the right to use the Mosaic name to a number of companies. By the end of the summer, Spyglass had become the exclusive licensee, in a deal potentially worth millions of dollars, both to the university and to Spyglass. Clearly, the name Mosaic had huge economic value to the university.

But by then NCSA officials believed that Jim Clark had diluted the power of the Mosaic brand by giving his start-up the same name as the university's property. Larry Smarr remembered hearing complaints from a number of the Mosaic licensees who "called up the university and said, 'Hey, you can't charge us, but not them, for using the name.'"

The university's lawyers investigated the situation. They feared that if they failed to defend the Mosaic code as proprietary intellectual property, it would set a bad precedent. "If you don't defend your intellectual property on something as big as Mosaic, how can you claim intellectual property on anything else?" Smarr said later. "The university would cease to have credibility."

NCSA contacted Clark to ask him if he wanted to license the Mosaic name. After he declined, the university poured on the heat. There were rumblings about the possibility of a lawsuit. It was a nasty subtheme—on top of Will-we-get-our-code-out-the-door-on-time?and Will-it-work?—that gave managers like Paquin the sweats.

Barksdale's First Steps

Doerr and Clark stayed in close contact with Barksdale as the AT&T deal closed in the early fall of 1994. Barksdale had agreed to stay on at AT&T through the end of the year to make the transition smoother for both companies. But after that? All bets were off. To give Barksdale more information about Mosaic Communications without forcing him to commit to taking the job, Doerr and Clark offered him a seat on the company's board of directors. As one of the council of corporate elders, Barksdale would get the down-and-dirty he needed. Barksdale agreed.

From his fence-post seat, what Barksdale saw was both exciting—and deeply disturbing. The company was quickly approaching a day of reckoning. The burn rate—the rate at which it was spending Clark and Doerr's $9 million in seed money—threatened to consume Mosaic Communications within the next four months. (Your typical Silicon Valley start-up combusts roughly $1 million a month; in this instance, Mosaic was typical.)

But where would revenue come from? With Andreessen's plan to give away the product for free, the company couldn't expect much money to come in from the client-side application that home and business users would use to scan the Net. Of course, Mosaic Communications already was showing early success in licensing the browser to businesses—Clark was close to closing a major deal with telecommunications giant MCI—but the company would need many more large customers like that to show a profit. The real money-making opportunity could come from the server side—selling companies (like Knight-Ridder) the code to create their own websites and serve them to the public. That would mean broadening the product base in two ways. First, Mosaic Communications would have to inject new features into subsequent generations of the browser to appeal to businesses. Second, the company would have to expand the product line, creating a suite of software applications to market to businesses.

Would it work? Remember, this was the Internet, a kind of public welfare system for geeks and academics who had demonstrated a real animosity toward paying for anything. How many paying customers were out there? Even Doerr would admit that the market question—would anyone pay for the product?—was the most dangerous variable in any start-up. As he once told *The New Yorker,* it was the fundamental question, the acid test: "Will the dogs eat the dog food?" Of all the risks—technical (Will the thing work?), financing (Can we raise the money to keep the enterprise going?), and people (Will the brain trust stick around?)—the market risk was the most gut-wrenching because it became apparent only after all those millions of dollars had been invested. Before they could answer the market question, Mosaic Communications would need to raise more short-term operating capital—immediately.

Then there was the threat of a lawsuit. Shortly after Barksdale visited Mountain View, the National Center for Supercomputing Applications began to make noises about suing Mosaic Communications, charging that the company was illegally using the Mosaic name.

The tension from the legal battle was palpable since Andreessen and his compatriots maintained that their alma mater had gotten it backwards. The way they saw it, the college kids created Mosaic against all odds and figured out its awesome commercial potential—despite the school's bureaucratic meddlings. It was a mess.

All this was playing out against a backdrop of intense competition to get the browser out the door by the end of the year. Meanwhile, a number of other companies had licensed the original NCSA code and were racing to release commercial versions. Spry was working on Air Mosaic. Spyglass was developing Enhanced Mosaic. Netcom had Netcruiser. Even Apple had announced plans to include a web browser in future versions of the company's basic software.

And say Mosaic Communications did get the thing out the door. And say it even worked. And imagine, just for a wild, carefree moment, that companies and newspapers and magazines and hospitals and banks and who-knows-who-all would actually pay real money to buy and install Mosaic's server code. That there's a real market for the thing.

As Barksdale could see clearly, that would be the moment Bill Gates would notice Mosaic Communications. And after that? Who would dominate the Internet in the long run? Would Barksdale bet against Microsoft? Would you?

The Big Night
(October 1994 Beta Launch)

They were doomed, unavoidably and tragically doomed. They would die a slow death of a billion clicks. They would be remembered, if they were remembered at all, as losers. Their beta would not launch on time; it wouldn't launch at all. If it did, they would look like idiots in front of thousands of their peers. Their code was full of bugs. Soon enough, they would be unemployable. People would laugh at them and jab them with sticks. It was what they deserved.

Mosaic Communications was at last releasing Mozilla publicly. Not on CD-ROMs, packed in boxes trucked to CompUSA—nothing so industrial-age as that. Instead, for the first time, a major piece of commercial software would be distributed over the Net, in its native ethereal zeros and ones, unconstrained by space. And Andreessen had prevailed: The code would be free.

While what was going out the door (out the server port?) was technically called a beta release—Mozilla version 0.9, for anyone keeping score—the events unfolding were far more important than a last dress rehearsal.

Zawinski was doing what he did best: finishing the builds on six different Unix platforms, finding the show-stopping bugs, and squashing them. At 11 A.M., he figured it would take him a half hour to get his work over to an ftp server (a computer connected to the Net that was publicly accessible to anyone who wanted to download the server's programs, text files, whatever). At 1:50 P.M., Zawinski handed off the code to testers and promptly fell asleep.

Screams of horror and disbelief awakened him at 2 P.M. The building's power had conked out. Zawinski, too exhausted by the past week's push to even care anymore, went back to sleep. The beta release would be postponed a few more hours.

The doomed started to trickle into the conference room late in the evening. They were zombified from weeks of little sleep that had given way to days of none. If Andreessen had been a pinch more charismatic and of dubious spirituality, he could have had them all out hawking roses by the roadside and drumming up recruits for the First Church of Mozilla by now.

Someone hooked a wide-screen TV into one of the Indigo workstations so they could watch the ftp logs scroll by. That way they could see if anyone was actually downloading the program when it was at last released at midnight. John Giannandrea, a charter member of the doomed, wrote a little script that caused the Indy, through a pair of stereo speakers, to produce different sounds for certain events. A cannon shot signaled all downloads. A bell rang for a Unix download. A glass shattered for any Macintosh version. And downloads of the Windows version would cause a stentorian frog croak.

At midnight, Mozilla was uploaded to the ftp server, and before Andreessen or Paquin could hit Usenet, that commons of the Net, to post an announcement to the newsgroup called comp.infosystems.www.browsers to tell the public that Mozilla was available, thousands of the faithful converged on the ftp server.

They sat in unrepentant awe. A person in Japan was the first customer served. They could only deduce this later from the logs because now people from all over the world were trying to grab the thing. Fifty of them at once (thankfully, fifty is all the server would allow at one time, otherwise the computer itself might crash from the load). A user from England—"sprocter" according to his user name— came onto the server and, apparently confused by all the names in the ftp directory, left without downloading Mozilla . . . then he came back! Someone urged him on. "Go, Sprocter!" "Sprocter! Sprocter!" they chanted, begging him to download the file.

Cannons fired! Glasses smashed! Bells jangled! Frogs croaked. A cacophonous, riotous tintinnabulation rippled across the room. It sounded like a pirate ship trying to commandeer a pet shop. And in the darkened conference room, sleep-dumb and humbled by hard work, celebrating with a few beers, the doomed watched their hard work fly off into the night on the Net.

Zawinski could hardly believe it. He checked a few Usenet groups to see if anyone was posting any reaction to Mozilla 0.9. They were. In EXCLAMATORY CAPS!! MOZILLA was AWE-SOME!!!!!! He looked down at his throbbing arms. The word *void* was clearly spelled out on the inside of his right wrist. He vaguely recalled going to a concert and getting the generic hand stamp a week ago. After the show, he immediately returned to work. He'd been there ever since.

Building a Better Mousetrap

Given the legal skirmishing between NCSA and Mosaic Communications, Clark wanted to make sure the university could never claim that his company had stolen any of the original Mosaic code. He hired independent auditors in Oregon, who compared the Mozilla code to Mosaic, line by line. Clark was sure Mozilla was written from scratch and bore no resemblance to the university's code. Still, "The first time the guy in Oregon called back and said, 'Oh, yeah, your stuff isn't anything like theirs,' you wanted to wipe the sweat off your brow and say 'Good!'" Paquin remembered.

But the university and Spyglass continued to keep the heat on Mosaic Communications after the beta release. The public accusations were starting to have an impact—Matoza told Clark that the folks from Digital were getting nervous about closing the OEM deal—so Clark flew out to Illinois to meet at Chicago's O'Hare Airport with Spyglass CEO Doug Colbeth.

"We accused them of stealing the name," Colbeth said. "Jim knew what he was doing. He knew he would use the name short-term. His thing all along was, 'I'm going to use it until I'm ready to crush it.'"

Clark agreed to settle the dispute out of court, offering the university fifty thousand shares of stock in his company. The university turned that down. Cash was the only settlement the university would accept. It was expensive for Mosaic Communications. "Onerous," recalled Rosanne Siino. "But it was time to get on with business." Although financial terms of the December 1994 settlement were not disclosed under a confidentiality clause, James Wallace reported in his 1997 book *Overdrive* that Clark agreed to pay the university $2.2 million in damages, plus up to $1.4 million in additional payments, depending on licensing deals that materialized in the future. In the end, Clark ended up paying the university $2.7 million, which the school split with Spyglass.

"In hindsight, the price we paid to get the settlement done was well worth it," Siino remembered, "because now it was the end of the year, and the products could go out and they were *ours*."

Another thing Clark agreed to was giving up the Mosaic moniker. That caused a last-minute scramble to rename the company. At first, Siino wanted to come up with an *M* name to salvage the coporate logo. The little *M* with the tiles around it had cost thousands of dollars. Various *M* names were duly considered and rejected. MetroCom? What did that stand for?

Then someone recalled the name Greg Sands, a manager, had thought up a few months ago: Netscape. His idea was that just as a landscape allows you to see everything on the horizon, a browser allows you to see everything on the Net. Not a landscape, not a seascape—a netscape. Clark liked it. All that remained was for Rosanne Siino to scramble to change the company's entire identity—in the few days left before Comdex.

Comdex, in November, is the world's biggest annual computer trade show, attracting a zillion vendors and twice as many press people. It was the yearly cotillion, a place for new companies to eye the competition—and to be seen by everyone else. Siino knew, as always, the start-up would make good copy. What better place to announce the name change and generate more buzz for the upcoming end-of-year commercial release of the browser?

But there was no time to replace the little *M* with an *N* on the browser. At least, Siino figured, she could get the signs for the trade-show booth changed. She also had new T-shirts printed up. And of course she issued a press release, a royal decree announcing that henceforth and for all time the company formerly known as Mosaic had a new name: Netscape Communications.

The Night of the Flying Chairs

One day, Aleks and Zawinski were talking and Aleks told him that, for the record, he thought Jamie had been picking on Lou Montulli too much. And it was true, the two of them were bickering even more than usual. But just to clear the air, Zawinski fired off a message to the engineering group:

> *Aleks just said that he thinks I've been picking on Lou a lot*
> *lately. Well, I just want to make it clear that I think you're all*

*idiots, and I hate each and every one of you. I don't mean to
single anyone out.*

Love,

Jamie

The short days of November clicked by at hyperspeed. Everyone at the company had been working ungodly hours—for so long
that the place resembled an airport. People slept wherever they could
find space. The engineers had streamlined their plans for Netscape
1.0—they had been told in no uncertain terms to finish only the essential features, just *finish;* there was plenty of time to add bells and
whistles in the next version—because Clark had promised mighty MCI
Communications that a commercial version of the software would be
ready by the end of the year. The $12 billion telecommunications
company had agreed to partner with Netscape, to distribute the
browser to customers on its new internetMCI service, scheduled to
launch in January 1995. MCI wanted both the client browser and the
Netsite Commerce Server that the McCool brothers were writing, to
ensure on-line security for customers browsing in the marketplaceMCI
on-line shopping mall. The plan called for Netscape's Secure Sockets
Layer to guarantee MCI's customers safe credit-card transactions if
they bought something from the mall's stores.

The MCI deal loomed big. Signing a major customer like
MCI was a milestone—if only they could get the code out the door
on time. No wonder the patience had run out weeks ago. It was
Edge City around here now, raw egos bumping against raw egos.

A few days before December 15, the ship date of the commercial version of Netscape 1.0, Zawinski and Montulli were at each
other's throats again. The matter at hand was some code Montulli
had written that Zawinski had publicly disparaged. Instead of sending
a private E-mail, Zawinski sent a message to the engineers' group,
complaining.

Montulli, who usually resisted flame bait, had been working for thirty-six hours straight (like everyone else) and decided to vent a bit. Besides, he looked at the code and it seemed fine to him. So he fired off a message to Jamie—copied to the engineering group, of course—that said, "If you bothered to look at your own code you would know *you* are screwing up. I feel sorry for the people who have to work with it."

Later, he realized that was the wrong thing to do. Zawinski was, after all, working on something like eleven different Unix builds and was frantically trying to rout the various subtle bugs he was finding. "I shouldn't have done it. But I had a lot of endorphins going through me at the time," Montulli said later. At the time, he knew his little flame would spark a massive war of words, and frankly he relished the idea. In anticipation of the firestorm, he sneaked over to Garrett Blyth's cube ("Read your E-mail! Read your mail!"), which was one away from Zawinski's. He wanted to be at ground zero when the explosion occurred.

Sure enough, he heard furious typing coming from Zawinski's keyboard. ("Oh, boy, oh, boy, this is going to be a good one.") It sounded like the *\$#*&^%**! in cartoon curses. Let the flame war begin!

But then came a noise that neither he nor anyone else expected, a sound that made their spleens contract and blood shoot out to all appendages in the classic fight-or-flight response: the sound of Zawinski's Sun rebooting.

His machine had crashed. At the worst possible time. Fightus interruptus.

Zawinski had been piqued and baited, and his one method of retribution—his tongue—had been electronically severed.

"What!? What The Fuck!?" erupted from Zawinski's cube, followed almost at once by the lightning and thunder of a huge wall of empty Coke cans flying from his desk into the aisle. Zawinski leapt from his seat and kicked the wall; then he threw his desk chair. Eric Bina came around the corner to see what all the commotion was about and almost got hit. He jumped back as the chair flew past and dented the wall. (A number of engineers noted later that Zawinski would have done the whole *company* great damage if he'd hit Bina.) Zawinski grabbed his coat and left.

He didn't come back for two weeks.

Navigator über Alles

December was the bleakest month. The company's seed money was all but gone, and until they could ship a product, no new money would come in. Clark bit the bullet and laid off fifteen people—part-timers and freelancers for the most part.

But then, just before Christmas, Netscape shipped the first commercial version of its browser, called Navigator. The software was compatible with Windows, Macintosh, and Unix machines running X Windows. Just before Christmas, an all-hands meeting was held in the company cafeteria. Marc Andreessen entered, tentative on Rollerblades, resplendent in spandex shorts. Then he ate a gag reflex–inspiring mouthful of tofu, to great doomed cheers. Netscape's Navigator, shipped on December 15, 1994, was a breakaway smash hit, arguably the first "killer application" to conquer the Net.

On Castro Street, everyone watched the daily logs, which showed how many people were downloading Navigator. But a more interesting statistic came from watching the characteristics of the users who hit Netscape's home page, the front door to the site. At first, virtually everyone who visited used the NCSA Mosaic browser or one of its offshoots. More quickly than anyone could have imagined, a great conversion occurred—and most users were running Navigator.

The unscientific sample turned out to be no fluke. Navigator was destined to become one of the most wildly popular software programs ever unleashed on the planet. A stunningly broad cross-section of users anointed Netscape Navigator 1.0 as universally cool. Its applicability was as obvious to a first-time home user as it was to a computer-savvy college student, business person, or academic re-searcher. Within four months of Navigator's launch, more than 75 percent of the people on the Net would use the Netscape browser. The former market leader, NCSA Mosaic, would claim an ever-dwindling 5 percent. An astounding six million copies of Navigator would be downloaded. "If we had been six months later, we would have been lost in the noise," Clark later told a reporter for the magazine *Fast Company*.

And that was just the free stuff, the razors—or the *temporarily* free stuff. In a confusing turn of events, people who downloaded Navigator were told that their copy could be used for three months, after which they were expected to pay. If they didn't pay, they'd be violating the license agreement. Would anyone really pay? Surprisingly, many of them did. Not surprisingly, though, lots of them didn't—and bitched miserably about the company's about-face. Still, within the first two weeks of the 1.0 release, the company sold $365,000's worth of product. Server code was selling briskly for $1,500 a unit; a version designed for secure electronic commerce, including credit-card transactions, would soon be selling for $5,000 a pop. Even Netscape T-shirts, complete with a lizardlike Mozilla monster, were moving like iced beer at a ball game. Netscape was selling them from an on-line "company store."

In a few short months Netscape had changed the way the software industry did business. Its speed set a pace that was even faster than the eighteen-month cycle dictated by the steadily evolving microchip, forcing the rest of the industry to adopt some of the same business strategies that Netscape pioneered.

Taken singly, each of Netscape's strategic innovations had been relatively simple, borrowed in part from the lessons that Andreessen had learned from his days at NCSA. The difference was that the methods of academia were now being applied to a commercial product. The first radical idea Andreessen had pushed—to give away Navigator for free—had been a logical outgrowth of his experience in Illinois, where he had watched as a grass-roots groundswell embraced the original Mosaic's giveaway. His second suggestion, that the company use the Net to distribute the browser, fast and cheap, instead of wasting untold amounts of time and money to create a retail product in a pretty box, had been just as logical. A third smart move had been to release in beta form code that was raw, bug-ridden, early-early-early, more unformed than any commercial beta previously released.

Overall, Andreessen's strategy paid off, popularizing the new browser. Netscape began to wrest users away from competitors weeks before the team in Mountain View even had a finished product on the market. The public beta also allowed the cash-strapped start-up to harness the intellect of millions of users around the world, who happily sent back—for free!—bug reports that became an instant ad hoc addition to the work the monkey testers were performing in Netscape's tiny quality-assurance lab.

For a moment, at least, even the doomed were optimistic. During all-hands meetings with Clark and Andreessen, the programmers allowed themselves to play the What If game: What if we do really, really well? What if we sell $1 million's worth of server code during the first quarter of 1995?

In other ways, the commercial release felt anticlimactic. Compared to the night in October when the public beta was unleashed— *Cannon boom! Bell! Whistle!*—the commercial version of the code entered the world with little drama. Weeks earlier, Paquin had instituted a code freeze, pulling the plug on any ideas they had about cramming in just-one-more-feature-please-it-would-be-so-cool, so the programmers had been concentrating instead on the relatively low-stress business of fixing bugs.

When Netscape Communications uploaded the commercial code to its ftp site, the predominant emotion at 650 Castro Street was relief.

Paquin went on vacation with his family. Everybody else went home for a few days. To sleep. And to wait to hear whether Barksdale would sign on with the company.

CHAPTER TEN

Owning the Boardwalk
and Park Place

What the Netscape team didn't know yet was that by the end of 1994 time had run out. The irony of the situation was that the very success of Navigator 1.0 had made it harder for Netscape to survive. That's because the enormous popularity of Netscape's browser proved to Bill Gates and his top deputies that the Internet had the kind of mass appeal that could form the basis for a lucrative new software market.

No one outside Microsoft was aware of it yet, but Bill Gates's mammoth company had begun to gear up to conquer the Internet— and to trounce competitors. Up in Redmond, momentum for creating a browser had been building quietly for months, sparked by a Microsoft Systems Group plan for including a concept called Integrated Net Browsing in the Windows 95 operating system.

Microsoft's ideological shift may have seemed slow by the go-go start-up standards that prevailed in Silicon Valley. But consider the fact that the federal government had been diverting much of Microsoft's energies since 1990 with a grueling antitrust investigation, and consider that the company's CEO, Bill Gates, had been sidetracked for months by the hype of interactive TV. Despite those distractions, Microsoft was still evolving. Even back in 1993, when Gates was meeting with executives at Time Warner and TCI to discuss how Microsoft might provide software for the coming age of fiber-optic networks and video on demand, some of his brightest deputies were already discovering the power of the Internet.

By the time Barksdale had gone on his fact-finding mission to Mountain View in August of 1994, one of Gates's senior engineers had been assigned to design a browser for Microsoft. A few months later, around the time that Netscape released its 1.0 browser, Microsoft had struck a deal to license the commercial version of the Mosaic code from Spyglass.

At what moment did Netscape's client browser became truly vulnerable—in danger of becoming eclipsed in the marketplace by Microsoft's browser? It's difficult to pinpoint an exact date, but in retrospect Andreessen said he and Clark had known from the day their company was incorporated that they couldn't fight Microsoft's superior firepower head-on in the browser market. They knew that Microsoft's monopoly over the operating-system market for most of the personal computers in the world gave the company enormous power to leverage a Microsoft browser onto the desktop as well. So Netscape's plan, Andreessen said, had always been to use its own browser to establish a beachhead on the desktops of the hundreds of thousands of computers around the world that employees use every day in the course of their work. The reasoning was that if the Netscape Navigator icon sat on all the desktops in a company's shop, a systems administrator would at least consider Netscape's full line of products when it came time to buy other Internet software.

And there lay the real challenge for the Netscape brain trust—to anticipate the emerging needs of the business market and quickly bring to market a comprehensive line of Internet software to meet those needs. Of course that sounds like a gargantuan task. It was a company that had only focused on the basic, fundamental technology for navigating the Internet. Netscape had done that well, but to take it into the realm of business applications was another thing.

Why? Well, quite simply, Netscape had to—if the company had any hope of thriving.

Extend and Embrace

There was one wild card yet to be played that potentially could give Netscape a huge advantage. It was unclear at the end of 1994 exactly how the federal government's antitrust investigation against Microsoft would end. The only obvious thing was that the case—at least the current phase of the case—appeared to be headed for a climax within the next few months. How the case turned out would dictate Microsoft's future, the future of any machine that ran software, and the future of Silicon Valley.

The government believed that Microsoft had been walking a razor-thin line for years. With endlessly deep pockets *and* control of an operating system that drove more than 80 percent of the desktop computers in the world, it was possible for Microsoft to try to dominate the marketplace in ways that bordered on, if they did not cross, the limits of legality. The most common charge against Microsoft was that the company leveraged its operating system, forcing computer makers who needed MS-DOS to run their machines to buy other Microsoft products. Competitors complained about other Microsoft practices as well. The Silicon Valley start-up, Go, a pioneer in "pen-based" computing, accused Microsoft of coming down for a friendly visit and then turning around and stealing ideas. In still other cases, software developers alleged that Microsoft could scare off companies with vaporware simply by claiming that some future release of Microsoft software would do X, Y, or Z. If Microsoft is going to do it, why would I need your software?

It hadn't taken long for these stories to reach the ears of the federal government. Starting at the Federal Trade Commission in 1990 and handed off to the Justice Department in the summer of 1993, the federal antitrust investigation of Microsoft had been painful and grueling. The probe required Redmond's emissaries to meet dozens of times to answer investigators' questions and to produce more than half a million pages of company documents for the government to scrutinize. In fact, just a few weeks before Jim Barksdale traveled to Mountain View for his first look at Clark's company, Bill Gates's lawyers had been summoned to a summit meeting with the Justice Department in Washington, D.C.

The Meaning of Monopoly?

The world had changed since the days, centuries past, when the English monarchs exercised their power to grant exclusive monopolies. To millers, tanners, tailors, and others—the Stuarts handed out monopolies like county commissioners awarding highway contracts, and Parliament couldn't do a thing to stop the practice. The lessons were obvious. Monopolies stifle trade and innovation. They are inefficient, they inhibit creativity, and they deprive people of the chance to improve themselves.

A deep and abiding fear of monopolies came to characterize public policy, not only in England but, later, in the United States as well. A hundred years ago, in an era known as the Age of the Trusts, the U.S. Congress feared that the ascendancy of monopolies over such vital resources as the railroad system and the oil industry would destroy the freedom of the marketplace. The result: In 1890 the Sherman Antitrust Act was passed to eliminate monopolization and restraint of trade.

The Sherman Act's mandate was to ease a tension in society: the tug-of-war that ensues when a big and powerful company stops benefiting the marketplace and becomes a bully who chokes everyone else.

How does the Sherman Act relieve tension without destroying a successful business? For one thing, there's a distinction between a *monopoly* and the *act of monopolization*. It's OK under the law to have a monopoly—that sort of situation often arises when a company holds a patent for some particularly potent technology. That's how, for instance, AT&T built its monopoly over phone service in the United States. But it's illegal to use monopoly power to exclude competition or block innovation. That's where AT&T ran afoul of the law, during the decades when the monolithic utility became better known for keeping the cost of phone calls artificially high than for improving phone service.

In the early 1900s, Congress decided that the Sherman Act could use some reinforcement. So in 1914 the nation's second major piece of antitrust legislation, the Clayton Act, was passed. Under the Clayton Act, it became illegal for a company to leverage its monopoly into new industries by "tying" its products together.

While the government has brought hundreds of antitrust suits, they are among the law's most dangerous surgical tools. When they work, the suits keep markets open and free, promote competition and innovation, and spawn new jobs while keeping prices for services and products low. But a poorly conceived case can kill a company, throwing people out of work and jeopardizing an industry. It's dangerous stuff, no question, and it's no wonder that many citizens view their government's forays into antitrust law with the same hostility and suspicion that they reserve for the very monopolies in dispute.

That's especially true in the latter decades of the twentieth century, some economists argue. Can the old rules to govern monopolies, which were written back in the time of railroads and strip mining, be relevant in today's information economy? Nowadays, good ideas—instead of nonrenewable, finite natural resources—are at issue.

So what if Microsoft has a lock on the operating system? So what if it is a monopoly today? Regulating Microsoft could be worse for the global economy than allowing it to forge ahead and push its advantage and set the de facto standard for all things digital. After standards are set, we all benefit, right? Investment pours in because people like to invest in certainties, and standards are certain. Increased investment breeds more technology, and the whole shebang takes off. Especially on the infobahn, where, as ethernet inventor Bob Metcalfe told us, the power of the network is equal to the number of the end users squared. The more the merrier. But if half of us use one technology—Netscape Navigator, say—and the others use Microsoft's blend, and the Net world is halved, aren't we all a little bit poorer? Why not let the stronger player kill the weaker?

So what if the best technology doesn't always win. The Macintosh OS was clearly superior to Windows, WordPerfect kicked Word's butt, Betamax was finer than VHS, and the Dvorak typewriter keyboard was smarter than QWERTY. Japanese is a more efficient language than English. What of it? For whatever reason, one became ascendant. Do we really need the government to referee, to prop up the weak in the name of fairness?

Some economists say this argument is disingenuous because it fails to take into consideration the peculiar nature of high-tech industries. The high-tech marketplace tends unfairly to favor an ascendant product for two reasons that economists have identified. For one, high-tech products are dependent on each other to run properly. A word-processing software product is of limited use if it isn't compatible with the operating system on your computer. Microsoft's Word has an undeniable edge over the competition because it works so seamlessly with Microsoft's Windows 95. (WordPerfect, on the other hand, lost market share by failing to update in tandem with the Microsoft operating system.) The other peculiar feature of the high-tech marketplace is the fact that its products are increasingly hooked into— and dependent on—a network. So the more people who use a particular product, the more that product assumes the power of a de facto network standard. When any standard reigns, it can choke off competitive products' entrance into the marketplace.

Despite those concerns, the prevalent cry in this country during the past fifty years or so has been: Let the technology sort itself out. The free market will correct itself, goes the argument promoted by the so-called Chicago School of thinkers, whose ranks include the Nobel laureate Milton Friedman and the prominent legal philosopher Robert Bork. By tomorrow, a new innovation in the marketplace might render Microsoft's technology obsolete.

You could easily learn that lesson by looking at the history of another historically powerful computer company, IBM. Founded in 1911, IBM managed during the better part of this century to gain dominance in no fewer than four technology markets: accounting machines, early mainframes, mainframe systems, and early personal computers.

What happened to IBM in each instance? The company got bloated and bureaucratic and lost its monopoly as smart, innovative competitors created technology that left IBM in the dust.

Could the same fate be waiting around the corner for Microsoft?

By the 1990s, through its operating system—the mighty information engine that runs desktop computers—Microsoft enjoyed an absolute monopoly, running as it did on the vast majority of personal computers worldwide. But was Microsoft using its control of MS-DOS and, later, Windows to exclude competition? To stifle innovation? Was it violating the Clayton Act by tying its operating system to other software, forcing customers to buy more than one product when all they really wanted was MS-DOS? That's what the feds had been trying to find out.

How the Feds Jumped
from IBM to Microsoft

The investigation was not the first time the government poked its long antitrust nose into the computer industry. Perhaps the most infamous earlier attempt, which ended in a debacle for the authorities, was an investigation of IBM that the government had launched back in the dark ages of the mainframe era. Ironically, the government's probe would jump from IBM to Microsoft.

IBM was no novice at defending itself against antitrust charges. It seemed as if the government had been accusing the company of one thing or another since 1931, before modern computers had been invented and IBM's monopoly was over the accounting machines industry. IBM controlled the market for tabulators, keypunches, and sorters. The government case put an end to the company's practice of leasing machines instead of selling them—and then forcing customers to buy cards to use in the machines only from IBM. Another government antitrust investigation ended with a settlement in the 1950s, when IBM executives signed a consent decree agreeing to grant licenses to competitors who wanted to develop similar accounting machines.

By the late 1960s, when it dominated the mainframe computer industry, IBM had become adept at defending itself from antitrust charges. The Justice Department launched an investigation into whether the company was advertising "phantom" models of computers that had not yet been developed, in order to discourage customers from buying competitors' computers. Kind of a vapor-hardware case.

The government also was concerned about whether businesses that bought IBM computers were pressured into paying for a wide range of accoutrements (also IBM products) to maximize the machines' potential.

The government made no secret of the fact that it would have liked to break IBM into two or more smaller, discrete companies. The government's antitrust investigation dragged on for more than a decade before it was abandoned in the early 1980s. Whatever monopoly IBM seemed to have had was gone by then; during the 1970s, competitors such as DEC thrived in the marketplace, manufacturing and selling mainframes.

The investigation took a toll on Big Blue, where management had begun to reorganize the company, anticipating a time when IBM might be split up. By the 1980s, IBM ended up with a number of separate divisions—responsible for independent products—that didn't communicate or interact well. As a result, many of the company's computers were simply incompatible. There was a widespread perception in the industry that the omnipresent threat of a government-forced breakup was at least partially to blame for the bureaucratic mess.

By contrast, look at smoothly running, perfectly integrated Microsoft, which, by 1990, enjoyed a monopoly of its own in the operating system. (The courts have ruled over the years, in fact, that owning a mere 70 percent of a particular market gives you a monopoly.)

Bill Gates's monopoly, ironically, blossomed because he was an agile businessman who ten years earlier had stood on the cusp of the personal computer era and had negotiated a particularly prescient deal with IBM. In 1980, Gates licensed an operating system called MS-DOS to IBM to preinstall on the new personal computers that Big Blue was manufacturing. The terms of the license, now legend, were extraordinarily favorable to Microsoft and enabled the company to maintain control over MS-DOS and to license the software to other computer makers as well.

In 1990, it was a planned venture between IBM and Microsoft that attracted the attention of the government's antitrust investigators and brought them for the first time to Microsoft's door. At Comdex, the annual computer industry trade show in late 1989, Microsoft and IBM issued a joint statement announcing that the two major companies would work together to develop future generations of their operating systems.

At that time, IBM was developing its OS/2 operating system for PCs, and Microsoft was manufacturing its DOS system. Microsoft's Windows software, in those days, was an overlay to DOS; it provided a front-end graphical interface to make DOS more user-friendly.

Staff at the Federal Trade Commission were concerned that the powerhouse partnership would stifle competition in the software industry, so they embarked on an investigation to gather information about Microsoft's business practices. Concerned by what investigators heard about Microsoft from its partners and competitors, the FTC continued to investigate Bill Gates's company even after Microsoft decided to abandon its partnership with IBM and focus instead on developing Windows.

At the heart of the federal investigation was Microsoft's way of doing business—a strategy that not only perpetuated the company's monopoly on operating-system software but also propelled Bill Gates's products inexorably into other segments of the industry.

Microsoft's business strategy was, at its core, breathtakingly simple. What the company did was to *link* its operating system to all its other software programs. Keep in mind that operating-system software is not just another software product; rather, it is the heart and soul of a personal computer because it controls all the basic functions of the machine. All the other applications—word processors, spreadsheets, shoot-'em-up ray-gun games, you name it—run on top of an operating system and must be able to interact with it.

Microsoft's product line included a wide array of applications, and they all interacted with the operating system. The operating system had little "hooks," known as applications programming interfaces, or APIs, to optimize the functionality of Microsoft's other products, making Microsoft's software run seamlessly and quickly in conjunction with the operating system.

Competitors who wrote software applications for PCs had to update their products every time Microsoft updated its operating system if they hoped to stay current. Even then, their products lagged behind Microsoft's own in taking advantage of the latest properties of its operating system. Competitors complained to the FTC that they learned about crucial operating-system updates long after Microsoft's own developers.

The FTC also was concerned about the licensing arrangement that Microsoft had with all the computer makers who shipped new machines with preinstalled copies of Microsoft's MS-DOS 6 and Windows 3.1 operating systems. Since 1988, Microsoft had required the manufacturers to pay royalties for each computer sold whether or not Microsoft's operating system was preinstalled on the machine. Also, the license agreements required the computer makers to agree to large minimum commitments, with unused balances credited to future license agreements. The licensing arrangement discouraged manufacturers from installing other operating systems on their machines because they had to pay Microsoft anyway.

And, the government believed, computer makers who offered a choice of operating systems would have to charge customers a higher price for the machine to cover the "double royalty."

Bill Gates strongly denied that Microsoft's way of doing business created an anticompetitive stranglehold in the marketplace. He argued that the tight interdependency of the operating system and other applications is necessary to give customers added value. But from the federal government's point of view, Microsoft's method of maintaining its monopoly smacked of illegal anticompetitive tactics.

The government's approach was much more cautious by the time it looked into Microsoft's business practices, a decade after the shambles of the IBM antitrust investigation. While there were some FTC investigators who advocated breaking up Gates's company into two—one that manufactured operating-system software and another for applications—the government eventually narrowed the focus of the case considerably, hoping that this time it would get a win.

The FTC investigation culminated in a 205-page report in late 1992 that recommended seeking a court injunction against Microsoft to force Gates to change his business practices. But the commission stalemated in 1993, unable to decide whether or not to go to court.

Enter the Justice Department. Anne Bingaman had just been named assistant attorney general in charge of the antitrust division in the new Clinton administration and was looking for a case that would revitalize the demoralized department, whose ranks had dwindled during the Reagan-Bush years. On June 20, 1994, Bingaman called Microsoft's attorney, William Neukom, to a meeting in Washington.

Neukom and Richard Urowsky, another Microsoft attorney, were ushered into the antitrust division's main conference room at a little before 1 P.M. the next day. Bingaman and her principal deputy, Robert Litan, were friendly and cordial; Bingaman told Microsoft's lawyers that a few days earlier she had met with U.S. Attorney General Janet Reno. Reno had said this was "a big case" and had authorized Bingaman to discuss a settlement with Microsoft.

Bingaman told Microsoft's lawyers that the government wanted to "open up the market." Next to the conference table in the meeting room was an easel on which Bingaman had placed a written outline of a comprehensive settlement—called a consent decree.

According to its terms, the government wanted Microsoft to agree not to force computer makers to preinstall other products as a condition to installing Microsoft's operating-system software, not to force computer makers to make minimum commitments, and not to impose onerously long time frames on contracts.

Over the next three weeks, the government and Microsoft negotiated the terms of the proposed settlement. In the final days, Bingaman and Gates negotiated directly with each other for hours at a time over the phone. Gates agreed to sign an agreement that would prohibit Microsoft from tying products to the operating system— but at the eleventh hour, during a conversation with his lawyers on July 13, 1994, he insisted that a clause be struck from the section about tying. The original clause read: "This shall not be construed to prohibit Microsoft from developing integrated products which offer technological advantages." Gates insisted that the last four words be stricken on the grounds that "Microsoft would not accept any limitations on its right to design new products," a Microsoft lawyer later said in a deposition.

The next day, both the government and Microsoft signed the proposed consent decree, which Attorney General Janet Reno hailed as a major success that "leveled the playing field" in the software industry. The only hurdle left was to get a judge to approve the settlement.

Gates and company were free to do business, more or less as usual—provided, of course, that anything Microsoft tied to the operating system was *integrated*.

A Detour on the Information Highway

By then, the giant had awakened. Down at the lower extremities of the corporate body in Redmond, a number of people who worked for Bill Gates had begun to sound the alarm that this Web craze was big. And the nervous impulses were being relayed, up, up the corporate corpus to its brain. Things were starting to happen. Years later, Microsoft would submit confidential documents to a federal judge to show that Gates's company had begun as early as 1993 to work on some of the technologies that would eventually be included in its Internet Explorer browser.

Microsoft was growing at a phenomenal rate, with sales tripling from 1990 to 1993 and a payroll that grew during the same period from 5,600 employees to 14,400.

But for the most part, the portion of Gates's attention that wasn't consumed by the upcoming release of Windows 95 was focused elsewhere. By 1993, he had begun to think in earnest about how Microsoft could take advantage of the growing phenomenon known as the information highway.

He was in good company. Major companies like Time Warner and Tele-Communications Inc. (TCI) were developing strategies for delivering "information on demand" to consumers via cable and interactive TV. Gates, particularly intrigued by Time Warner's pilot project to bring interactive TV to five thousand homes in Orlando, Florida, began to meet with Time Warner head Gerald Levin in 1993.

The talks had an on-again, off-again quality, stalling and then restarting throughout late 1993. Gates also met frequently with John Malone, TCI's chairman, who planned to build a nationwide fiber-optic network to deliver interactive TV.

In the meantime, Gates had authorized Microsoft to start work on another on-line project. In mid-1993, the way that most home PC users accessed the Internet was through one of the big proprietary on-line services. Between them, America Online, CompuServe, and Prodigy had more than three million customers.

Seeing the growth potential of that industry, Gates told his staff to begin work on an on-line service, code-named Marvel, to compete with the big three, and Gates directed them to create the on-line service, which would eventually be named the Microsoft Network, in time to launch in tandem with Windows 95, the successor to the MS-DOS operating system.

By the winter of 1993–94, in the months before Clark and Andreessen met and founded their company, several people in the Microsoft camp began to understand the growing importance of the Internet. The Net tied together everything, from commerce to communications, and offered many opportunities to a company that currently controlled the desktop.

As early as December 1993, Rob Glaser, Microsoft's former vice president in charge of multimedia development efforts and one of the top thinkers at the company, took the Marvel development team on a virtual tour of the World Wide Web, using the Mosaic browser that Andreessen and his colleagues at NCSA had created. Later, in January 1994, James "J" Allard, a Microsoft program manager who had followed the development of the Mosaic browser from its very inception on a mailing list called WWW-Talk, wrote a sixteen-page memo called "Windows: The Next Killer Application for the Internet." The memo, which got the attention of Gates himself, urged Microsoft to take advantage of the Internet and "capture this user base by positioning Windows as the ideal information system."

At around the same time, Steven Sinofsky, Gates's personal technical adviser, had been on a recruiting trip to Cornell University, in upstate New York, and come away filled with Net zeal. Cornell had always been on the bleeding edge of the Internet—in a curious way, the mother of all networks reached the public's consciousness for the first time after a Cornell student named Robert Morris unleashed a notorious "worm," a program that caused the nascent Net to grind to a halt in 1988. By early 1994, all kinds of interesting Internet-related work was going on, including the development of a program

called CU-SeeMe, a free program that transmitted video in real time.
It was totally cool and the whole campus was deeply into the Net and
the Web, with queues of kids lined up at public terminals to read their
E-mail.

Sinofsky was struck by it and told his boss. When he returned
to Redmond, he booked time with Bill in February 1994, fired up
Mosaic, and gave Gates a guided tour of the World Wide Web.

Gates got it in a big way—so big, in fact, that over the next
few months, he directed some of his top lieutenants to develop a plan
for building a browser. The first concrete step in the process occurred
in April 1994—within a few weeks of the time Clark hired the NCSA
programming team—when Gates summoned his executive staff to a
retreat at the venerable Shumway Mansion, in Kirkland, Washington,
to discuss the threat of the Net. At the retreat, Sinofsky explained the
importance of the Internet.

By the end of the retreat, Microsoft's top managers had
reached consensus: The Windows 95 operating system must include
a number of technologies that would make it easy to use the Internet.
If they weren't yet sure how to go about that task, at least the team
emerged from the retreat intending to incorporate some kind of
web-browsing capabilities in the software package that would launch
with Windows 95.

A few days later, Gates went off to his second home on the
Olympic Peninsula to spend a week brainstorming. On April 16,
1994, he sent a now-famous memo to his staff, announcing a "sea
change" and stating, "Microsoft has decided that the Internet will be
very important." In the memo, Gates discussed a number of specific
"action plans" for his deputies to carry out. In particular, he directed
Allard and Sinofsky to come up with a plan for creating a browser—
which he referred to as a "viewer"—to launch in conjunction with
Windows 95. In the memo, Gates made it clear that the project
would be expected to grow in importance after it got under way.
He wrote:

J Allard in the TCP/IP team along with Steven Sinofsky will propose an architecture and plan for accomplishing this goal and integrating these services. J Allard and the networking team will also implement this, and if additonal resources are required this will be part of the plan.

Thus he decreed. And thus would a Microsoft browser be integrated—not perfectly, not brilliantly, but just in time to be cobbled onto Windows 95.

Momentum slowly began to build. By the end of April, Microsoft's Systems Group, which was responsible for developing Windows 95, had prepared a three-year plan stating that Windows 95 would include "Integrated Net Browsing."

The company quietly began to signal customers that Microsoft was on the case. During that spring, Sinofsky found himself having discussions with members of Microsoft's marketing staff, trying to decide how much of the still-emerging Internet plans to reveal publicly. It was a delicate situation; on the one hand, it would be good to reassure customers and developers; on the other, it would be unwise to promise something that Microsoft couldn't deliver. One day late in April, Sinofsky received an E-mail from the Microsoft employee whose job was to promote Windows 95's Internet capabilities, asking "exactly what it is that we have committed to support" (on the Internet). As the details had not yet been worked out, Sinofsky recommended telling independent software developers who worked with Microsoft something vague: that Microsoft was "committed to providing the 'plumbing' necessary to connect to the Internet." His reasoning was simple. Sinofsky wanted third-party developers to "know that they could build products that connected to the Internet without having to duplicate that 'plumbing.'"

Microsoft's Internet initiatives got more specific in July 1994, after a senior software engineer named Benjamin Slivka took his first tour of the World Wide Web. Slivka, whose code for Windows 95 had already been written and was being debugged, was looking for another challenge. He found himself "immediately intrigued by the possibilities it presented for making huge quantities of information available to computer users."

The next month, Slivka was assigned to the project to develop Web-browsing capability. He wasted no time and began thinking about the look and feel that the new browser should embody—and about how it should differ from the NCSA version of Mosaic that was then the most popular browser.

On August 22, 1994, Slivka sent E-mail to the Windows planning team, saying he had "made a start on the design by cataloging all the Mosaic" user interface features and "starting to write down what improvements/changes we would make."

By November, Microsoft had begun negotiating to buy browser code from a company called Booklink. But Microsoft decided instead to license the commercial version of the Mosaic code from Spyglass. Negotiations dragged on for months, with Microsoft originally offering Spyglass a mere $100,000. In the end, however, Microsoft agreed to pay Spyglass $2 million for the right to license the Mosaic code to create a browser that would run on the Windows 95 platform. Of course, that wouldn't entirely solve Microsoft's problem; while Netscape's browser ran on nearly two dozen different platforms, Microsoft still had no firm plans to create versions that would run on operating systems other than Windows 95. That meant any home computer user who was still running, say, Windows 3.1 on the desktop would be unable to run Microsoft's browser. For now.

And yet, as Microsoft's plans to create a browser got under way, the bulk of Microsoft's Internet efforts were directed toward launching the Microsoft Network in conjunction with Windows 95. At the annual Comdex trade show in November 1994, where Jim Clark's company announced its name change to Netscape Communications Corp., Microsoft had an announcement of its own to make:

The company would include Microsoft Network access software as a feature of Windows 95.

It was clear that Gates and company couldn't afford to stay out of the emerging on-line market. They may have been behind on the curve, but it would soon become clear that Microsoft would do whatever it took to embrace the Net and its emerging market.

PART THREE

Barksdale Builds a Business

CHAPTER ELEVEN

Following the Money

Over the Christmas holidays in 1994, Barksdale took a vacation with his family at his second home in Colorado. He packed his laptop so he could experiment with the Netscape browser; he still was trying to decide whether or not to join the company.

One afternoon, he showed his three children the browser, to get their reactions to what the software could accomplish. His daughter Susan, a law student, asked if the browser could track down information on the Web about a certain case she was interested in. Just like that, Barksdale found some data points about it on the Web. His other daughter, Betsy, was a third-grade teacher. For her, Barksdale located a ton of lesson plans out there in cyberspace. His son, David, a high school student, wanted to know when the Grateful Dead would be in New Orleans. The answer was April, it turned out.

"All three of them had totally random questions, and we could answer them. Simply," he recalled much later. His children were impressed. They told him, "If you're going to do something stupid like leave your nice secure job, at least it looks like you'll be doing something fun."

Just like that, Barksdale made up his mind. "It pleased me that they liked it. I decided to take the job," and a few weeks later, he showed in Mountain View for his first day.

By January 1995, Netscape had outgrown the Castro Street offices and moved to more spacious quarters in a glass-sided building on Middlefield Road. Most people were still unpacking their desks on the morning Barksdale arrived.

He had a twofold agenda. He understood that, in the long term, competition from Microsoft would be the company's biggest challenge, and he expected to engage on that battlefront soon. But first Barksdale wanted to win an important internal battle: to define Netscape as a company.

He hit the ground running, calling an 8 A.M. senior staff meeting on his first day at work. Clark wasn't there; in fact, as soon as Barksdale showed up to take over the company, Clark began to distance himself from day-to-day operations. Marc slipped into the room late, as usual. All the vice presidents showed up on time, expectant, relieved to have a pro at the helm. The senior management team had taken the young company as far as it could; now it was up to Barksdale to make the transition from start-up to mature business.

Barksdale understood the principles of leadership. Managing ninety thousand employees at Federal Express had taught him a lot about how to be top dog. He'd watched how his own boss, Fred Smith, operated; Smith showed him that the boss must put himself last, not first. Barksdale told people that, in many respects, managers of information technology companies were on the *bottom* of the pyramid, not the top. The customer was at the top of the pyramid, and the second level consisted of the employees who served the customers most directly. By the time you got down to the bottom level of the pyramid, where the CEO was, you were pretty far removed from the customers—and the day-to-day generation of sales revenues. With the distributed technology of the Net, a good manager could put everything he knew out there, sharing with his staff. A good manager gave his people the stuff they needed to do their job and cut through red tape rather than creating it.

Barksdale told his key managers that he'd spend some time learning his way around. To that end he wanted everyone to know he welcomed their advice and counsel. Yet he also let it be known that he was the boss. "I love facts, and I love data," Barksdale told his senior managers, "but if we're going to use opinions and we can't agree, then we'll just use mine."

Defining the company would be a daunting task, despite the fine reception that Netscape's recently released Navigator 1.0 was enjoying in the marketplace. The fact was, Netscape's strategy so far had been to build a business based on a software program that a bunch of kids wrote for fun and once gave away for free. How long could that last?

Cash resources were at an all-time low. A number of contract workers had been let go in recent weeks to cut expenses. Where was the business in this business? Where was the money? Barksdale needed to find it. Netscape needed a message. What, exactly, did the company stand for? It struck Barksdale that the place was disorganized; indeed, it was unclear which market Netscape was pursuing. Was it the home user? The academic user? The business user? No one was sure.

The lack of clarity made the product ambiguous. Although Clark and Andreessen had been talking about selling Navigator to businesses, there was a penchant for "thinking your products were cool— with Mozilla dancing around on the screen," Barksdale said. That image wasn't going to capture too many Fortune 100 customers. Enough of this "what's cool" nonsense. He'd been around long enough to understand that the shelf life of "cool" wasn't so hot. Coolness could only take you so far.

So far, Netscape had proved to be, in the words of its new marketing VP, Mike Homer, "a one-trick pony," selling a relatively simple client-server line. That had been an obvious starting point for a start-up. But the product line didn't have enough depth to support a solid long-term business venture. If this company was going to succeed on its merits, Barksdale had to make sure that Netscape developed a viable product line—and fast. The company had to sell something that people genuinely needed and would pay for.

In a general way, Jim Clark and Marc Andreessen had known that even before they founded the company. Back in the days when

they sat on Clark's boat, spinning schemes, they had agreed that someday, somehow, their company would need to move from a consumer
market to a business market. But in the early months of 1994, it had
been impossible to know exactly how the burgeoning interest in the
Internet would translate into business terms.

By the time Barksdale arrived, more specific information was
emerging. For instance, in the month or so since Netscape started
selling Navigator 1.0, it had become clear that a surprising number of
businesses were starting to buy the software—to use on their corporate networks. Corporate customers were licensing multiple copies
of Navigator and installing the browser on all the desktops their employees used. How could Barksdale capitalize on that?

At the same time, informing Netscape's every move, Barksdale
would need to figure out how to keep the company alive long after it
turned up in Microsoft's crosshairs. That would require speed, agil-
ity, smarts, and scratch gamesmanship. There would be little room
for error. From the first time he met with Clark and Doerr, when the
pair flew up to Seattle in July 1994 to urge him to become Netscape's
CEO, he knew beating Microsoft was the name of the game. "Even
then there was never any question but that Microsoft would be our
principal competitor," he said. "If the business was any good, Microsoft
was going to be in it."

Barksdale knew that Netscape's early start was a fleeting advantage at best. To stay ahead of the giant, he would have to position
Netscape to take advantage of a market that Microsoft had—so far at
least—mostly overlooked. Barksdale believed his business could be
built around the open standards of the Internet. By contrast, Microsoft's
business revolved around the closed standards of its operating system.
"Our strategy was antithetical to Microsoft's business strategy," he
said. "So if we were going to stay in the open standards arena we
would have a defined market that, almost by definition, they were not
going to go after." At least, not right away.

Barksdale figured that if everybody else around him was doing
their job, he would be free to do his. So he wanted to convince every-

body who worked for him that they were on a team. "I try to tell folks, 'It's like basketball.' That's the most level sport, all the players being pretty equal. You have everyone working together, and then management's sort of like a coach."

Although he knew next to nothing about the Internet—and was happy to leave the role of visionary to Clark and Andreessen— Barksdale made a point of introducing himself to all the engineers who had hacked the code in the first place. "They dressed way down, in shorts; some of them had ponytails," he remembered.

But Barksdale wasn't averse to learning from kids—after all, his own three convinced him that the Web was a grand opportunity. "I had for over half my business career been responsible for people who wrote computer programs," he said. "I'm always impressed with people who can be so single-minded and work so long at a stretch on things that are just purely mentally wearing. I'm not that way; I tend to work on this, and then on that for a while."

Déjà Vu

Barksdale sounded relaxed and unthreatening, with that soothing Mississippi drawl. In fact, he was methodically gathering information. "If you're going to lead people on a specific mission, you have to know what they're doing, every one of them, and what they're capable of," he said later. He was trying to figure out the answers to his two favorite questions: Where's the money coming from? and How can we make more?

One of the key people Barksdale met on his rounds was Bill Kellinger, who helped run the sales department. Kellinger had joined the company a month earlier, on the day Netscape started shipping 1.0, which was auspicious enough. Like Barksdale, he was an experienced manager hired to help instill order in the disorganized sales division, and he took over the telephone-sales group, which employed all of three people. Never mind that by 1997, tele-sales would employ 112 people, making deals that would account for half of Netscape's business. Now the sales staff felt like bookies on the eve of Superbowl Sunday.

Navigator's wild popularity had swamped the three over-worked reps. "Total chaos" might be a better way to describe it—and that was how Kellinger described it to anyone who would listen. The three reps were handling a thousand calls a day. Another six people who were supposed to be keypunching orders were dragooned into simply answering the constantly ringing telephones, hoping to siphon off potential customers before they got sucked up into the voice E-mail void. People were working until 1 A.M. every morning.

The company had sold $365,000's worth of product in the two weeks after Netscape 1.0 started to ship. Those were strong numbers—plenty of software companies that would like to see $365,000's worth of sales in a quarter—but Kellinger knew the company could do better.

He knew his "abandon rate" was awful, for instance. That is, the number of people who would hang up—abandon the call—rather than subject themselves to voice mail. *Thanks for calling, someone will be with you in a few minutes.* Most people don't wait.

Kellinger was so sure that demand for Netscape software was greater than anyone imagined that he had just cut a private deal with Andreessen in which he had promised to generate $3 million in sales in the first quarter in exchange for a nice chunk of stock options to enrich his personal portfolio. Kellinger figured it was a safe bet. If you sat by the phones for an hour and saw prospective customers stacked up, waiting for a chance to spend their money, you'd know that the potential was there for far more sales than a measly $3 million. If Kellinger could get the resources—more bodies to answer the phones—the potential for sales was nearly unlimited.

This certainly answered one of Barksdale's golden questions (Where is the money coming from?) and might even lead to answering the other (How can we make more?). He scheduled a meeting with Kellinger.

At the predestined time, Kellinger sat down across from Barksdale in the "New York" conference room. (The place was growing so fast that all the conference rooms needed names, so just name them after—big cities! As more and more buildings went up, the naming conventions would change. By the time the Engineering Building went up, all the conference rooms were named after prisons—a Chris Houck inspiration.) A touch nervous, Kellinger had put together a presentation for the boss and started shuffling through his papers. While he was reviewing his notes, he handed Barksdale a little chart he'd drawn up to illustrate how many phone calls were coming in.

"Bill, close that book," Barksdale said.

Kellinger did.

It was déjà vu. Barksdale immediately saw that the short-term answers to both his favorite questions were right there in front of him. He'd learned the same lesson years earlier at FedEx: The company was limiting its own business by the number of incoming phone lines available.

"Look at me," Barksdale said. "You mean we are turning business away because we don't have enough people to answer the phones?"

Kellinger nodded. It was what he'd been trying to explain. "If I give you more people, how much more revenue can you do?" Barksdale asked.

"Right now we have three people. If you give me six people, I can triple the revenue."

"You mean you can do *nine million dollars* in the second quarter?" Barksdale asked.

"Yeah."

"You've got it." To Barksdale, it seemed like a rather simple thing to do: Hire enough people to answer all the damn phones. They shook hands. Kellinger made the hires.

In the second quarter, sales reached nearly $12 million.

The Kellinger conversation gave Barksdale an important piece of information: Interest in Netscape's products was bigger than what the company was supplying. While that sounds like good news—the dogs are eating the dog food—it had an ominous undertone. The dogs couldn't get enough dog food! When demand outstrips supply, customers may take their business elsewhere, someplace where people answer the phones and treat the customer like gold. Barksdale decided the next step was to hire two hundred more people, just as fast as the company could find good ones.

It's hard enough to hire one decent employee. But it was especially difficult to do in Silicon Valley because the big boom was just beginning in the early 1990s. Start-ups were snapping up everyone with the least bit of high-tech skill. The logistics were hellish, said Kandis Malefyt, Netscape's head of human resources. People always want to give notice on Mondays, so you want to make them offers on Fridays. "One day we had fifty-six offers to make on a Friday," she recalled. "It got pretty crazy."

Of course, there was one surefire way to hire lots of good people fast. You could buy up whole companies. Naturally, you'd need to buy companies whose businesses were complementary to your own. That would be the way to go. But it would cost money, lots of money.

There was only one place to get it: Wall Street. How soon could they make a play?

The Anti-Microsoft Antibodies

Barksdale thought his fledgling company was too small to compete head-on with Microsoft, which was why he was anxious to find another way to coexist. He favored a strategy of finding ways to work *with* Bill Gates. (Barksdale was new to Silicon Valley and its culture; maybe that's why he didn't share the prevailing local opinion that mighty Microsoft was the devil, ready to suck any unsuspecting smaller company down into the fiery pits of hell.)

In any case, when Barksdale ran into one of Gates's deputies at an industry conference in March 1995, he was happy to sit down and have a friendly talk. He and Dan Rosen, Microsoft's new senior director of strategic relationships, already knew each other from the not-so-distant days when they both had worked at AT&T. "We spent an hour or so over drinks swapping stories about AT&T and brainstorming about how Microsoft and Netscape could work together," Rosen remembered. "Jim said he would rather find a way to work with Microsoft than compete against us, so we agreed to try to scope something out."

Microsoft was developing an Internet server product. Rosen thought Barksdale was particularly eager to convince Microsoft to abandon its product in favor of licensing and distributing Netscape's Commerce Server. In addition, Barksdale told Rosen that Netscape and Microsoft should work together to support a single security protocol to facilitate financial transactions over the Internet.

"It seemed to me there was room for a good deal," Rosen said. So over the next few weeks, he and Barksdale and Mike Homer spoke over the phone a number of times to come up with a list of "areas where cooperation could result," Rosen said.

Then Barksdale invited Rosen to come to Mountain View with a team of negotiators for a daylong meeting.

It wasn't the first time that emissaries of the two companies had met face-to-face. The previous year, Microsoft had been briefly interested in licensing the Navigator code as a basis for creating its own browser to ship with Windows 95. But, as Rosen remembered it, Clark "rudely" rebuffed Redmond in its initial foray. The reasons for the alleged rudeness might have had something to do with the terms Microsoft proposed. In a written statement, Clark recalled that Microsoft wanted to license Netscape's code for $1 million, but Clark sent word to Redmond that he was "not even remotely interested in licensing this to Microsoft, because they would subsequently use it against us."

Clark wrote that he believed his company's best hope at that time was to push its early lead and the advantage it had in hiring Andreessen and the rest of the team of university students who had hacked the first version of Mosaic. Later, in the fall of 1994, Homer managed to convince Clark to hear Microsoft out; Homer traveled with a Netscape team up to Redmond to rekindle the possibility of licensing the code. But that deal never went through either.

According to Rosen, Microsoft was already in deep discussions with Spyglass and "too late" to license Netscape's browser code. Homer, though, had a different recollection: He said Microsoft's terms for licensing Navigator were, quite simply, unacceptable. "They wanted to pay a flat licensing fee for all rights to the product. We just walked away from the deal." There would have been no royalties. "We basically would have become a subcontractor to them," Homer concluded.

But Rosen and Homer, who also knew each other well from previous employment, had reopened a channel of communication, so it was only natural, when Rosen and his team arrived at Netscape headquarters one day in April 1995, for Homer and Andreessen to act as their hosts.

The Netscape team already had reviewed a proposal that Microsoft's negotiators had sent ahead, outlining a number of formal ways in which Microsoft executives felt they could work with Netscape.

Homer and Andreessen were suspicious of Microsoft's motives, fearful that Microsoft had sent spies to try to get information about Netscape. Rosen saw they were "openly distrustful," which surprised him, based on the cordial tenor of the earlier phone conversations. He later decided that the atmosphere at Netscape headquarters was so tense because of "the culture of Silicon Valley . . . the antibodies floating around in Mountain View just were too powerful to allow even a sensible business deal to blossom."

Most of the new discussion items were general. For instance, Microsoft was willing to make Netscape a development partner and provide advance product plans under nondisclosure to enable the Mountain View company to work with Windows 95.

But Homer felt the proposal raised more questions than it answered. For instance, how often would Netscape get updates on the plans? Homer felt that what Microsoft was really doing with that particular discussion item was making a subtle threat: If you don't become our partner, you won't have the benefit of the advance disclosure that our own internal developers have. Homer thought the implication was "work with us or get screwed."

Andreessen also was distrustful. He sat there with his IBM ThinkPad on his lap, taking notes and sensing that the proposal conveyed an implicit threat: If you don't cooperate, we will crush you. Andreessen would later turn his notes over to federal investigators.

After the formal meeting ended, a more interesting discussion occurred that day in Mountain View. Rosen and Barksdale met privately to discuss another offer: Microsoft wanted to buy a 15 to 20 percent stake in Netscape.

In addition, Microsoft wanted Netscape to put a Microsoft executive on the company's board of directors and asked for a guarantee that Netscape would report to Redmond regularly, keeping Microsoft up to date on all of the company's plans.

The round of financing that Netscape had just completed—selling shares to media companies—meant that the start-up was worth a hundred million and some odd dollars. So Microsoft was talking about a relatively small investment for a company with deep pockets: no more than, say, $40 million.

Barksdale told Rosen that "he would welcome it, if we got the business deal done at the same time," Rosen said. Having Microsoft on Netscape's side could be a good thing. But if Microsoft was not interested in helping Netscape, but merely was setting its claws into the company so it could eventually pull it down, that was bad.

Clark, who did not attend the sessions, recalled in a written statement that he was told Microsoft was unwilling to give Netscape information it needed to make the Netscape browser run properly with the forthcoming Windows 95 "without first discussing an investment and a board seat in our company." He recalled, "I felt this should be illegal, for otherwise no company could hope to build a new product on Windows if Microsoft was going to make such demands."

Rosen sat down with Homer to try to work out terms. They wrote a draft, but no final agreement was reached.

A few weeks later, Barksdale (who still lived in Seattle and commuted to Mountain View) visited Microsoft's offices to continue the discussions. Rosen had arranged a meeting between Barksdale and top Microsoft executives Paul Maritz and Nathan Myhrvold. "At the meeting, Jim still expressed a desire to work together," Rosen said.

Negotiations ended shortly afterward, as it became clear that the companies would pursue separate—and competitive—paths. This was no surprise to Homer, who had spent nine years at Apple Computer studying the ways of Microsoft. "I woke up every morning competing with Microsoft. I knew their tactics. The truth of the matter is, if you expect to build any successful software company, you have to compete with Microsoft."

Besides, Netscape was about to undergo a transformation that would vastly increase the cost of buying 20 percent of the company—from about $40 million to $400 million. Netscape would go public sooner than most anticipated. It was the only way to secure the capital to be able to grow fast enough to compete.

The Tent of Doom

Most of the programmers thought the move to Middlefield Road was a big mistake. How did Clark think they'd ever fill so much space? There was a fountain on the lawn, for God's sake! How much was this costing?

Zawinski for one had felt pretty lousy on moving day, crawling around on the floor under the unfriendly overhead glare of fluorescents, hunting for cables to hook up his computer, complaining all the while that the building's decorators must have watched too many episodes of *Star Trek*. How else could you explain that stupid red stripe that ran down the middle of the hallway walls? Let's not even discuss the annoying moiré pattern that snaked across the carpet. Beam me up, Scotty.

Something needed to be done to claim the space and personalize it. So Zawinski and Montulli drove over to a local army-surplus store to buy their own decorations. Fortified by five hundred square feet of camouflage netting, Zawinski started to feel a little better. By the time he'd unrolled the net on the office floor to discover a bunch of dried leaves inside—who knew this stuff would be *authentic?*—he realized he had the makings of an Insta-Theme Park.

He hung the netting above his desk, using little pieces of phone wire to fasten it to the ceiling, then draped it over the sides of his cubicle. (He found the multicolored phone wires had many excellent uses, including wrapping around one's dreadlocks.) The netting pooled down to the floor. Hmmmmm, not bad. It had a certain M.A.S.H. appeal, a kind of in-the-trenches, at-the-front-lines-of-the-war panache.

Voilà! The Tent of Doom.

Once installed, the netting muted the glare from the fluorescents. Sitting underneath, Zawinski could fantasize that he was in a real jungle. He just needed some audio to simulate the sounds of wildlife. Chattering monkeys, anyone?

In addition to being a unique addition to any corporate environ, the Tent of Doom had a hidden benefit. People who wanted to actually visit with Zawinski needed to pass a kind of intelligence test. They had to figure out how to get in. It wasn't that hard, of course. You just needed to reach down to the floor, here, and lift up a corner of the sinister netting, and duck through the makeshift doorway. You'd be surprised how many people, though, would try to just brush it aside to get in. They ended up caught like flies in Jamie's web—which was amusing, sometimes.

One person who passed the intelligence test was Marc. Indeed, in hindsight, Andreessen had been acing all sorts of intelligence tests. Along with Barksdale and Clark, he was looking at the horizon, trying to figure out how to make the browser take the company right into the heart of corporate America and the rest of the world. And he came up with some decent solutions.

All hands were currently engaged in hacking the next version of the Netscape browser, version 2.0. The new release would be a radical upgrade. Where Navigator 1.0 was all about connecting people to the Net, version 2.0 would be all about connecting people to each other.

That's because Andreessen and the rest of Barksdale's executive team had figured out how to capitalize on the fact that businesses were buying Netscape's products. Increasing sales to these so-called enterprise customers provided a perfect opportunity for Netscape to commercialize certain Internet protocols that were applicable in a business environment. File transfers, reading newsgroups, sending and receiving E-mail—wouldn't it be useful to customers if Navigator could accomplish all those tasks with a simple click?

That's how the idea for SuiteSpot—Netscape's expanded line of server products—was born. SuiteSpot would propel the server line far beyond the 1.0 generation of products, which had included only two web servers, secure and nonsecure.

"We decided, 'Jeez, we should do a mail server and a news server and look at the other functions,'" Homer said. In early 1995, a plan emerged to include all the separate servers' functions into a single integrated client: Navigator 2.0.

None of the established software product lines that sold applications to businesses, such as Lotus Notes, included a browser. In fact, none of the software that corporate America licensed for its employees' use was Internet-compatible. The software that businesses bought was called groupware, a catchall term to describe programs that allowed colleagues to work together from remote locations on a single shared document. Groupware allowed businesses to update meeting schedules on-line. Groupware also routed workers' E-mail

messages almost instantaneously over intranets, avoiding the traffic
tie-ups that delay communication on the increasingly data-clogged
public Internet.

The groupware market was dominated by Lotus Notes, which
originally had been designed in the mid-1980s, back when a business
operated a "local area network" (LAN) that connected employees' computers to each other but not to the outside world. Groupware software
had been designed for *closed* systems. Any groupware package worked
fine within the artificially insular universe of its particular LAN. Most of
the groupware currently on the market (such as Notes, or the more
compact Novell Groupwise, or Microsoft's Windows for Workgroups)
couldn't even talk to each other. It worked fine for the groupware makers as well, because, once entrenched, the proprietary software tended
to perpetuate itself. Systems administrators would return to the same
groupware maker for upgrades; it was cheaper than scrapping the whole
damn system and starting from scratch with another product.

Groupware customers were starting to realize there was a
growing trove of information beyond the LAN that employees needed
to access—information on the Net, for instance. To enable its users to
connect to that vast network of data, groupware was going to have to
undergo a transformation. Enter Netscape.

It would be tough for Netscape to compete against heavy hitter
Lotus Notes, which had grown from its 1989 inception into
a $200-million-a-year product. (During the summer of 1995, IBM would
buy Lotus for $3.2 billion, primarily to get its hands on Notes.) But
Andreessen thought there was room for a competitive, less-expensive
product—Notes cost companies an average of $155 per user—one that
used the browser as the wedge to get in the office door.

One day Andreessen arrived at the Tent of Doom to explain
the future and give Jamie his marching orders in the grand plan.
E-mail, said Andreessen, was the first step in a fundamental shift in
how Netscape should market its products. He explained that the
Internet phenomenon was clearly here to stay, and businesses were

nearly frantic to figure out a way to integrate the new technology into the workplace. E-mail was an obvious entry point. E-mail was, in the parlance of the Net, a killer app—an application that every computer user embraced on a daily basis. It was an application indispensable to everyone who got on-line.

So Andreessen assigned Zawinski to create an E-mail component. The idea was to graft E-mail onto the browser so that anyone running Navigator could send and receive E-mail without firing up a separate program. Andreessen also realized that E-mail was an obvious first step toward transforming the Navigator browser into an essential workplace tool.

Jamie spent most of early 1995 inside his lair, toiling night and day on an E-mail program for the 2.0 version of Navigator. He got to design it from scratch, sitting in cafes in Berkeley for weeks while he thought of features and wrote them down on long wish lists. It was a lot of work, but it was fun too.

When he finally unveiled his design for the other engineers to pick apart, he endured heated arguments. Everyone had an opinion about every feature, and by the end of a meeting the whiteboard in the conference room would be covered with the angry black scrawls of dissent. But Zawinski prevailed, for the most part, holding his ground on subjects as esoteric as the necessity for a three-pane model. The rest of the engineers were smart, and Zawinski really had to be on his toes to defend his ideas, which was fun too.

Around the time Zawinski started the actual coding, Netscape hired Terry Weissman to do half the project. Weissman was swell; he jumped right in, and the two of them worked splendidly together. They didn't get territorial. They met every other day or so to check on each other's progress, and the rest of the time they worked as hard as they could to get the thing done.

The program was on target to launch with the 2.0 beta. No sweat! Nothing doomed about it!

Then one day in the early summer of 1995, the camouflage webbing parted and in came Andreessen. "We have our eye on this other company," he said. "They have a mail product." The company was called Collabra, and it was headquartered right around the corner in Mountain View.

"Why are you thinking of doing that? We already have a mail product," said Zawinski, "and ours is better. And ours is already done." And ours, Marc, is *ours*.

Andreessen said Collabra had a lot more to offer than just an E-mail product. Talk about connecting people to people: Collabra was all over the groupware market. Groupware could be the salvation of Netscape, Andreessen said. This could be the magic bullet. The company was in the software *communications* business; that's how people were using their computers. Let Microsoft dominate the world of spreadsheets and word processing. Communicating in the business place—*that* was where the killer apps were.

Pairing groupware software with Navigator would broaden the product line significantly. It could be a perfect fit: The world of the Internet was based on client programs like Netscape's talking to server programs (also Netscape's, God willing) scattered around the world. The same kind of model could be set up inside a business, on a proprietary network. Instead of an Internet, it would be an intranet. Companies could publish corporate "Web" pages (for employee access only) on their intranets.

For Netscape to get a jump on the burgeoning new market, it made sense to buy a company like Collabra, which already had a groupware product. It would be much faster than developing the software from scratch, in-house.

Zawinski had to agree it sounded reasonable. But it sure didn't sound like fun.

Abracadabra ... Collabra?

Andreessen first saw a demonstration of Collabra's main product, Collabra Share, at the popular Demo conference in early 1995. He sat in the audience at the conference and watched as, up on stage,

Collabra went head to head against Lotus Notes—and performed faster than the heavyweight champion. Marc was attuned to the vast potential of groupware. He remembered that Bina, after all, worked on Collage back at NCSA, which was a pioneering groupware effort.

Collabra's software had been getting favorable reviews ever since its debut in 1994, and the company had a good pedigree as well. It also had been partially backed by Kleiner, Perkins money when it went into business in 1993. Indeed, Doerr himself had recently suggested that Netscape and Collabra might have something to gain from each other. Collabra also was attracting attention from Novell and Microsoft, as those companies started to investigate potential ways to broaden their groupware presences.

A few days after the Collabra-Lotus bakeoff, on a quiet Saturday, Andreessen parked his red '94 Mustang—littered with empty soda cans, half-gnawed pieces of abandoned pizza, and magazines greasy from popcorn butter—in the lot outside Eric Hahn's office. Hahn, president and CEO of Collabra, had promised to give Andreessen an impromptu tour of Collabra's weekend-quiet offices, though he wasn't sure what the kid in khaki shorts and rumpled shirt had in mind. Hahn had never met Andreessen before, but he'd read the same glowing magazine stories as everyone else. He figured the youngster probably owed 70 percent of his success to being in the right place at the right time and 30 percent to smarts.

When the two had scheduled the meeting via E-mail, Andreessen hadn't said anything about wanting to buy Hahn's company. In fact, Hahn was talking to Netscape mainly because Doerr had urged him to do so: You two could help each other. Maybe there's some business you could do together.

Hahn understood the upside, of course. Netscape could get its groupware ticket punched; Collabra needed to integrate Internet compatibility into its product. Maybe there was some cross-marketing effort the two companies could launch.

But in Hahn's mind, Collabra wasn't for sale. The company was his baby, and it was doing so well he was hoping to take it public in the next year and a half.

That said, Hahn wasn't naive; he had nearly fifteen years of experience on Andreessen and knew that an acquisition was one of, say, about ten possible outcomes if the two companies hit it off.

Andreessen didn't say much that day. Hahn demonstrated the company's flagship product, Collabra Share. Hahn was impressed that he only had to explain things once to Andreessen, including the arcane technical details of the program's main architectural breakthrough, which enabled dozens of people to have a single collaborative on-line discussion even if they all were using different groupware packages.

Hahn told Andreessen that one of the company's best customers had in fact bought Collabra Share to ease the transition after taking over a smaller business. Collabra's mission in that workplace was to enable the five hundred employees using Microsoft Mail to communicate seamlessly with the two hundred employees who were using a completely different E-mail package, cc:Mail.

Andreessen asked a question here and there, and listened intently to the answers. He's on a research mission, Hahn thought. Within twenty minutes, Hahn was convinced that Andreessen understood Collabra's business totally. He reversed his previous calculation about the kid: Andreessen was 70 percent smarts, 30 percent right-place-and-time.

Andreessen, too, was assessing Hahn. The Collabra founder's résumé was impressive; on paper he sounded like just the kind of guy that Netscape needed to recruit. He was seasoned and could provide adult supervision to the younger engineers. Likewise, he seemed the kind of boss who'd build a decent team. And since acquiring Collabra would also mean acquiring its forty-seven employees, that was an important consideration.

Andreessen learned that Hahn's job experience had prepared him, rather uniquely, to understand just how to propel a company into the groupware market using the Internet. At a time when the concept of an Internet industry was still a novel idea to many Valley entrepreneurs, Hahn was a Net vet. His first job after graduating from college in 1980 had been at Bolt Baranek and Newman, the legendary Cambridge consultants who had designed and built the original sub-network of routers that moved packets of data across the early ARPANET, decades before the government-sponsored network grew into the Internet.

During his tenure at BBN, Hahn had been the lead architect on a major project to overhaul what Hahn politely referred to as the ARPANET's "very mature technology." Known as the C-30 project, the renovation was a critical step that enabled the ARPANET in 1983 to adopt the TCP/IP standard that transmits information across the Internet today.

After two years at BBN, Hahn left Massachusetts for California, seduced by what he thought of as the "virulent capitalism" of Silicon Valley. Lured by the frantic pace of the start-up culture, he got a job at Convergent Technologies, a leading manufacturer of the Unix workstations and servers that dominated workplace computing in the days before the ascendancy of the IBM personal computer. Convergent was so successful, in fact, that it had earned the moniker of being "the fastest growing hardware company in history," a reign that was supplanted by the success of upstart Compaq after the advent of PCs.

Hahn's eight years at Convergent, as an engineer and later as vice president and general manager of the company's server products division, were a wild ride. He saw firsthand what it felt like to be in the middle of a classic Silicon Valley story: a crazy no-holds-barred we-own-the-world growth spurt, followed by—well, a rather precipitous drop-off as soon the industry paradigm shifted.

Eager to abandon the world of management and return to programming, Hahn went to work in 1990 for a small company with an electronic mail product—cc:Mail. That's where Hahn became an expert on electronic mail. Within a year, Lotus Development bought cc:Mail. Hahn, the company's vice president of engineering and general manager, left in 1992.

Hahn dabbled next in the venture capital business, where he met the Kleiner, Perkins team who helped fund his Collabra start-up a few months later. After writing some prototype software and a business plan for Collabra, he convinced the venture capital community that groupware offered a lucrative opportunity. "A lot of money came our way," he remembers, "and the company got into high gear very quickly." Not unlike Netscape.

Marc was impressed. He told Barksdale, who agreed.

"Groupware was the logical extension of our architecture, sort of the next big thing to do with it," Barksdale would tell people later. "Once you've got publishing and business—which were what the first applications of our technology were—what do you do next?"

A few weeks later, Barksdale invited Hahn to a friendly breakfast at Hobee's, a popular Tiffany-lamp-and-tofu diner-style restaurant across the street from Ricky's Hyatt in Palo Alto. Barksdale just wanted to meet Hahn to see if he could work with him.

Guerrilla War

Navigator 2.0 was well on its way to connecting people to people. E-mail and groupware were clearly fine ways to extend the browser. But how did the addition of new features and applications do anything to protect them from Microsoft? Even if they were successful, it was just more bits and bytes for the Redmond giant to gobble up.

For Andreessen, Barksdale, and the rest of the executive staff, the fun had ended a long time ago. They spent most of 1995 just trying to think of ways for Netscape to maintain its head start over Microsoft.

But how? Microsoft was big and powerful; Netscape was little. Microsoft had deep pockets; Netscape was nearly broke. Microsoft controlled the operating system; Netscape controlled legions of loyal browser users who would continue to be loyal, until someone asked them to pay for their software. Microsoft had unlimited resources, with thousands of the industry's best computer programmers ready to take on any task; Netscape had the doomed.

Netscape did have a few advantages, however. For one thing, Netscape owned its market and wrote the rules for conducting business on the Net, at least for now. While the client-side browser, which sat on the Microsoft-dominated desktop, was clearly vulnerable, Netscape's SuiteSpot would add significant value to the *server* side, which was not yet a market that Redmond had conquered. Microsoft would have to fight the battle on Netscape's turf—the open-standards turf of the Net. And it would be guerrilla warfare, the Netscape team decided, because, to stay one step ahead, they would keep changing the rules.

Then there was the Justice Department case. It refused to die, despite the 1994 consent decree.

Critics saw the consent decree as a victory for Microsoft because it did nothing to restrain the company's monopoly over operating-system software. In fact, the settlement did nothing to hurt Gates's business or break apart his company. It was too early for Gates to heave a sigh of relief, though, because the settlement would not become final until a federal judge ruled that the terms were in the public interest.

Back in 1994, Federal District Court Justice Stanley Sporkin, who had a reputation for being irascible and for closely questioning the facts of any case that came before him, had asked tough questions about Microsoft's business practices, questions that the proposed consent decree didn't answer. Sporkin was particularly concerned that the consent decree didn't address the vaporware issue—scaring off potential competitors with hypothetical new-product announcements.

In court, assistant AG Anne Bingaman tried to reassure Sporkin that the terms of the settlement were the best the government could hope to get. "I'd sue them on vaporware. I'd sue them on anything if I thought I could win the case," she said. "But, your Honor, I didn't think I could win these other claims at that time. Now, if somebody comes to me with the evidence and shows me I can win it, hey, I sort of like suing these guys."

In fact, the Justice Department already had begun a new phase of the Microsoft investigation. In October 1994, Bingaman's staff began to investigate another Microsoft action: Gates had announced he planned to pay $1.5 billion to buy software maker Intuit, whose banking software program, Quicken, dominated 70 percent of the financial software market. If the Intuit deal went through, Gates would have bought his company a monopoly in another segment of the software industry.

The government also asked a Silicon Valley lawyer named Gary Reback if he wanted to file a white paper on the proposed merger, for the court record. Reback, forty-five, was a partner in the influential firm of Wilson, Sonsini, Goodrich & Rosati and was well-known to the Justice Department.

His roster of high-paying clients included many of the major Silicon Valley software firms—including Netscape—who were terrified of Microsoft's power, and he had repeatedly urged the government to take action against Microsoft.

After filing the white paper in November 1994, Reback had worked over the Christmas holidays on another brief: urging Sporkin to reject the proposed settlement between the government and Microsoft because the terms were too favorable to Microsoft. Reback also had submitted a number of documents relating to Microsoft's practice of announcing vaporware. Three of Reback's high-profile clients—Apple, Sybase, and Sun Microsystems—bankrolled his work on the brief but requested anonymity because they feared retaliation from Microsoft.

In February 1995, Sporkin had rejected the proposed settlement between the government and Microsoft because it was too lenient. Later that spring, however, the U.S. Court of Appeals removed

Sporkin from the case, criticizing him for second-guessing the Justice Department.

The case was reassigned to U.S. District Judge Thomas Penfield Jackson, who finally would approve the consent decree on August 21, 1995. But by then the Justice Department had embarked quietly on a second investigation of Microsoft. Its investigators had begun once again to travel around the country to interview Microsoft's competitors. And this time around, the investigators would hear about how Gates had begun to use his monopoly in the operating-systems software market to try to control another arena: the Internet.

The Justice Department would hear a lot about that from Netscape. Clark was more than happy to tell interviewers what he thought. "Break the company apart. There needs to be an operating systems company. But it shouldn't be the same as the applications company," he told *Upside* magazine in July 1995. In other words, prohibit Microsoft from leveraging its control of the operating system by giving its new browser features that competing browsers such as Navigator couldn't offer. That same solution that had been proposed by the FTC in its earlier investigation of Microsoft. The FTC got nowhere.

Would the Justice Department be able to do what the FTC couldn't? If so, would it intervene in time?

No one at Netscape knew the specifics of what Microsoft was up to now. All they knew was that Microsoft had licensed the Spyglass code and planned to incorporate a browser into the Windows 95 package. Gates realized he had been on the wrong track with the new Microsoft Network he had planned to launch as a proprietary on-line service. Instead, Gates refocused the Microsoft Network to take advantage of the Internet; he already had issued a directive that the service should be compatible with the technical protocols that governed the Internet.

No one at Netscape knew whether Microsoft's browser would be any good. In a way, the quality of it didn't really matter. If the first generation flopped, Gates could assign a team of his best and brightest programmers to write an improved model. If that one failed too, he could hire even better programmers and try again. And again. And again. He had nearly unlimited resources. Some people referred to Microsoft as the Chinese army: It could simply swamp any competitors.

In the meantime, Netscape had other, more short-term business problems to solve. Despite its phenomenal growth rate—in the first half of 1995, Netscape had unexpectedly large sales of $16.6 million—the company was still in the red, reporting a loss of $4.31 million for the period.

Luckily, Clark and the board of directors had enough to keep his company afloat temporarily, after arranging for a cash infusion from a private sale of company stock in April.

Selling 11 percent of the company to a group of leading publishing and technology companies, including Knight-Ridder, Hearst, Times Mirror, Adobe Systems, TCI, and International Data Group, raised $17.3 million. That was Clark's idea. He figured it was win-win. "Who can be the main beneficiaries of the Web today?" he asked, and answered his question: "All the publishers in the world." The Web was mainly text and images, after all, the same media as newspapers and magazines. The print business, already ransacked by television and stung by an abortive foray into Videotext, knew the world was changing fast. It wouldn't be long before the courts would lift restrictions on the telephone companies and allow them to get into the information business. A lot of newspaper publishers were terrified by that prospect, since the phone companies and their yellow pages seemed poised to take away the bread-and-butter of the local papers: classified and display advertising. Of course they were ready to make an investment in new media.

By the end of the first quarter of 1995, Netscape had on hand an additional $14.7 million in working capital. Netscape had bought itself some breathing space.

Now it was time to change one of the big rules.

Disarming the Operating System

One day in May 1995, Sun Microsystems introduced Java, a programming language whose very existence threatened to end Microsoft's power over the computer industry.

On its face, Java promised to immediately bring bells and whistles like animation to the Web—media techniques that were sorely needed in the static, two-dimensional on-line world.

But Java was far more important than that. The unusual thing about Java was that it could run on almost any kind of computer—Mac, PC, Unix box, OS/2 machine; it was a great equalizer. Programmers writing in Java no longer needed to create code that catered to the vast majority of computer users running the Windows operating system. They wrote for a generic machine, a so-called virtual machine.

Java accomplished this because it was an interpretative language. That gave it some unique characteristics that made it perfect for Web programmers and set it apart from a compiled language like C++. A software vendor typically locked the source code of a compiled language deep inside a particular computer, most typically a personal computer running Windows.

But Java was interpreted, or translated, line by line *in real time* into any user's computer. Java's source code was translated to a virtual computer that allowed programmers to create applications that weren't wed to a specific type of computer. Because Java could be translated into any kind of machine, its programs could in theory live anywhere—like, say, out on the Web—and be downloaded by a computer user as needed.

The potential for change was enormous: Someday Java might eliminate the need for all operating systems. All software programs could be written as compact Java "applets" and archived publicly on the Web. Then, instead of storing software on big hard drives on the desktop, computer users could summon the compact applets from the Web as needed.

Spin out the theory, and suddenly you realize: A computer user wouldn't need a $1,500 desktop computer with mega-memory and a huge hard drive anymore. You could carry around a tiny, cheap "NetPC" whose main function was to hook up to the Net and scarf down anything you needed, from your E-mail to a word-processing applet to whatever. All it needed, of course, was a browser to interface with the Net. You could put that browser on a chip; no full-blown operating system was necessary.

Needless to say, under that kind of a scenario the browser would become king. The browser could *replace* the operating system. It would be the organizing principle, collating your files, finding what you need, summoning applets—everything, in fact, that Windows does now.

The Network, then, would become the computer, as Sun's CEO Scott McNealy was fond of saying. The impact could be enormous, with economic reverberations that would hit the stock prices of the major software and hardware companies. It could affect the fortunes of every technology company in the world, every analyst, every computer owner, every baby boomer with a retirement portfolio, every computer retailer, and, yes, every venture capitalist who gambles on where to invest next.

John Doerr, of course, had heard about Java first. Just as he had been introduced to Mosaic, the peripatetic venture capitalist learned about the development of Java from one of Sun's founders, his old friend Bill Joy. As soon as he saw it, he knew Java was something that would benefit Netscape.

For a while, Java was all Joy talked about. And no wonder. The creation of Java represented the culmination of a five-year quest that Joy had embarked on in 1990. Fed up with the proliferation of clunky, stuffed-with-awkward-features software that he saw coming to dominate the industry, Joy had moved to Aspen to launch a software microbrewery he called Sun Aspen Smallworks. Often cited as one of the great minds of the software industry, Joy had hoped to create innovative, compact programs that would replace gluttonous memory hogs.

While Joy was out of town, Sun spun out a Silicon Valley subsidiary called FirstPerson Inc. Spurred by the hype surrounding the launch of Apple's personal digital assistant, Newton, First-Person's mandate was to create a compact programming language that would run on personal digital assistants (PDAs) and other consumer electronics devices. After the Newton's failure soured the consumer market, FirstPerson had shifted focus and attempted to pursue the mythical interactive TV market. But by 1994, Sun's chief technical officer, Eric Schmidt, realized that the FirstPerson venture was in chaos.

Schmidt convinced Joy to take control of the foundering FirstPerson team. Once back from Colorado, Joy quickly realized that the programming language (then called Oak) could achieve many of his personal goals for revolutionizing the software industry. Within a matter of months Oak had become Java, a new kind of language that made it possible to run any kind of application—or animation—on the Web. With the aid of Java, objects suddenly could dance across a Web page.

Soon after Joy told Doerr about Java, Doerr found himself on a business trip with Jim Clark. The two, who frequently stumped around the country trying to raise interest in Netscape, were holed up in a hotel in Minnesota one night when Doerr told Clark about Java.

Clark wanted to talk to Joy about the project, so Doerr dialed the phone. Clark and Joy talked for more than an hour, and by the time they hung up, Clark was convinced that Java was just the thing they needed.

Clark and Doerr wasted no time. They quickly made sure that Andreessen, whose mandate was to investigate new technologies, was on the Java trail.

Andreessen had heard of Java before, it turned out. In fact, back in early 1994, when he was working as a lowly programmer at EIT, he had entertained a job offer from FirstPerson but turned it down because the offer wasn't lucrative enough. "They couldn't really make me an attractive job offer because they couldn't offer FirstPerson stock. They could only offer Sun stock and not very much at that," Andreessen remembered.

Ironically, soon after Clark and Andreessen had launched their new company back in early 1994, some of the staff at FirstPerson had again approached Andreessen, this time about the possibility of coming to work for Netscape. "FirstPerson was started to do interactive TV devices early on, this whole class of consumer devices with no connection to the Internet," Andreessen recalled. "But when they started to realize the potential relevance of what they were doing to the Internet, they had this huge debate inside Sun. Some of those people actually approached me and said, 'Can we jump ship to Netscape? Can we just get out of Sun and do this?'"

But Netscape had been too small at the time to consider such a thing, Andreessen said.

In hindsight, Andreessen said the decision to pass up acquiring the Java project had been a good one. Andreessen liked the fact that Netscape didn't *own* Java. "Then it would be a Netscape thing, and it would have been difficult because it would have been perceived as a Netscape proprietary thing," he said.

Sun, however, was the perfect company to front for the language. With revenues of more than $5 billion a year, Sun was one of the world's leading manufactuers of workstations and servers, but the hardware manufacturer was not perceived as a threat to software makers in the Valley. Andreessen had high hopes that other software companies would quickly adopt the language as well.

As Andreessen studied Java in early 1995, he saw it had obvious benefits. The language would enable developers around the world to easily write code to work with Netscape's browser. In addition, if Java worked the way it was supposed to, it promised to be a boon to encouraging business transactions over the Web; its applets could be coupled with Netscape's security protocol, the Secure Sockets Layer (SSL), to repel hacker attacks.

Then there was the speed issue. Java could be a godsend in that department. It was a given that Netscape needed to maintain its frantic pace of development to compete with Microsoft. But Andreessen knew that *maintaining* the pace would not be enough to win the war, not if Microsoft ramped up and assigned hundreds of engineers to write its own version of a browser. To beat Microsoft under those circumstances, Netscape would have to increase the pace and go even faster, releasing subsequent versions of Navigator as quickly as possible.

Faster? Such a goal was almost impossible in the world of 1995, a world in which software programs like browsers inevitably grew bigger and clumsier with each successive release, a world in which engineers struggled to graft new features onto a mammoth product without causing the whole damn thing to implode, a world in which code bugs from previous versions lurked deep within the guts of software.

Java could transform that world, because the language was platform-independent.

Netscape's engineers were spending a lot of time tailoring a number of different versions of the browser's user interface to the specific kind of computer that would run the browser. They wrote a front end for Mac users. They wrote a front end for Unix boxes. They wrote a front end for Windows. But if the program were written in Java someday, then they would only need a single front end. It could save a significant amount of development time—perhaps two-thirds of the time they spent coding the front end.

There was a potential downside to Java, though. Licensing the new technology represented a big risk, Andreessen thought. What if the new language didn't work as promised? It could take as long as a year and a half to fix technical problems. Or what if they couldn't be fixed? What if Netscape had to scrap Java two years down the road?

In the end, Andreessen relied on favorable technical reviews of Java's source code for reassurance. So on the day in May 1995 when Sun unveiled Java to the world, Netscape simultaneously announced that it had licensed the language and would incorporate it in future versions of the Navigator browser. Later, and together,

Netscape and Sun set out to create a derivative language called JavaScript, which as a scripting language would enable developers to express in two or three compact lines of code things that would take twenty or thirty lines of code to express in Java. Think of it as Java Lite. Learning to do JavaScript was far easier than Java itself, so it would be adopted by thousands of Web heads who lacked the expertise to hack Java itself.

The Netscape-Sun alliance represented a powerful threat to Microsoft—one that Gates was not be able to ignore. In fact, six months later, in December 1995, Microsoft would sign its own deal with Sun.

CHAPTER TWELVE

IPO Days

Something big was in the air. Word flew around the office one day in June 1995: There's an all-hands meeting tomorrow at 4 P.M.

At the appointed time, everybody who worked for Netscape, more than two hundred people by now, filed into an empty warehouse of a building—Building 7, the dark, dingy one where the engineers liked to play roller hockey. They perched on the edges of folding chairs. They talked in low voices. They thought of new homes and cars and even sailboats and tropical vacations and all the things that money can buy. . . .

Jim Clark stood up front to get his staff's attention. "Is there anyone who hasn't guessed why we're here today?"

A nervous titter. Get on with it, Jim.

"The company is going public," Clark said.

He explained what that meant. Netscape had retained the investment bank Morgan Stanley to be the lead underwriters to take the company through the process of selling an initial public offering. IPO: the magic acronym. In the next few weeks, Netscape would be filing all the necessary documents with the Securities and Exchange Commission; the expected date for the offering was August 9. In the meantime, Clark warned his employees: keep your mouth shut. We're entering the SEC-enforced quiet period, and we don't want to derail the whole deal with loose lips.

A Quiet Period

It's crazy, thought the Doomed. It's too soon! You don't take a start-up public for at least five years! There was little precedent for this kind of speed in taking such a young company public. Just look at the most successful technology IPOs of the past decade. Why, Microsoft was founded in 1975 as a partnership, didn't even incorporate until 1981, the year that MS-DOS launched, and finally went public in 1986.

Even Clark's last company, Silicon Graphics, didn't go public until 1986, a full four years after it was founded. And that was considered a wildly successful IPO. Not to mention the fact that Professor Clark and his students had previously done years of research that led to the idea of a geometry engine to drive three-dimensional computer graphics before he even created SGI.

But if Netscape was to survive, the company needed to grow— and fast. For that, Clark needed money.

The timing was right. Most people in the room were aware, at least vaguely, that Internet fever had seized Wall Street this year. The number of technology companies that were going public was astonishing, and stock prices were soaring. The last time Wall Street's appetite for technology stocks had been so rabid was almost ten years earlier, back in 1986 when Microsoft and SGI and Oracle and Novell all went public. But by comparison, that earlier generation of companies had been much more mature—they had proven track records, at least!—than this year's crop.

That was a major difference between 1995 and 1986. In 1986, you had to be a big established company with a solid history before you went public. In the decade since, the investors' habits had changed. For one thing, by the early 1990s interest rates had declined steadily from the double digits of a decade earlier down to short-term rates of 3 percent or less. Short-term money market securities—a darling of the 1980s—no longer looked as attractive as they once had. Investment dollars had shifted back to the stock market, in the form of investments into equity mutual funds, whose managers tend to buy common stock issues and new public offerings.

At the same time, the flood of mergers and acquisitions that was so fashionable throughout the 1980s had slowed. Investors no longer were so willing to gamble on earning high returns from undervalued stocks.

Meanwhile, an aging generation of baby boomers had begun to invest in stocks in unprecedented numbers. No longer content to sock away retirement savings in low-interest certificates of deposit, they knew from history that, long-term, the stock market would only go one way—up—and at much faster rates than CDs. In unheard-of numbers, boomers were flooding institutional investors such as mutual fund companies with a glut of orders.

To meet the demand, the public offerings of relatively small and new companies were being snapped up. Uunet Technologies Inc., an Internet access provider, went public in May 1995 at $14 a share. And everyone at Netscape was keenly aware of the fact that Spyglass was going public this month, for God's sake, mainly on the strength of the original Mosaic browser code! Ah, but Spyglass had one thing going for it that Netscape didn't; Spyglass had made money in 1994, $1.3 million on revenues of $3.6 million. Spyglass was in the black.

And Netscape? While its revenues were much higher, Netscape would still be in the red. So was this really the best time to go public? Privately, everybody in the room had their own personal reactions to the news.

Lou Montulli had already heard about the plan, because of his relationships with higher-ups (he was dating Clark's daughter). He had kept the information a secret, since he considered it out of channel. But he had given his friends a subtle hint recently when they all were sitting around dinner wondering when the company might go public. Everybody had predicted a date, and Lou had offered one that at the time seemed crazy: I bet we go public by the end of the year.

Paquin was sitting on a folding chair. This is the same building I played hockey in all winter long, and now I'm hearing this? Wow, this is really so, so . . . *Clark*. Everything Clark does comes with urgency, Paquin thought.

They're insane, thought Jamie Zawinski. Just insane. He started to think about how the stock would be priced. Let's say Morgan Stanley tried to sell it to the public at $5 a share. Now, the earliest employees of Netscape had tens of thousands of shares of stock, which Clark had sold to them outright at about a tenth of a cent per share. On top of that, the company had given out plenty of bonuses, in the form of tens of thousands of shares per employee.

So let's see, tens of thousands of shares of stock—OK, let's say hundreds of thousands of shares of stock in the case of a few lucky early employees—and let's calculate them at $5 a share, and we come up with . . . Jamie looked around the room at all the people doing the math in their heads. Jesus. It was a fortune. Maybe even millions.

No way.

The Window of Opportunity

The idea to go public had actually been hatched weeks earlier by Netscape's board of directors. The entire board was there—including Barksdale, Clark, and Andreessen. Doerr was there. So were Frank Quattrone, of Morgan Stanley, and Quattrone's colleague, Bill Brady.

Morgan Stanley had been acting as Netscape's financial advisers for months, helping the company to place the private offering that gave an 11 percent share to a group of media and publishing companies in exchange for $17.3 million.

Quattrone, an enormously influential investment banker who managed Morgan Stanley's Global Technology Group, had been encouraged during that deal by the level of enthusiasm that investors showed for Netscape. "That was something that gave us confidence, made us think we had something special, because of the number of companies who were extremely interested in making an investment," Quattrone said later.

Quattrone, as the lead banker for the company's underwriters, would be responsible for the success or the failure of the venture. His team at Morgan Stanley would help determine the price of the stock shares. The underwriters would purchase the shares to be offered to the public and then resell them to institutional investors. If Quattrone had not been so confident, Netscape probably wouldn't have gone public so soon.

The start-up could not have picked a more experienced banker to guide it through the process. With fourteen years of experience in taking technology companies public, Quattrone had one of the strongest résumés in the Valley. The roster of companies who went public under his guidance included Intuit, SynOptics, 3Com, Cisco—and, in the dark ages of 1986, Jim Clark's Silicon Graphics.

As a young man fresh out of Stanford University's M.B.A. program, Quattrone had been one of the very first investment bankers to realize that the coming growth of Silicon Valley could someday change how the world did business. Quattrone still remembered the time in 1980 when Steve Jobs came to preach the high-tech gospel to his investments class, soon after Morgan Stanley took Apple public.

In 1981, with his brand-new M.B.A. in hand, Quattrone had been hired as an associate in Morgan Stanley's San Francisco office. This was back when the Wall Street powerhouse was starting to build a Technology Group to specialize in taking computer-industry companies public. "Morgan Stanley didn't have anyone on the West Coast doing it, so I got in on the ground floor," he remembered.

Quattrone learned about the technology business the hard way: "We were real, real excited when we were named the lead manager of the VisiCorp IPO, which never saw the light of day," he said. But some of the other early projects that Morgan Stanley's Technology Group handled helped create the mystique of Silicon Valley. Quattrone worked on the initial public offerings of companies like Quantum, Bridge Communications, and Mentor Graphics—big deals at the time.

Back in those days, the investment climate had been more restrained than it became in the techno-giddy 1990s. For instance, Quattrone learned that investors' demand for the technology market was intensely cyclical. Certain windows of opportunity opened when interest was high and companies could fashion attractive deals for themselves; then, suddenly, investors would turn fickle and the market would sour for months. During those downturns, people just didn't want to hear about technology, and you couldn't get a deal done to save your life.

Quattrone met Clark in late 1985 or early 1986, during the period when the professor was deciding to take Silicon Graphics public. Needing a cash infusion, Clark interviewed bankers, searching for an underwriting team who could predict, among other things, the most opportune time to launch an offering.

"I thought right away that Clark was brilliant, very passionate, telling us how the chips would calculate floating point operations at billions and billions of operations per second," Quattrone said. "Later, we teased him about sounding a lot like Carl Sagan. But he really explained, for the first time, the process of what it takes from a mathematical point of view to render an object, a real object, in color, in real time, at a speed that makes sense on a computer, and then he kind of backed it up to what the chip requirements were to do that and made it clear that what Silicon Graphics had done was very, very special."

Silicon Graphics chose Morgan Stanley to underwrite the deal, which was scheduled to go off in mid-1986. But Morgan Stanley soon postponed the offering; the summer of 1986 marked one of those cyclical downturns when no one wanted to hear about technology. Both Sun and Apollo—which had gone public a few months earlier to great fanfare—had slipped from the prices set at their initial public offerings.

Quattrone went off to the Cotswolds on vacation with his family, figuring it would be a long hiatus. Wrong. A few days into the vacation he got a call: Get home *fast,* the market was heating up. What Quattrone's colleagues had noticed during his absence was that demand had increased for shares of already-public technology companies. With investors snapping up stock, tech companies' price/earnings ratios were rocketing. To the bankers, the situation was a classic sign that the environment had turned receptive to new issues, whose shares—sold at a discount relative to companies with proven track records—could look like bargains to tech-hungry investors. The window was opening. The underwriters had a hunch that the timing was right to revive the SGI deal.

So Quattrone traveled with the Silicon Graphics team—Clark, CEO Ed McCracken, and Mark Perry, the company's chief financial officer—around Europe and throughout the United States, touting SGI's stock to potential investors at half a dozen meetings a day. At night, exhausted, sometimes they would have a drink together in the hotel bar. That's when Quattrone learned that the esoteric professor also had a talent for telling the kind of "disgusting" jokes that Quattrone and just about everyone else loved to collect.

The bankers' hunch had been right. SGI's public offering was a success, with demand so high that the stock opened about $1 higher than its offering price. After that, Clark and Quattrone stayed in touch. Subsequently, Quattrone and Morgan Stanley ended up doing about a dozen more transactions for SGI—financings, corporate strategic partnerships, acquisitions. And of course, whenever they ran into each other at a party, Quattrone could count on Clark for a good joke.

Quattrone had seen the press release that Rosanne Siino wrote in 1994 to announce Clark's resignation from SGI. Soon after, Quattrone heard rumors that Clark was about to launch a start-up. Quattrone was excited. He considered Clark a kind of a Pied Piper who attracted technical talent. With Clark's reputation as a visionary, the buzz in the Valley was that "whatever he was going to do was going to be exciting . . . and it probably was going to have great, great technical talent associated with it," Quattrone said.

So after Clark set up shop on Castro Street, "I was probably the first banker that called on him," Quattrone said.

Quattrone was attracted by a combination of factors: Clark's reputation, the fact that John Doerr had invested substantially in the company, the fact that Clark seemed to be in the forefront of creating a whole new segment of the technology industry.

Down on Castro Street, Clark was lit up, talking a mile a minute about the possibilities of the Internet, about the information highway, about the jump that he'd gotten on this brand-new industry.

Clark talked to Quattrone about teams, about how excited he was with Andreessen and the rest of the crew. He told Frank he thought he had an *unfair* number of the people who really understand what was going on with the Net and Internet-based software. He told the banker he had an interesting business model, that he was going to proliferate the new thing called a browser and have it become an industry standard.

Quattrone was hooked. The success of the private offering that Morgan Stanley had underwritten for Netscape the following April merely confirmed his suspicions. Now, at the meeting of Netscape's board of directors, he thought it was appropriate for the discussion to turn to the future: What was the next logical step to keep the flow of money coming in so the company could continue to grow?

The conversation at Netscape's board meeting naturally turned to the idea of going public. Clark raised the issue, and the discussion turned into a free-for-all. Barksdale's position was that Clark had the most money invested in this venture and therefore had the right to push the company in that direction. John Doerr's view was, Let's put the puck on the ice and see what happens. Peter Currie, the former McCaw CFO whom Barksdale had lured to Netscape in April, dissented, noting that it was really early in the company's development to be considering such a move and, all things being equal, maybe it wasn't advisable to go public.

But were all things equal? A number of benefits could accrue as a result of a successful public offering. For one thing, going public creates a trading currency with which you can make strategic acquisitions—of other companies, such as Collabra, and technologies— to continue boosting your company's growth. Second, going public can be very helpful from a public relations standpoint, creating a buzz about how hot your company is and turning its name into a household brand.

And the time was certainly ripe for technology companies to take advantage of Wall Street's interest. When should Netscape do it, in 1997? If so, should it be early in the year or late? Or would it be better to wait until 1998?

The decision to take a company public is never made lightly. Going public changes the whole universe. One minute you're this little private company; the next, you're required to put all your history on display for the world to inspect, dissect, pick apart. You become a public spectacle. You'd better not have any skeletons in the closet.

The question was, Would the benefits outweigh the risks in this case? Currie had worked previously as an investment banker at Morgan Stanley and had seen what happened when companies tried to go public too early. A premature IPO could be distracting for a young start-up. When an unseasoned management team took its eye off business, and a chief executive started waltzing around the world for months to hawk his stock, the business could falter fatally. But Currie felt that Netscape's management team was experienced enough to handle the pressure.

Undoubtedly, a successful public offering would create a huge cash infusion, mainly from institutional investors, who buy thousands of shares of public stock in a company. But the impact of raising so much money so fast can have negative side effects on a company that isn't positioned properly to take advantage of the situation. That's why you proceed carefully. If millions of dollars flow into a company's coffers, virtually overnight, the company has to spend that money: hiring, expansion, new products. It sounds like a dream scenario, but it also can spell disaster if a company's top management isn't strong enough to orchestrate the growth, or if a company's business plan isn't sound enough, or if the vision of what the company should become isn't clear enough.

There's another potential drawback to going public, as well, one that hits the company's founders. It was a drawback that Clark already had experienced at Silicon Graphics: If you sell big chunks of your company to other people, you lose control. Was Clark really ready to take the same risk with his new baby?

Of course, there was also a huge risk in doing nothing. Bill Gates was getting ready to launch his long-awaited and much-trumpeted Windows 95 operating system. The Netscape team felt some urgency. Already, Microsoft had distributed thousands of beta copies of Windows 95 to users around the world. After months and months of delays in getting the operating system to market, Microsoft was orchestrating a smart marketing and press campaign. Newspaper and magazine columnists who covered technology stories were focused on little else. Interest was at a fever pitch; Windows 95 must be revolutionary. The operating system would have to be far more than a mere upgrade. To live up to the hype surrounding it, Windows 95 should transform the personal computer into a magical, musical instrument that played beautiful sonatas. To live up to the hype, Windows 95 would have to be able to cook dinner and vacuum the rugs while you were out of the house. How else could Microsoft justify such a long wait for the product?

In the Netscape boardroom that day, the big fear was this: What if Bill Gates had been prescient enough to use the Spyglass Mosaic code as the basis for a killer browser? What if Windows 95, soon to be factory-loaded onto every brand-new personal computer in America before it even reached the consumer, was going to include a super browser able to compete head-on with puny Netscape? What if?

Good-bye, market share, that's what. Good-bye, 85 percent hold on the browser market—*pfft*. Overnight.—And, maybe, good-bye Netscape.

Windows 95 was going to launch sometime in August. Well, someone said, if we're going to go public, why don't we do it around the same time? Maybe we should come out right after Windows 95, right after Labor Day. Wait a minute, someone else said. Maybe we should come out *before* Windows 95 hits the marketplace. That way *we* set the agenda, not Microsoft. If we go public before Microsoft makes its move, before Bill Gates weighs in, we'll be playing from a position of strength.

Barksdale was thinking about how Microsoft would be pulling out all the stops in August to promote Windows 95, no matter what. It could be extraordinarily helpful to Netscape's effort to go public if they were to ride the coattails of the Microsoft public relations juggernaut. Redmond's PR campaign would almost certainly create general interest in technology companies, and that could only be useful to Netscape's own IPO.

Great plan, in theory. But that would mean—well, that would mean going public in the summer, the worst time of year, because Wall Street's attention is focused elsewhere, on vacations and summer homes and the heat, not on tiny tech companies that want to raise cash. And if you're going to pick the absolute worst time of the worst season to go public—well, that would be August. A good many of the institutional investors you want to sell stock to are from overseas, for one thing, and everybody knows that in August Europe basically closes down. Everybody goes on vacation. An August offering should be avoided like a Boston tent wedding in winter.

Besides, there wasn't enough time to put the deal together, not between now and the end of summer. For one thing, there was the required SEC registration statement, reams and reams of documentation describing the company, describing the risks, describing the business, pulling together detailed financial information, audited statements of the company's finances, detailed descriptions of all out-standing contracts the company has. It usually takes at least six weeks to get those filings finished, even if you're going full speed.

For another, there was the road show. The road show is the glitz; it's when the investment bank that's taking a company public trots out the company's principals to meet with potential investors and to field questions, to reassure the marketplace that the company would be a wise place to park your money. A road show is a grueling world trip; it's more exhausting than a Grateful Dead tour; it's as many as thirteen meetings a day, for weeks. It's hopping from New York to London to Chicago to Munich to Minneapolis—by lunch. It's impossible to prep a company's management team—they have to know the answers to any conceivable question a skeptic might raise—and set up appointments in so many cities so fast. Especially if all the people you want to meet are on vacation.

But if we could pull it off? Then we'd beat Windows 95 to the punch, no matter what.

Microsoft is the thing to beat.

Quattrone weighed in. "With this company, and in this market, I think people will give up their vacations to see the road show."

He and Brady also pointed out that they already were so familiar with the financial minutiae of the Netscape company, they could get the SEC filings done at warp speed. Because of the private placement in April, Netscape already had pulled together and recorded an enormous hunk of the financial information that would be needed to complete a comprehensive S-11 filing.

Both Currie and Quattrone thought Netscape could probably shave the filing time significantly, complete the process at an accelerated pace, if the company was willing to take its culture of speed, which had evolved as a strategy to get software products out the door quickly, and superimpose that same efficiency onto the IPO process.

Barksdale wasn't worried about that part of it. John Doerr was a veteran; he'd taken maybe four dozen companies public. And Netscape had recently brought Peter Currie and Roberta Katz, the company's legal counsel, on board. Those two knew as much about taking companies public as anyone alive. Why, Katz probably did a hundred acquisitions back when she worked with Barksdale at McCaw. Barksdale thought, We have people who know what they're doing. It's not like six guys in a garage, sitting around, shooting the breeze. We've been through this process before.

Of course, it would mean working around the clock for the next few weeks . . .

When does the filing need to be done? Barksdale asked.

Quattrone said, Oh, in about three weeks.

Nineteen days later, Currie and his financial team filed the documentation with the SEC.

At Netscape, they prided themselves on not knowing the meaning of time.

Netscape Road Tour: Summer of 1995

Zurich, Paris, Glasgow, Edinburgh, London, Chicago, New York, Minneapolis, Boston, Los Angeles, San Francisco, Portland. By the end of July, the designated hitters on the road show, Barksdale and Currie, were starting to feel more like trained seals.

The Netscape board had been adamant that management not get caught up in an IPO frenzy that would divert everyone from the business of running a business. For the most part, Mike Homer and Todd Rulon-Miller, from marketing and sales, stayed back in Mountain View, to handle day-to-day operations. Andreessen kept away from the road show as much as possible too, but he was trotted out for a few of the high-profile stops in such places as San Francisco and New York.

A road show may sound glamorous, but it's like running for president. In your quest to raise money and build interest in your public offering, how many cities can you hit, how many banquet halls can you fill, how much chicken Kiev can you eat before you crash? A typical day began with a breakfast meeting in one city, a luncheon speech in another, and a late-afternoon pitch in a third—and given the heightened excitement of the Netscape offering, it wasn't unusual to be out of the country for dinner. They'd give the presentation and a twenty-minute slide show to two or three large groups and shoehorn in a dozen one-on-one meetings in between. Multiply that schedule by two and a half weeks. That's a lot of chicken Kiev.

Handlers escorted the Netscape team, of course: the investment bankers who set up the meetings in the first place. Barksdale and Currie were coached on what to say, but really, after a day or two, none of the questions took anyone by surprise. What are your projections for the future? What are your revenues so far this year? How are you going to compete against Microsoft?

A more welcome series of questions began to surface, too. The potential investors were as interested about the Internet phenomenon as about Netscape. What's the future of business on the Internet? How much will the Internet industry grow? How much money will it be worth in a year? Two years? Five years? What's the business model for the next decade? The Netscape team began to be seen as the prophets of the Net; and everywhere they went, everyone was bullish about its prospects.

They heard variations of the same questions everywhere, whether they were in a one-on-one meeting with Fred Kittler, the portfolio manager at J. P. Morgan, who was so gracious you wanted to go out to dinner with him and meet his whole family, or in a standing-room-only conference room at the headquarters of a big mutual fund family, being peppered with questions simultaneously by twelve blunt portfolio managers and three analysts screaming to be heard.

No matter the forum, it quickly became clear that Wall Street was wildly enthusiastic about the Internet's future—and that Wall Street regarded Netscape as the standard bearer for the Net. By the time they got to New York City, the road show felt like a feeding frenzy. Investors were treating Barksdale and Currie like celebrities. At meeting after meeting—at breakfasts, lunches, dinners, hotel conference rooms crammed with hundreds of people, high-stress phone conversations early in the morning—the demand for Netscape's stock was running high. And it just kept building.

Investors were turned away from one luncheon where a capacity crowd of five hundred filled a New York hotel ballroom. Morgan Stanley had to set up a toll-free number to handle phone inquiries about the deal.

The investment bankers had never experienced anything like it. Before the road show, Morgan Stanley had prepared Barksdale and Currie to answer tough questions and face skeptical investors leery of committing to such a young company. But just the opposite was happening. In New York, investors would plead, "Make sure you put in a good word for me with the underwriters so I can get my allocation."

The Morgan Stanley bankers told them the offering was wildly oversubscribed—potential investors had placed orders for far more shares than were being offered. In fact, demand was so high that Netscape increased the number of shares for sale, from the original filing of 3.5 million shares to 5 million.

That increase did little to satisfy the hunger, however: investors placed orders for 100 million shares!

The underwriters and Netscape decided to raise the price of the stock. After filing documents with the SEC indicating that it planned to offer the shares for $14 apiece, Morgan Stanley increased the share price, first to $21, and then to $24. Even that number wasn't firm. It sounded crazy, such a high price, but with so much enthusiasm the share price might climb even more before the actual day of the offering.

Barksdale and Currie started to get a little punchy. Jet lag took its toll. At their last stop in London, in a hot room crowded with men wearing navy-blue chalk-striped wool suits in the middle of summer, someone from the back of the room called out a question for Barksdale.

"What effect will Microsoft's bundling of its own browser into the Windows Ninety-five package have on Netscape's business?"

It was a softball question, really: basic, one that Barksdale had answered dozens of times before.

This time, however, he looked at the crowd and said, in a serious sugar-coated Mississippi drawl, "There are only two ways in this world a man can make a dollar." He held up one finger and said, "You can bundle."

He held up a second finger and said, "Or you can unbundle."

And then—instead of answering the question—he said, "Thank you very much, ladies and gentlemen."

The room was quiet. The men in their heavy suits cocked their heads as if to say, huh? Barksdale and Currie rushed out of the room. They had a plane to catch.

On the Offering's Eve

August 8 was a scorcher in Maryland. A handful of late-model black sedans, carrying men in business suits, pulled over to the side of the road in a small rural town.

The passengers jumped out to hunt for telephones. A couple of the men in suits scurried into a fast-food restaurant nearby. A couple more found pay phones at a filling station on the corner. Two others huddled over public phones that were catty-corner to each other, across the street.

Their drivers got out of the cars, wearing sunglasses, and leaned against the hoods, arms folded, waiting.

One of the passengers who ran to a pay phone was Jim Barksdale. It was late on the afternoon before his company was scheduled to go public. This looks like a mafia deal, he thought. I mean, these people who live here are probably scared to death. It looks like six guys and their bodyguards.

He had no time to worry about it. This was a historic moment. Barksdale phoned Morgan Stanley's war room—the Equity Capital Markets Desk in Manhattan, where all the action would go down the next day—to make a final, momentous decision. He had to decide what price to set for Netscape's shares when the stock opened the next morning.

Netscape's board of directors had authorized the board's pricing committee—including Barksdale and Peter Currie, who was standing at a nearby phone—to make the call.

Barksdale had been hoping the call would be quick, a formality almost, accomplished via cell phone from the backseat of his car as he whizzed through rural Maryland after finishing a final one-on-one meeting with a potential customer. He had expected to phone in from the comfort of air-conditioning, to talk to the guy who was running the book, get Morgan Stanley's estimate of what the price should be, and then dicker with the investment bankers up or down, depending on circumstances. Thanks very much, and we'll be on our way.

The problem was that the principal actors in Netscape's road show—standard-bearers of the information revolution!—were driving through a part of rural America where cellular coverage was spotty. Cordless phones wouldn't work in the heartland. So there they stood at that momentous juncture: at a bank of pay phones in the middle of God knows where, sun beating down, finalizing a deal that could be worth—what, hundreds of millions?

At Morgan Stanley, demand for Netscape's shares was so high, so frenzied, so over the top, that the investment banker recommended opening at $31 a share.

Barksdale thought that was a mistake; $31 was too high. And in the end, it was Barksdale's decision to make.

He said, "No, I want to bring it out at twenty-eight."

His reasons were simple. He would rather have Netscape remembered as a $20 stock than a $30 stock, for one. It was more a matter of perception than anything else, but on Wall Street, the only thing that counts more than perception is hindsight. Also, Barksdale figured that $28 was twice as much as the $14 per share that Netscape had identified in recent SEC filings as the top of the projected price range. This was the first time anybody had filed for a 100 percent increase, and Barksdale just didn't want to push it anymore. He felt he should leave a little money on the table.

So after all the tens of thousands of miles traveled around the world selling Netscape to potential customers, after all the board-rooms and rich restaurant meals, and after the revival-meeting atmosphere of the sold-out stops on the road show, this is what it came down to: a half dozen men in dark suits, sweating in the heat on the side of a dusty road, cupping their hands over their ears and trying to hear a phone conversation over the noise of passing traffic.

Their drivers kept the engines idling. Air conditioners hummed. They were anxious to be on their way.

Twenty-eight dollars a share, said Barksdale.

He could have set it higher, but even at $28, Netscape stock had the distinction of being the only offering in history that doubled its price before it even hit the market.

The Day Wall Street Went Nuts for the Net

Barksdale flew home to California that night and was in Peter Currie's cubicle first thing the following morning.

Currie was on the phone with ground zero—the investment bankers in Morgan Stanley's war room in New York. Frank Quattrone, who was in New Jersey for his mother's birthday, also was hooked into the office via conference call.

The stock should have been trading briskly by now. By now, they should know whether the $28 a share was holding.

It wasn't. Indeed, it wasn't trading at all.

Demand was so high for Netscape's stock that, an hour and a half later, a floor still hadn't been found for the price. Barksdale's fears about overpricing the stock had been unfounded. When it finally did trade on the NASDAQ market, Netscape was selling for an unprec-

edented $71 a share. The reason the stock opened so high was simple:
There was absolutely no supply to staunch the incredible demand.
Huge numbers of investors had placed orders to buy the stock at any
price, and even large institutions were trolling for big pieces; they
told Morgan Stanley that they were going to be trying to hit the bid at
prices anywhere up to $70 a share.

For Barksdale, the situation was "surreal. When they gave us
the number, it was exciting in one way, worrisome in another. It was
a bit confusing. I didn't understand. I thought to myself, Well, *now*
what are you going to do?"

Answer: Well, nothing. Just sit back and enjoy the ride.

Things were going crazy at Morgan Stanley's Equity Capital
Markets Desk. Imagine a room where the phones are always ringing
off the hook, where that level of mayhem represents normalcy. Then
ratchet up the noise level by a factor of ten on a day like this. Picture
a dozen rows of desks, with fifteen or twenty stations in each row,
with hundreds of phone extensions that people can push buttons to
get onto. Try to imagine the cacophony, with the Equity Capital Markets people sandwiched between sales and trading on one side and
corporate finance clients on the other, trying to balance the interests
of each.

In the center of the chaos was the Equity Capital Markets syndicate manager, charged with holding the whole thing together, trying to answer a number of questions: How much of the deal could be
handled centrally, in the institutional pot? How much should be moved
by other managers? Within the portion of the shares reserved for institutional investors, how much should be allocated to each one of the
institutions?

Meanwhile, the salespeople were on the phones with the buyers, confirming the new and astronomical price range. The buyers
were screaming back at the salespeople—not complaining about the
price but trying to jockey for position, to ensure that they got a big
enough piece of the pot!

More than two hundred large institutions wanted on the order of 10 percent of the shares for themselves. They all were good customers. Most of them were going to be disappointed. The syndicate manager was trying to figure out who should get an allocation, basing the decision in part on who attended the road show luncheons and who attended the one-on-ones, and which portfolio managers and analysts had visited the company, and were they asking good questions, and did these people flip the last couple of offerings or did they hold them?

Did they really want to own this, and how much were they willing to pay in the aftermarket; how many shares were they willing to buy later?

The situation was unheard-of for a company that only had $16.6 million in revenue the first half of the year. Nothing like this had ever happened before on Wall Street. Even more astounding, the price kept rising.

At one point, Quattrone heard from the syndicate manager that the shares were trading for $72. Only one day earlier, the syndicate manager had recommended selling the shares for $27. "Seventy-two? Not twenty-seven?" Quattrone yelled gleefully into the phone. "Are you sure you don't have dyslexia?"

By lunchtime, the money managers at big mutual funds who had been lucky enough to buy shares when it opened could have turned around and sold them—at a 150 percent profit.

Of course, those weren't the kinds of investors that Morgan Stanley wanted. The firm preferred to sell to investors who would hold on to their shares until after the dust had settled. That's because, after leading the offering, the investment banker would have to stand firm behind Netscape and be ready in the aftermarket to make bids for stock that people wanted to sell back. To do that, Morgan Stanley would have to put its capital at risk. If too many people wanted to sell, and there weren't enough buyers to absorb the shares, the stock could plummet.

That was the last thing anyone wanted.

At the time, the frenzy seemed like an act of nature—unexplainable and undeniable in its pure momentum. But in the aftermath of the deal, Quattrone discovered that an unusual amount of demand had been coming from retail investors, fueling the fire. Discount brokerage Charles Schwab had changed the recording on its 800 number to say, *Press one if you're calling about Netscape.* The discount brokerages hadn't specified a price ceiling on orders, so they were obligated to buy the stock at whatever price they could get it, driving share prices higher and higher and higher.

Netscape had become a trophy stock. Nobody wanted to part with it! More typically, in an IPO, you might see a third of the shares just acquired trading on the first day by sellers happy to get a 10 or 15 percent return on their investment, sold off to institutions willing to pay a little bit of a premium to build their positions for the longer term. But this time, most buyers were hanging on to their shares—even irrationally—ignoring the profit they could have made.

By the close of trading, based on the 38.1 million shares of Netscape stock in existence, the company's value had been set by the market: $4.4 billion. No other IPO had ever come close.

The last time the IPO tech climate had merited the description "frenzied" had been back in 1986, when Microsoft, Oracle, and Novell went public. But in those days, frenzied had meant that Microsoft sold 2.8 million shares for $21 apiece. Wild success meant that Microsoft's shares sold for a mere $2 higher than the upper end of its filing range.

After its IPO, Microsoft had been worth a mere $519 million. Netscape, however, had ushered in a new era.

In retrospect, Quattrone described it as "a once-in-a-lifetime kind of offering. Overall, it turned out to be an important event not only for the company but for the Internet as a whole. We felt like we had just witnessed an inflection point in time, which was really the formal ushering in of the new Internet era."

Clark and Barksdale threw a big party that night for all the company's employees at a local nightclub in nearby Sunnyvale. Everyone gave speeches. Clark called all the company's original employees up on stage—he loved to do that—and Montulli went with his cell phone in a back pocket. Of course, someone (not Zawinski) had to call him while he was onstage, just to embarrass him with the ringing.

The reverberations of Netscape's good fortune were felt far beyond the glass-walled buildings on Middlefield Road in Mountain View. Indeed, in the years to come, people around the world would always point back to Netscape's offering as the day the Internet captured the imagination, not only of Wall Street, but the rest of the world as well.

The Internet was, pure and simple, the big winner. Pundits declared the Internet the future, the next big wave, the savior of the economy.

One big loser was the old paradigm of five-hundred-channel interactive TV. According to that now-defunct dream, put forth by people like Sumner Redstone of Viacom and John Malone of Tele-Communications Inc. and Ray Smith of Bell Atlantic, the television set was supposed to morph into the center of the universe. The "viewer" would be able to accomplish everything from ordering groceries to paying bills to watching heavyweight boxing on the small screen. Of course, interactive TV would have been possible only in a world where the corporate big boys could control the pipeline via high-speed cable hookups, pay-per-view entertainment, and monthly fees.

The Internet had made that vision obsolete. The Net was the great equalizer, offering unlimited access over already-extant phone lines to unlimited amounts of information. And most of it was free.

Forget five hundred channels. Try five million channels. Or five billion. The Internet was limited only by the bounds of the imagination.

The Internet was, unmistakably, the information highway. And Netscape's Navigator was the vehicle that propelled you over the asphalt.

Acquiring Collabra

Barksdale phoned Hahn a week after Netscape went public, and they agreed to meet to talk about an acquisition of Collabra; in early September the deal was sealed by Barksdale in a slightly more intimidating venue than Hobee's had been—the formal rococo-paneled conference room at Morgan Stanley's Sand Hill Road office. To determine the specific price at which he was willing to sell his company, Hahn had taken into consideration the fact that Collabra would in another fourteen months be in a position to go public on its own. He had obtained an estimate of how much Collabra would be worth on that date and then, using standard accounting practices, calculated the company's current worth, adjusting a little bit for risk. He told Barksdale the number.

Barksdale had said, "Fine, let me go off for a little while to think about it."

At Morgan Stanley, there was a flurry of lawyers, investment bankers, lawyers, venture capitalists, and lawyers. They all hovered anxiously around Barksdale, who sat at the head of an imposing conference table amid the starched shirts.

The warm, let's-make-it-work feeling that Hahn had earlier gotten from Barksdale had disappeared. This was a roomful of adversarial bullies, screaming at each other at the top of their lungs, waving their big Rolex wristwatches in each other's faces. The scene had more drama than a Broadway play, Hahn thought.

Barksdale's initial offer was a bit lower than Hahn's minimum, so they haggled back and forth, with the parties excusing themselves for various private discussions. It was nerve-racking, but for Hahn, who loves a good bargaining session so much that friends often take him along to help negotiate the purchase of a new car, it was also a lot of fun.

In the end, Hahn accepted Netscape's offer to purchase Collabra for 1.85 million shares of Netscape stock, at the time worth roughly $100 million.

The only catch was that Collabra's investors wouldn't be able to sell their Netscape shares for several months. At about $52 a share, Netscape's stock was considered ridiculously overpriced, and Collabra's board of directors had directed Hahn to try to negotiate a collar on the deal that would force Netscape to make up the difference if its stock price went below a specified price in the interim.

Peter Currie told Hahn that Netscape really didn't want to agree to the collar, and Hahn conceded the point.

It turned out to be a smart move, because a collar usually has a cap as well. And by the time Collabra's original investors were able to liquidate their Netscape stock, shares were trading at an unbelievable high around $150—an amount that would have been well above a cap.

Netscape's stock continued to soar throughout the fall and winter. After the price peaked at $170 a share in December, the stock split two-for-one on January 23, 1996.

From a corporate standpoint, the Netscape acquisition of Collabra was an unmitigated success: Hahn and the other Collabra investors got rich, and Netscape got instant entrée into the groupware business and dozens of seasoned employees. All but two of Collabra's staff agreed to stay on to work for Netscape. Seven of Collabra's managers—including Hahn—signed key employee agreements, promising not to compete with Netscape for the next two years even if they chose to leave the company before that period elapsed.

"They're the people who run our company today," Barksdale said in an interview in late 1997.

A team of six of Collabra's top engineers had moved to Netscape's offices even before the deal officially closed. Their job was to start integrating the new generation of Collabra's software with Netscape's products. Meanwhile, Andreessen and Hahn wrote a three-page document that described in detail the integration of Netscape and Collabra, laying out how Netscape would launch the new products within eighteen months.

It's a Business

By the end of 1995, Netscape had begun to fulfill its business strategy. A number of corporate customers—including Lockheed-
Martin, H-P, Eli Lilly, McDonnell-Douglas, SGI, Wells Fargo
Bank, National Semiconductor, EDS, CNN, and Dow Jones—had
signed on.

But it was only a start. To keep its new customers happy and
attract more, Netscape needed a broader product line. The goal was
to create a mature line of Net-compatible applications, both clients
and servers, that would appeal to business customers. Acquiring companies, rather than devoting precious time and resources to creating
products from scratch, seemed to be the way to go. The Collabra
acquisition had been an important first step; the success of that deal
created a blueprint for those that were to follow over the next few
months.

Netscape went shopping for properties with characteristics
that mirrored Collabra's: small companies with fewer than a hundred employees but with a proven proprietary software product that
could be reworked to sit on top of the open protocols that made the
Net equally accessible to any kind of user on any kind of computer.

But the next company that Netscape bought—InSoft—
wasn't as smooth a fit as Collabra had been. In January 1996, Netscape bought the maker of multimedia conferencing software for
$160 million.

As with the Collabra deal, Netscape's two-pronged strategy
was to acquire both the company's code and the valuable employees
who had written it. But the InSoft deal fell short of Netscape's expectations on both fronts. "This acquisition didn't work very well," remembered Marketing VP Mike Homer.

For one thing, InSoft's headquarters were located far away
from Silicon Valley, in Mechanicsburg, Pennsylvania. Although
Netscape offered a relocation package, "of the eighty-two people at

that company, I bet that less than twenty are left now at Netscape," Homer said in late 1997. "A lot of them didn't want to move."

The InSoft software was problematic as well. InSoft made two products, called CoolView and CoolTalk, which Netscape bought to add real-time video conferencing to its product line. Even then, the feature was considered "a real gamble," Homer said. "And as you know, real-time video conferencing has only caught on slowly. Those features of our products were never really attractive to that many of our users. But we took the gamble, because if it caught on it could be a real differentiator for our products."

In the end, InSoft's software became the foundation for Netscape LiveMedia and Netscape Media Server.

The next company that Netscape bought was Paper Software, a provider of distributed three-dimensional graphics that made WebFX Virtual Reality Markup Language software. Unlike the employees of InSoft, the majority of the seventeen people who worked for Paper Software in Woodstock, New York, were willing to move to Silicon Valley, along with the company's code.

Paper Software had created a valuable proprietary three-dimensional plug-in based on VRML, the standard for creating three-dimensional images on the Internet. The Paper Software code became the core technology for Netscape Live3D, which enabled people who used Navigator to see VRML graphics on-screen. The feature was extremely useful for browsing games and entertainment sites and was also useful for displaying and rendering engineering drawings.

In April 1996, Netscape announced its decision to support the Lightweight Directory Access Protocol (LDAP), a standard that enabled a systems administrator to create a central directory of authorized users and E-mail addresses. LDAP, which was created at the University of Michigan, eliminated the need for maintaining separate directories on each server on an intranet.

During the spring of 1996, Netscape also acquired Netcode, a Menlo Park company of about fifteen employees that had created a

Java-based object toolkit and visual interface builder for developing Java applications.

Netscape had just shipped Navigator 2.0, the first product to hit the market with Java. In its infant state, Java created some challenges for developers. It was somewhat difficult to write programs in the newborn language, for one thing, because there existed no trove of Java components to plug into new programs. Instead of browsing through libraries filled with components of Java code that could be inserted, wholesale, into various programs, developers had to write from scratch.

That's what made Netcode's toolkit so valuable—the company had built libraries of user interface components written in Java, to speed the development process of Java programs. With Netcode's core team of engineers agreeing to come to work for Netscape, Netscape was quickly able to integrate the Netcode code into its Open Network Environment (Netscape ONE) to provide a framework for developers to build cross-platform network-based applications.

As Netscape grew and diversified, the company tried to balance a number of competing interests. Growth, for instance. It was one thing to hire people every day, expand into this new building today and that new building tomorrow, and order office chairs for a third one down the street as well. But at the same time, you had to try to hire only really good engineers, which limited the available number, which in turn limited the number of projects that the core engineering team could handle at any one time.

But Barksdale and his managers didn't want to pass up any promising business opportunities. The market was changing, the world was changing, the whole universe was changing so fast that if they let something good slip away just because Netscape didn't have enough bodies to throw at a project, the long-term ramifications could be devastating.

That's why Netscape paired with General Electric, in April 1996, to announce the joint creation of Actra Business Systems, a venture to develop and market software that would enable businesses to do transactions with each other over the Internet.

The business of business-to-business transactions looked like too good an opportunity to pass up. The people who ran GE's Information Services unit, a leading seller of electronic data exchange software, had seen that the Internet market would widen and wanted to develop products to meet the coming demand.

There were a number of obvious applications to create. Say you were a big company, and you wanted to buy some software you could put up onto your network to enable your customers to log in and place on-line orders. You'd need a software package tailored for the way you do business—taking into consideration the fact that all your customers probably already had contracts in place, each with special terms and idiosyncratic pricing structures. Actra was created to develop software that would take care of those situations.

Or say you were a large corporation that wanted to make it possible for all divisions of the company to streamline the process of ordering office supplies and equipment. You'd want a software product that would walk a staffer through the process of ordering, providing on-screen a list of recommended suppliers and preapproved items. You'd want that software to keep track of who was ordering what and when. Actra was developing a product like that, too.

The partnership between GE and Netscape worked well. Pairing Netscape's software with GE's expertise enabled Netscape to leverage itself into a new initiative without distracting the company's core engineering team.

Netscape relied on the same approach to enter the consumer devices market. Ever since the company's founding, a number of consumer electronics companies had approached Netscape from time to time to propose building a version of the Navigator browser to run on a future generation of Net-connected television sets. While it would be some years before anyone could reasonably expect to see such devices running in a majority of households, the venture clearly represented an opportunity that Netscape didn't want to miss. Clark, who had distanced himself from the day-to-day operations at Netscape, was interested in this new venture.

So in August 1996, Netscape joined with IBM, Oracle, and four Japanese consumer electronics giants to create Navio Corp. Navio's mandate was to develop a new operating system to run consumer devices. Netscape's contribution to the venture consisted, essentially, of the Navigator code, which Navio planned to use as a base for creating new products. "It was a clever contribution to get a stake in Navio, with no money, and have a position in the marketplace," Mike Homer remembered. Clark remained on Netscape's board, but by 1996 was involved in new ideas—again. He formed Healtheon, a service to use the Web to make health care services more accessible.

Space Crunch

The company continued to grow and grow and grow. By the summer of 1996, you couldn't even walk on the sidewalk near Netscape's loading dock on most afternoons. Since early morning, the trucks would have pulled up, one after another, unloading orders, and by 3 P.M. the walkway would be thoroughly stoppered by an endless pile of cardboard boxes, deliveries that the overworked shipping and receiving department hadn't yet had time to unpack. They didn't even have room inside to stack all the boxes. So the deliveries snaked around the building, waiting their turn to get into one of the three cramped buildings that the company occupied on Middlefield Road.

Inside the boxes were computers and office chairs and modems and paper clips and reams of printer paper and pens—the supply line that fed the courageous new enlistees at the front. New hires were arriving every day, and there was no expectation they would stop anytime soon. In fact, in 1996 the company's head count tripled to nearly two thousand employees.

Ironically, the supervisor of buildings, Ed Axelsen, who was Netscape's director of real estate, and his staff of half a dozen had set up shop behind the corrugated roll-up door of the loading dock. So the newer receiving area itself became prime real estate, a few thousand square feet of floor space hastily converted into offices and occupied by the very people who were supposed to find more space.

Hired in January 1996, Axelsen had spent his first few weeks at Netscape in a corner near the CFO's office. He moved down to the loading dock because it was the only place in the whole damn complex where his staff could spread out. At a company where space was at such a premium that management was debating whether to eliminate parking spaces to make room for temporary office trailers in the back lot, the loading dock wasn't such a bad place. There was no carpet, of course, but at least there was breathing room. You could wheel your chair around on the smooth bare floor and have chair races whenever you felt like it. Another nice thing about a loading dock was that on balmy days you could pop the overhead door and get plenty of natural ventilation.

Inside the buildings, many of Netscape's employees were working two to a cube—if they were lucky. Engineers were doubled up, coding for eighteen hours a day, neighbors in a space that might be as small as a hundred square feet. It would have been worse if they weren't used to it. After all, the company had quadrupled in size in 1995, with the number of employees increasing from 150 to 600.

Axelsen, who was employee number 595, had to find places for them all to sit. Sometimes he'd tour a cube he thought was empty and available, only to find that some space-crazed and wily employee had stuck an unused computer on the desk to make Axelsen think the place was already inhabited. A fake name would be tacked up on the entryway and a few papers strewn across the desktop for added authenticity.

For dozens of temporary employees—the contract employees, the part-timers, the sixty-seven college interns hired for the summer—the space situation was even more dire. They were in tighter quarters, packed up against each other like sardines in former meeting rooms where rows of desks had been installed.

Former meeting rooms? People still needed to have meetings. Well, go outside and sit at a picnic table on the grass. That was the only alternative, so after a while the administrative assistants started to schedule meetings outdoors. It was only a problem when it rained.

During bad weather, meetings moved to the cafeteria. When he walked through at lunchtime, Axelsen could see that most of the tables were taken up not by diners but by groups in deep discussions— or by managers conducting ever more job interviews.

Axelsen and his staff were working insanely long hours trying to relieve the space crunch. When he was hired, the entire company was crammed into three little buildings on Middlefield Road. Netscape had just leased another three buildings on the street, planning to move into them over the next year. On his first day on the job, Axelsen took stock of the situation and said, "You need all three of those buildings today—and let's get working on the next three."

Usually it takes six months to bring a newly leased building on-line. You have to meet with the architects, design the space, get the general contractors to configure it properly, order the office equipment, assign seats, and move employees to their new locations.

Axelsen compressed that time line. He opened Building No. 4 in April, Building No. 5 in June, Building No. 6 shortly thereafter. How did he do it? From Axelsen's perspective, the main thing was to increase space. "Forget about aesthetics for now," he said. "We have to breathe." It was a philosophy that trickled down from Barksdale: Focus on what's important today, and keep the main thing the main thing. Space was the main thing.

A bunch of employees made bets about when their new offices would be ready. The programmers kept track of who won and who lost the bets. Kandis Malefyt, vice president of human resources, bet they'd all be in offices by July. She lost that one, so she went over to See's candy store and bought a whole bunch of truffles, the good kind, and left them on the winner's desk.

Axelsen was unfazed by the phenomenal pace of growth. This was Silicon Valley, after all, during its peak. Also, he'd worked at

Silicon Graphics and SynOptics before those companies went public; both had doubled their workforces in a single year while he was there. The interesting thing Axelsen had learned from those jobs was that nobody at a company believes unexpected growth is sustainable, even as it occurs. So instead of planning to accommodate future space needs, managers keep saying that it's got to end soon.

Axelsen knew from experience that the growth wasn't going to slow down anytime soon at Netscape. He had surveyed other software companies—places like Microsoft and Oracle—and learned they allocated an average 250 or 275 square feet of space to each employee. At Netscape, the luckiest staffers got 150 square feet to call their own.

And forget about parking. Each of Netscape's buildings had been designed to follow the civilized convention of allotting 250 square feet of parking per employee, four spaces per thousand square feet of space. Axelsen needed to figure out a way to cram *six* cars into four spaces.

It didn't work too well. Would valet parking help? The people who came in at 7 A.M.—mostly administrators—could park without a problem. But by 1 P.M., when the programmers typically would roll into the office, there wasn't a spot to be found. So they parked along the curbs, ignoring the red-paint pain-of-death-or-towing warnings. They parked on the grass. They parked behind other employees' cars. They even started parking in a neighboring company's lot. A programmer who was lucky enough to get a "legal" spot would sometimes sleep overnight at the office to avoid giving it up.

A Toehold

By mid-1996, Netscape was firmly in the black. The company had earned $55 million, more than expected, and realized a profit of $4.7 million.

Netscape's decision to focus on the intranet market was ratified by a study that showed 89 percent of Fortune 500 companies planned to set up an intranet by mid-1997. The study, conducted by Forrester

Research of Cambridge, Massachusetts, predicted that $8.5 billion would be spent on intranet and Internet software in the year 1999.

In fact, more than two thirds of the Fortune 500 companies that already had intranets had purchased Netscape's server products to manage the networks, sales that accounted for more than 70 percent of Netscape's sales for the first half of the year.

While Netscape had successfully gained a toehold in the intranet market, there was one problem. The rest of the world didn't seem to notice.

That's because the world was focused on a sexier story, Netscape vs. Microsoft.

On August 24, 1995, two weeks after the Netscape IPO, Microsoft released Windows 95, which contained version 1.0 of the company's own browser, Internet Explorer. Bill Gates had assigned, by then, a mere eight people to work on Explorer.

The small team belied the huge effort that was already underway in Redmond. As everyone from *Time* magazine to the *Seattle Times* was quick to proclaim, the battle had been joined.

The browser wars were under way.

PART FOUR

The Giant Strikes Back

CHAPTER THIRTEEN

The Netscape Problem

One of Bill Gates's top lieutenants prepared a reconnaissance report on the enemy during the winter of 1995–96. Paul Maritz, the executive in charge of Microsoft's operating system, had been gathering bits and pieces of information about Netscape for months. He hoped to understand how the smaller company operated, so that Microsoft could capitalize on Netscape's perceived weaknesses.

During the same period, Microsoft had been moving ahead with its own plans for a browser that would dominate desktops in the same fashion as Windows 95. Soon after the release of Internet Explorer 1.0 in August 1995, it had become clear to the world that Bill Gates planned to aggressively pursue the Internet market. Gates announced it himself, at a speech on December 7, 1995, in which he gave what later came to be known as his Pearl Harbor Day speech. The sleeping giant had awakened, Gates told journalists and industry analysts. He described his company's Internet strategy, which included a plan to give away the Microsoft browser for free, and announced that Microsoft had made a deal with Sun to license the Java programming language. Realizing that its browser had to run on multiple platforms to compete with Netscape's Navigator, Microsoft also negotiated a second deal with Spyglass, to license the Mosaic code to build versions of the Internet Explorer browser that would run on Macintosh machines and on computers using the older Windows 3.1 operating system. Also, Microsoft began to focus on expanding its

Internet-compatible business applications. After all, anyone could see that there was a growing market for selling intranet software.

Against that backdrop Maritz wrote a confidential thirty-six-page report in February 1996, in which he described his observations about Netscape. He called the report "The Problem: Browser Market Share." He distributed the document—which described Netscape as "obsessed with MS"—to other managers at Microsoft to study. As part of his fieldwork, Maritz had compiled a detailed dossier on Netscape's finances and background. The document described Netscape's history, including a pie-chart breakdown showing who owned the biggest chunks of the company (Clark, Barksdale, Doerr, and "others").

Maritz described the "key people" at Netscape, evaluating Netscape as a company:

- Able to scale up quickly.
- Clark, Barksdale, Doerr—know how to work "system."
- Andreessen—giving good direction on browser.
- Hahn (Collabra) will drive good workgroup direction.
- Schell, Sha—good technical managers.
- Able to react quickly.

After studying Netscape's "organizational characteristics," Maritz reported that Netscape had a "fast response—shared mindset, quick decisions processes, delegation." He wrote that Netscape was "high risk—initiatives announced with little followthru thinking." And, he noted, Netscape was "anti-Microsoft—reactive to MS strategy."

After evaluating Netscape's products, Maritz wrote that he believed the Navigator browser represented "excellent work." Netscape's tools and server products he deemed "OK."

In his report, Maritz laid out a long-term strategy called "How to Win" that described how Microsoft could wrest market share away from Netscape. "Browser share needs to be a top priority for our sales teams and the customer units," Maritz wrote. He also recommended that Microsoft focus its future browser strategy on an effort to "tie back to Windows," and thereby transform the Windows operating system into "the Intra/Internet browser."

In addition, Maritz recommended that Microsoft's marketing team launch a broad advertising campaign to do "massive seeding of IE." He recommended that Microsoft promote its browser in magazines, at trade shows, through business partners, and at high-profile events. "IE being free is a key advantage," Maritz wrote. Microsoft should capitalize on its partnerships with computer makers who licensed the Windows operating system for their personal computers by "encouraging them to ship Windows with all their systems since IE is a part of it."

Maritz also recommended that Microsoft compete head-to-head with Netscape in the newly emerging intranet market. In the report, he wrote that, to "own the intranet," Microsoft would need to educate its sales and marketing forces about how to "use the intranet." He also recommended marketing a package of Microsoft software products—including the high-end NT operating system and the new Internet Information Server—as "the intranet solution."

The Compaq Compact

Barksdale had considered it an important coup when Compaq Computer Corporation, the world's largest supplier of personal computers, struck a deal with Netscape to install the Navigator browser onto the desktop of every new Presario personal computer shipped.

After all, Compaq sold $10.9 billion's worth of computers a year, and the Presario line (launched in 1993) was the flagship of the Houston-based company's consumer products division. The computer maker had its own reputation for creating revolutionary products that snatched market share away from a reigning giant. Compaq had shocked the staid assumptions of mighty IBM back in 1982 when the tiny new company rocketed to success with a new kind of portable computer that a user could close up—keyboard and all—and carry around. It took IBM the better part of the decade to catch up.

In April 1995, months before Microsoft would roll out its own first-generation browser, Compaq announced that it would broaden and improve its Presarios, manufacturing a new, easy-to-use line aimed directly at the novice home user. So Compaq's decision in 1995 to package the Navigator browser with its computers was a valuable endorsement for Netscape. It meant the browser would be directly distributed to a whole new market of consumers. Forget about figuring out how to get onto the Web, how to get to Netscape's website, how to download the browser onto a hard drive. Instead, any computer user who bought a Presario would find Netscape Navigator already in residence. Just click on the little Navigator icon onscreen to launch the browser.

The consumers who bought the Presarios were likely to use Navigator rather than replace it with another flavor of browser. Unlike the corporate customers who wanted to customize computers after they bought them—loading specific software applications onto the hard drives to optimize the machines for a specific workplace's requirements—consumers expected their machines to arrive preconfigured. Compaq's Presario marketing campaign boasted that the machines came "ready to run" and could be set up in under ten minutes.

The Presario operating system was Windows, of course, the industry standard. When it came to choose a browser to include in the Presario software package, Netscape's Navigator had been the obvious choice. It was far and away the industry leader; heavy-hitter Microsoft didn't even have a browser.

But then, in 1996, the world changed.

Microsoft's browser development efforts had hit high gear by midyear. In Microsoft's new Internet Platform & Tools Division, there already were twenty-five hundred people working away on Net products. By now, Bill Gates had assigned eight hundred employees just to work on Internet Explorer.

Hard at work on the third generation of its browser, Microsoft expected its Internet Explorer 3.0 to catch up to—or surpass—Netscape's browser. The new browser would be showcased in the Windows 95 package, which was configured to automatically load the Internet Explorer icon onto the Windows desktop when the computer booted up.

Microsoft didn't much like the terms of Compaq's agreement with Netscape. Compaq had replaced the Internet Explorer desktop button with a Navigator button. Compaq didn't go so far as to *reject* Internet Explorer totally; the Microsoft browser was still preinstalled on the Presario hard drives, and a savvy user could find it in a file folder on the computer.

But the Netscape browser was the default choice on the Compaq desktop.

To Microsoft, that situation was unacceptable. Compaq's contract to license Windows 95 required Compaq to preinstall the *whole package* of Microsoft's software as it arrived. "Customers prefer a consistent Windows experience. If they sit down at a Windows PC, the look and feel and behavior of the product should be consistent," explained Claudia Husemann, a spokeswoman for Microsoft. To maintain consistency, Microsoft prohibited computer makers from removing any portion of the Windows package—and that included the browser desktop button. The way Microsoft read the Windows licensing agreement, Compaq didn't have the option to customize the Microsoft package—or to remove the Internet Explorer icon from the desktop.

Microsoft sent a letter to Compaq threatening to terminate its Windows licensing agreement. Needless to say, losing the right to preinstall Windows 95 on its Presarios would be devastating to Compaq's business. What consumer would buy an IBM clone that didn't have Windows? Compaq quickly restored the Internet Explorer launch button to the desktop.

For the next few months, Compaq shipped its Presarios with both browser icons displayed on the desktop. When Mike Homer found out about the situation, he wasn't happy—nor was he surprised. There was nothing he could do. Compaq's decision to display both icons on the desktop didn't violate the computer maker's contract with Netscape. "Microsoft took their strongest weapon—the monopoly over the operating system—and tied Internet Explorer to it," he said.

By early 1997, however, Compaq decided that it made more sense to streamline the desktop and display a single browser icon on-screen.

It decided to drop the Navigator browser altogether from the PCs it shipped.

When Barksdale heard that computer makers were dropping Navigator in favor of Internet Explorer, he knew the situation had gone too far. He was as well versed in the 1994 Microsoft consent decree as anyone, and it specifically forbade them from tying sales of the operating system to sales of other products. He knew immediately that this "could not be lawful. You cannot take one product and tie another one to it, or else the logical conclusion is all products would be tied to the monopoly operating system."

It was time to act. Barksdale summoned Roberta Katz. She was a fighter. She was the one he wanted to lead the lawyers' brigade against the putative monopolists.

Katz Fights

As McCaw's general counsel, Katz had answered directly to Barksdale since 1992, when the two arrived at the cellular phone company within months of each other. Katz had come to McCaw—and to lawyering—by a circuitous route. As an undergraduate at Stanford in the 1960s, she had switched her major from mathematics to anthropology because "this math stuff is really dry." After earning a doctorate in the 1970s and before deciding to go to law school, Katz did fieldwork in the Mexican town of Tonalá, where she studied living cultures in the throes of change.

That experience would turn out to be especially pertinent, two decades later, to working at Netscape, where the corporate ethos was constantly evolving and new ways of looking at the world emerged overnight. Her fieldwork would serve her well as she once again embarked on the study of another kind of culture: the culture of Microsoft.

She didn't focus solely on Microsoft, though. Her day-to-day job was running the legal department, which meant more than just knowing how to negotiate product distribution agreements. It meant making up the rules as she went along. "Every time we turned around we had to invent something from whole cloth," Katz said. "No one knew what the market would be for Net software."

After arriving at Netscape in May 1995, Katz quickly learned that every license required a unique negotiation technique. A company that wanted to license the Navigator browser to help establish a business on the Internet might have a vague idea of what the business would be—an on-line shopping mall, say—and a vague idea of what they wanted to charge customers. But the rest of the business plan would develop in the course of licensing negotiations. "There was no model," Katz remembered.

This meant that Katz and her growing staff—by the end of 1997 she would supervise a legal department that numbered thirty-five, including seventeen lawyers—would have to make decisions on the fly. If they licensed the browser to a customer with particular specifications, whose engineers were responsible for making any necessary code changes? How would Netscape's software interrelate with the other software that a customer was buying? How much should Netscape charge individual customers, and should that depend on how much individual customers could expect to charge their own clients once they got the business up and running?

Beyond running the legal department, Netscape's general counsel had to be a policy expert as well. Katz quickly got involved in the legal arguments to block the federal government's proposed Communications Decency Act in 1995. She also became an expert on encryption policy, so she could lobby legislators to ease export controls on software that protected users' privacy.

But in the course of carrying out these more typical aspects of her job, Katz never lost sight of the fact that one of Barksdale's top priorities was to build a successful business in the shadow of the giant. "Microsoft has been a part of our business from the beginning. They made no bones about the fact that they wanted to kill us," Katz said.

So in 1995 Katz began, quietly, to investigate the legality of how Microsoft did business. Knowing that the federal government already had targeted Bill Gates's company for anticompetitive practices, Katz "made an effort to learn what Microsoft did in the past."

How did she start to gather information? Although new to the software industry, Katz had heard the rampant rumors about how Microsoft tried to buy up competitors to neutralize them. She knew, of course, that, early on, Microsoft had made an offer to buy a portion of Netscape. She also had heard rumors about Microsoft's unusually stringent license agreements.

So Katz contacted the general counsels at several other Silicon Valley companies and began to question them about Microsoft. "I tried to learn why the industry felt they didn't play by the rules," she said. "It's reasonably uniform in the Valley: The view is you can't trust those guys; they will cross the line."

During the first few months that Katz worked at Netscape, before Microsoft even launched the earliest version of its Internet Explorer software, a channel to Washington had serendipitously opened: Investigators from the Department of Justice contacted Katz with their own questions about Microsoft. The government's lawyers said they were investigating whether the Microsoft Network, scheduled to launch in conjunction with Windows 95, would violate antitrust law.

That summer, Katz met with the federal investigators at Netscape's offices in Mountain View, where the investigators were clearly more focused on the Microsoft Network than on Microsoft's belated entry into the browser market. Initially, they were especially concerned about whether Microsoft's Network would spell the demise of the reigning king of on-line services, America Online. The Microsoft network, like AOL, would be a gated community on the Net that one would reach through a direct dial-up phone number. They "wanted to evaluate the market for on-line services and wanted to know if the Net represented competition to on-line services," Katz remembered.

But after her first conversations with the half-dozen Justice investigators, Katz began to hear disturbing anecdotes from Netscape's sales staff and other employees about how Microsoft was trying to gain market share in the browser industry.

"There were a lot of days when I heard about what Microsoft did and that made my jaw drop. When I started seeing some of these things, at first I didn't believe it," Katz said. "They seemed so far over the line—the things they would do with customers that would harm us."

Katz directed the company's outside counsel, the venerable Silicon Valley law firm of Wilson, Sonsini, Goodrich & Rosati, to inform the Justice Department of Microsoft's tactics. Who better to enlist than the firm's notorious anti-Microsoft crusader, attorney Gary Reback? Of course, through her contacts with the Justice Department, Katz knew exactly who would be interested—and, by the summer of 1996, Barksdale's troops had amassed a lot of war stories.

In an August 8, 1996, letter that Reback wrote to the government, Netscape complained that Microsoft embedded secret hooks in its operating systems to enable its own web server to run faster than those of its competitors. The result was software reviews— such as one published in *PC Week*'s March 1996 issue—that reported Microsoft's speed superiority. By the time Netscape's products caught up, most reviewers already were writing about the next generation of software.

Netscape's letter also said Microsoft was offering Internet service providers "side payments" of up to $400,000 if the providers would agree to make Netscape Navigator inaccessible to customers. In other instances, Barksdale's staff believed that Microsoft offered freebies to corporate customers—including software upgrades and consulting services—if the customer bought the Internet Explorer browser. Netscape even suspected that Microsoft paid a bounty to kill copies of Netscape's browser. Microsoft "offered international telecommunications customers $5 for every installed Netscape Navigator that they removed from their corporation and installed with Internet Explorer," Netscape's letter to the Justice Department alleged.

Meanwhile, Netscape's sales staff started to hear disturbing stories about Microsoft's business tactics from customers. In its letter, Netscape complained that one customer said Microsoft "gave me a deal that I couldn't refuse. Free dialer, browser, developer's kit, free distributable, etc. . . . I know Netscape is better, but $0 vs. $18 K is impossible to beat."

Netscape's letter, addressed to Deputy Assistant Attorney General Joel Klein, asserted that the money to support such pot sweeteners came "directly from Microsoft's monopoly over the operating system." Netscape was concerned about Microsoft's recent decision to bundle its server software free with its $895 NT operating system; the letter accused Microsoft of threatening suppliers who wanted to couple a cheaper version of NT with Netscape's software.

Microsoft was engaging in unfair business practices by using its dominance in the operating-system business to take advantage of competitors in the Internet market, it charged. Netscape beseeched the Justice Department to crack down once again on Microsoft by opening a new inquiry into Microsoft's business practices, paying specific attention to how Bill Gates was moving to dominate the Internet software industry.

After the letter was made public, Microsoft called Netscape's charges "false" and "bizarre" and accused Netscape of launching "a calculated attempt . . . to enlist the government and the media in its marketing campaigns."

In Washington, after he got Netscape's letter, Assistant Attorney General Joel Klein kept his silence about the government's plans. A Justice Department spokesman issued a neutral "No comment." For now.

The Great Communicator

In the weeks following the 1996 releases of the 3.0 versions of both Netscape's Navigator and Microsoft's Internet Explorer, hundreds of press accounts had focused exclusively on the race between "tiny" Netscape and big-strong-smart giant Microsoft to dominate the Net. Reviews of the two companies' browsers had said that Internet Explorer had caught up to—and in some cases surpassed—the prowess of Navigator.

Barksdale and his team worried that dramatic press reports about the browser wars could, in the long term, damage Netscape's relationships with key customers at a critical juncture in the company's growth. As Netscape continued to make the transition from "cool browser company" to "intranet solution provider," the company in 1996 needed to define itself as a serious contender in a field already dominated by such established competitors as Lotus Notes. To succeed, it was necessary to convince potential customers not only of the superiority of its own products but also of the fact that Netscape would grow and thrive over time. In the business software market, you don't survive on the kind of quick-hit sales that you make to individuals who just want the latest version of the client browser. In the business market, Barksdale believed, you sell yourself—your company's reputation, your long-term reliability, your long-term promise to provide support, upgrades, and compatible add-ons.

Increasingly, however, the media had embraced the idea that Netscape could not survive. That kind of talk gave Netscape's sales reps a fit. How do you convince an IS manager to gamble hundreds of thousands of dollars of his employer's money on software from a manufacturer who everyone thinks is on the verge of going out of business?

So, while "browser wars" was the headline, Barksdale and his marketing team had been quietly working to reposition the company as something else: an "enterprise" software shop whose groupware catered to intra- and interbusiness communicating. Barksdale wanted Netscape to be known as a company that was poised to take advantage of the untapped groupware market, which had grown by the end of 1995 into a $450 million market. Groupware leader Lotus Notes, recently acquired by IBM, had more than 5 million users around the world, a number expected to grow to 25 million during the next three years. By the year 2000, analysts predicted that 180 million workers would be using intranets. Barksdale wanted those customers to think of "groupware" as a synonym for "Netscape."

Best of all, the message was simple: Beyond the browser! Version 4.0, to be released in early 1997, wouldn't be just a piddly browser; it would be a whole suite of applications! Employee bulletin boards, real-time conferencing, HTML authoring, scheduling software, and centralized management software would be among its new client features. It would be a new way of doing business. And it would be aimed squarely at IBM, rather than Microsoft.

The shift made sense because Netscape's core business was no longer the consumer market, where the company was fighting Microsoft directly, but rather the corporate groupware market. The numbers supported that contention: By mid-1996, intranet customers represented more than 70 percent of Netscape's sales.

Homer's marketing team had seen as early as the summer of 1996 that "browser war" had outlived its usefulness and was in fact becoming a negative. Within months, by the time the 4.0 generation of software hit the market, the Collabra groupware would be fully integrated into Netscape's software. It would make sense for the company to convey the message that E-mail and group discussion were as integral to the package as the browser was.

Seeking a strategy to shift the marketing message, Netscape staffers had surveyed customers for input. "Over and over, we heard from them that the really hard thing to do no longer was to create information; the hard thing to do was to share it in the workplace, to communicate it," said Bob Lisbonne, who headed the company's client marketing team.

The 4.0 marketing team had decided that the name Navigator simply could not effectively convey the shift to groupware. But changing the name of the product line sounded risky. What if customers around the world associated the word *Navigator* with Netscape's entire product line?

Lisbonne said focus groups disclosed that what customers confused with the product itself was the company name—which was limiting and unhealthy for future growth. "We learned that while Navigator was well known, what was really exceptionally well known was Netscape. More often than not, people in computer stores would say, 'Which aisle is Netscape in?' Not, 'Which aisle is Navigator in?'"

So the team came up with a list of possible candidates to replace Navigator as the umbrella name for the product line. Each potential name had to be screened both by the legal department (to make sure it wasn't already in use somewhere else) and by an international screening team to make sure that a potential name didn't have negative connotations in overseas markets, which accounted for more than 27 percent of Netscape's sales revenues. One name that the marketing team liked was "Collaborator." But that would be a terrible name for a product in many European countries, where a collaborator meant someone who had worked with the Nazis in World War II.

Finally, the obvious choice surfaced: Communicator.

Now would come the hard part: making the sales. First, though, it was time to communicate the Communicator message. And for this one, Barksdale handed the ball off to the pro: Andreessen.

Groupware Man

The elevators in the lobby of the grand Equitable Building in midtown Manhattan whisk passengers up to the fiftieth floor, to a meeting room that feels as large as a football field—if a football field could be decorated with majestic columns, swagged silk drapes, and hundreds of tiny lights winking down from a high vaulted ceiling.

Up in front of the room was a stage flanked by whiz-bang technological props like a huge-screen TV, dueling slide projectors that looked like missile launchers, and a satellite link to London. Concealed behind black drapes, dozens of Netscape staffers sat backstage, murmuring into headphones, watching the lights on their audio equipment wink red and green.

Onstage was the Net's most recognizable celebrity, Marc Andreessen, ready to deliver the new message. The ceiling lights shone down on him, like stars in the night sky.

Andreessen, dressed casually in his signature crumpled khaki pants and a blue button-down shirt, faced an expectant audience: hundreds of print journalists sitting in red-upholstered chairs with notepads on their knees. At the back of the room, two dozen television crews had set up their cameras, pointing yawning lenses and oversized microphones right into Andreessen's face.

If Andreessen looked smooth and relaxed, it could have been because he knew his audience well. Most of these same journalists had already interviewed him for past stories, driven around with him in his Mustang, trailed him at software conferences, written glowingly about the young entrepreneur and his company.

Andreessen cleared his throat. With any luck, Web Boy was about to evolve into Groupware Man.

"The killer app for 1997," Andreessen said dramatically, "will be E-mail and groupware as rich as the Web." The message was direct: We're not just a browser company anymore.

The lights went down, the projectors fired up, and Andreessen clicked through slide after slide that unveiled the components and focus of Netscape's forthcoming product line. The 4.0 version of Netscape's client products—which weren't even scheduled to hit the market for several more months—would be the first generation of Netscape software aimed squarely at business users and corporate customers.

As compared to the 3.0 version of software released a few weeks earlier, which had contained only minor improvements and updates, the 4.0 version would offer a whole new line of products.

The bundle would include group discussion software (the first version of Collabra fully optimized for Netscape), real-time conferencing software (Netscape Conference), a new electronic mail program (Netscape Messenger), and HTML authoring software (Netscape Composer).

For intranet users, the 4.0 version would also have scheduling software (Netscape Calendar) and centralized management software (Netscape AutoAdmin).

In addition, Netscape's new 3.0 SuiteSpot generation of servers would have six products, including major upgrades of the web server and mail server, a new streaming audio server (Netscape Media Server 1.0), and a new scheduling server (Netscape Calendar Server 1.0).

And, yes: The new generation of products would also include a browser, Netscape Navigator 4.0. But the product line would no longer be known collectively as "Navigator." Starting with the 4.0 generation, the Navigator browser would be relegated to a subsidiary position, a single tool in the toolbox, a mere program among many.

With 4.0, Netscape wanted to send a strong signal to the world that the company had become far bigger and far more wide-reaching than its past history would indicate: Good-bye, Mozilla; hello, corporate America. And to christen that transformation, Netscape had baptized its product line with a new name, a grander name that conveyed the vast scope of its landscape: Communicator.

Andreessen's announcement had a subtext that few in the audience missed: The browser war is over. "The story of the browser war was counterproductive to what we were trying to do, so we felt we had to do something dramatic to reposition ourselves," Mike Homer said. "That's why we did two things: We renamed the product Communicator, to make sure that people knew that the browser was only a part of the software, and we introduced SuiteSpot, to show a focused strategy and complete product line."

Andreessen's job on that day in October 1996 was neither to declare victory over Microsoft nor to concede defeat. He had a more delicate message to deliver: The browser war was over *because Netscape got bored with it*. What Andreessen was saying, in effect, was that if Microsoft finally wrested the majority of the consumer browser market away from Netscape, it wouldn't matter. The company had moved on to bigger and better things.

Truth be told, Netscape was doing better than ever financially. In the third quarter of 1996, Netscape continued to grow at a rapid pace, posting revenues of $100 million (an increase of 33.3 percent over the second quarter of 1996).

But the negative perceptions of a protracted battle with Microsoft were beginning to cast a pall. The stock price was trending downward. The glory days of February, back after Netscape split its stock and each share was still worth $85, seemed like a dim memory.

And it was only going to get dimmer.

Déjà Vu All Over Again

One day in October 1996, a manager in Netscape's engineering division logged onto a website called www.specbench.org. The site, which is run by the nonprofit Standard Performance Evaluation Corporation, measures how well software runs and then publishes the results for everyone to see.

Netscape's engineers, checking in regularly with SPEC, were accustomed to finding that their products ran faster and more efficiently than the competition's. But today the news on the SPEC website was not good. The results of a recent test showed that two of Netscape's server products—FastTrack and Enterprise—were performing poorly when compared with Microsoft's Internet Information Server.

Results like this could have a deadly effect on Netscape's long-term sales. Say a potential customer who was running a corporate network on Microsoft's NT operating system also had a public website that millions of people visited every week. The web server would naturally need to interact seamlessly with the NT software. But this very public nonpartisan benchmark was showing that Microsoft's own web server product—unveiled in February 1996—worked much better with NT than Netscape's web server code. According to the test results, Microsoft's server could process many more requests per second than Netscape's. "Microsoft's server was running significantly faster, like twenty to fifty percent, which makes a very real difference," recalled Netscape's Greg Sands.

How did this happen? Sands and his coworkers wondered. One obvious place to look was at the applications programming interfaces, the little hooks Microsoft builds into its operating systems so that web servers and other applications can run faster. Think of APIs as being the paved roads provided for software developers. Once the developer has a map and knows where the roads are, his apps will run faster than they would over undeveloped dirt trails.

When Netscape was hacking its latest web server, its engineers were doing it "blind"—the APIs they needed had not been disclosed. Microsoft had withheld the information about the existence of the hooks, so that Netscape's engineers weren't able to optimize the code in its FastTrack and Enterprise web servers, Sands claims.

Naturally, Sands says, Microsoft's web server developers knew all about the hooks—and wrote code to take advantage of them. "They knew what the hooks were, but we didn't. So we couldn't compete," Sands says.

Microsoft denies it withheld any information, maintaining that any APIs Netscape engineers needed were disclosed and available on the Web on November 25, 1995—a year earlier. Indeed, "Microsoft mailed a copy to Marc Andreessen" of the relevant APIs on December 5, 1995, says Claudia Husemann, a spokesperson for Microsoft.

But Netscape disputes her account, saying that Microsoft had told its own developers about the hooks in a routine update called a "service pack," published to let developers know about fixes and other changes in NT. But no one had sent this particular service pack to Netscape—or even notified them that it existed.

On November 4, 1996, Netscape sent E-mail to Microsoft, asking for the service pack. Soon after, a response arrived. "It said, 'You're right, this is included in Service Pack three, but only Service Pack one is available right now,'" Sands remembered. "'You'll have to wait for further service packs.' You know what? We actually got it in 1997."

In the months that passed before Netscape got access to the current service pack, Microsoft's own developers were able to optimize Microsoft's web server in incremental ways that made it perform better. And that, Netscape claimed, was unfair.

"The operating system is a common service on which everybody depends, and everybody should have access to the same functions, and they should have access at the same time," Sands said.

Microsoft's Internet Information Server "is part of the operating system," says Husemann. "Microsoft believes that http server functionality is just part of the common service Sands is referring to."

Barksdale wasn't pleased when word of the API stunt reached him. How much longer could this go on?

No Dogs Allowed

On the day the dogs were banned, anybody in the Valley could have told you that Netscape had officially outgrown its start-up phase. Only a full-grown bona fide corporation bans dogs at work; no self-respecting start-up would dare. It's a tradition, some would say, a point of pride throughout Silicon Valley, that employees who work those crazy-long start-up hours, one hundred hours a week, sleep-at-the-office-for-days hours, often bring their pets in with them. What are their alternatives, to leave the dog camped out alone in some barren apartment for days on end? (Chris Houck had tried that with Guido, the cat he'd brought along from Illinois when he'd moved back in May 1994. Guido protested in no uncertain terms; he ran away.)

It's common to see dogs roaming the aisles in a start-up, playing tag, wrestling with each other, getting territorial over who rules the cubes. It can be a bit of a problem if they start to growl at strangers who come by to ask a work-related question, but God knows nobody would dare to stand up in public and say, Could we just stop bringing these animals to work, please?

It's a freedom thing. It epitomizes the nature of start-up culture. Hey, I don't work for some tight-assed straight-laced corporation; no, I work here at this risky seat-of-the-pants venture because I am a free spirit, I am creative, I believe in the greater cause. I'm not an employee, I'm on the team. And so's my dog.

That pet-friendly attitude had pervaded Netscape since the company's founding, of course; look at the cult status that Lou Montulli's fishtank enjoyed. Marc had two Newfoundlands. Some employees even brought in cats once in a while, until there was a scare over some allergic feline-hater who was worried about going into anaphylactic shock.

But then some dog had to go and pee on somebody else's leg. It was a little Labrador retriever puppy that belonged to one of the engineers, and what do you expect from a puppy? A puppy gets excited, it pees, right? Well, the employee with the wet leg apparently expected a urine-free workplace, and complained to Human Resources. That's how the situation came to the attention of Kandis Malefyt and the rest of the executive staff.

That incident alone might not have been enough cause to institute a ban. Netscape was a company, after all, that prided itself on being loose, on making it fun to go to work—a company whose founder (Clark) was described as "wacko" by members of the executive staff because sometimes he would bring a Super-Soaker into the office and squirt employees. Malefyt even had a "budget for fun," which funded the purchase of thousands of superballs that bounced all over the walls and ceilings and desks for an entire afternoon.

And dogs certainly weren't the only animals raising a ruckus on campus. Certain staffers kept reptiles as pets. One time a huge iguana got loose in the engineering building and hid out in the women's bathroom, with predictable consequences after it scurried out from behind a toilet while someone was in the same stall. That iguana would have been evicted from the premises forever, but unfortunately no one could ever find it. Maybe it was so traumatized by the screams that it left town on its own.

No, the ban on dogs occurred after some dog had to go and trash a buffet meal that had been set up in a conference room, awaiting the arrival of customers. The carnage wasn't discovered until the hungry entourage arrived, ready for lunch.

That was going too far, Malefyt figured. But how to handle the problem? Barksdale had told her he didn't want the place to seem like a bureaucracy. Why not just go out there and tell people, in plain English, to leave their damn dogs at home? A company-wide directive went out one fall day, informing all employees far and wide: NO MORE DOGS AT WORK.

You would have thought, from the response, that Peter Currie was trying again to make people pay for soda from the machines. The E-mail server practically crashed. Scores of outraged messages zinged their way to Human Resources, protesting the draconian move, and dozens of staffers vented their displeasure to Bad Attitude, an internal newsgroup on the Netscape intranet. One employee protested the new antidog policy by putting a snake on his head before he had his photo taken for his company badge. The security department was livid, but the guy insisted; the snake sat coiled on top of his head in the picture.

This was no soda machine incident. This time the company held firm. With nearly two thousand employees, Netscape couldn't behave like a start-up anymore. The fishtank could stay, but no more

dogs. (Barksdale suggested to Malefyt that perhaps a solution was building some kennels back behind the employee parking lot, but she just
gave him a look.)

Of course, the protests continued. A few months later,
Human Resources received a tip that a dog was seen entering the
engineering building—disguised by a goldfish costume. Complete
with fins.

"We must leverage Windows more"

On December 20, 1996, four months after Microsoft released Internet
Explorer 3.0, Jim Allchin, Microsoft's senior vice president in charge
of the Personal and Business Systems Group, sent a one-page E-mail
message to his boss, Paul Maritz, to discuss "concerns for our future."
The E-mail said, in part:

> *1. Ensuring that we leverage Windows. I don't understand
> how IE is going to win. The current path is simply to copy
> everything that Netscape does packaging and product wise. . . .
> My conclusion is that we must leverage Windows more. Treat-
> ing IE as just an add-on to Windows which is cross-platform
> [is] losing our biggest advantage—Windows marketshare.
> We should dedicate a cross group team to come up with ways
> to leverage Windows technically more. . . . We should think
> first about an integrated solution—that is our strength.*

At the time, development was under way on Internet Explorer
4.0 that would so seamlessly integrate Windows and Internet Explorer that the two would use essentially the same user interface for
accessing information on the hard drive and for accessing information
on the Internet.

Allchin's E-mail suggestions made good business sense. The
only problem with using words like *leverage* was that, well, it's illegal
under antitrust law for a company to try to leverage a monopoly prod-

uct like the Windows operating system to gain broader distribution for software in another market. That is, it's illegal to leverage Windows to lock up the browser market for Internet Explorer.

Allchin later said in court documents that he didn't mean that Microsoft should leverage Windows to gain broader distribution for Internet Explorer. In response to government inquiries, he said the point he was trying to make in the E-mail message was that Microsoft should be "'leveraging' Windows as a matter of software engineering to build a better product."

The government didn't interpret it that way, as Microsoft would soon find out. The government would construe the message to mean that Allchin was urging his boss to leverage Windows to grab control of the browser market.

Design Wins / We All Win

Barksdale's company had just gone out and made a lot of noise about how its new Communicator product line would seize a significant share of the groupware market. So now it was time to put up or shut up, time to sell a significant amount of product and prove to the world that Netscape was a player.

But, realistically, how much groupware could Netscape sell? And to whom? And by when? Since the new generation of products wouldn't even hit the market until the second quarter of 1997, how could Barksdale motivate his sales department to go out there and close big deals now?

Barksdale believed he needed everyone on his team to help. The endeavor was so critical to the company's future success that every single one of the two thousand employees who now worked at Netscape should be directly involved. Barksdale needed to motivate his employees to *feel the need* to sell groupware. He wanted everybody—from the receptionist at the front desk in the 501 building to the sales rep in Europe to the forklift driver at the loading dock—to wake up every single morning and think: How can I help the company sell some groupware *today*?

The trick was, Netscape needed big-ticket sales: to Fortune 500 companies and government agencies and multinational corporations with sprawling operations. Barksdale wanted customers who would buy what Netscape called its "client-server solution"—not just individual copies of the client browser software but also the pricier server products to run the whole setup.

Netscape had to convince customers that Communicator 4.0 represented the first time that the company offered a full "client-server" solution. The sales reps would point out that the 4.0 products would ideally become a platform technology, the basic software architecture for customers' intranets, on which they could layer everything else. And Barksdale wanted his sales force to aim squarely at customers who would buy a minimum of "500 seats"—enough software to connect five hundred desktop computers—and he wanted those customers to install either Netscape E-mail (the communications backbone of a company) or some other Java or JavaScript application to run a similarly mission-critical application in the company.

By the end of 1996, Barksdale's staff developed a new way to license products, called the Enterprise License Program, to take advantage of those kinds of sales. An alternative to the company's standard retail model, the new licensing program charged customers on a per-seat basis. As a customer increased the number of users (added seats), it would have to pay Netscape additional incremental charges. The new licensing program was a gamble, though, or as Netscape explained it to the Securities and Exchange Commission in a 1997 document, "Any change in pricing . . . the company's products could have an adverse impact on product sales."

Barksdale was hopeful that his sales force would be able to land the big deals, known in the industry as "design wins." Once a customer was convinced to adopt Netscape's overall design to manage his shop, the product would become firmly entrenched. Back in the days when Barksdale worked at IBM, a design win meant selling an IBM mainframe to a company. When a company made that kind of financial commitment, then the customer's whole system *ran* on IBM. The customer would then turn to IBM to provide tens of thousands of dollars' worth of supporting computers and software as well.

Accepting Netscape's "client-server solution" was a design win in today's workplace. For a customer, it was a momentous business decision—equivalent to, say, buying Microsoft's Exchange and Back Office software to run the desktop network of a company or standardizing the whole company on Lotus Notes. A design win, in the groupware market, meant choosing the software that enabled you to do all your collaborative computing.

A design win would give Netscape, which built new products about every six months, hooks for future sales. For instance, in a few months a Netscape salesperson could just go into a customer's office and say, "Hey, I've got a new module for you to add to your platform. It works really well with what you already have, and you can use it to schedule your sales reps on calls worldwide." *We'll take it.*

So it was critical to get everyone who worked for Netscape focused on design wins. Barksdale mulled over the problem for a while and then, in early January 1997, called a meeting of his executive staff. He told them he was "playing with an idea" that would give employees an incentive for, well, basically for working their butts off for the next six months.

He looked at the expectant faces around the table—including Todd Rulon-Miller from sales, Mike Homer from marketing, and Rick Schell from client engineering—and said, "We've got to get our people behind us on this. And love and religion ain't gonna be enough to convince them."

"What do you mean?" asked Rulon-Miller.

"I think we should put some options behind this."

Barksdale believed the best way to motivate people was to dangle a carrot in front of them. And the best carrot that a successful Silicon Valley software maker has to offer its employees is *more stock options.*

"We'll set a goal for sales—and if we meet it, everybody in the whole company will get more options," Barksdale proposed. Offering options would be a greater incentive than offering, say, a $500 bonus to everyone on the staff. If the company did well, there was no limit to how much the stock price might increase and no limit to how much the options could be worth someday.

This tried-and-true approach made sense to the executive staff. Rick Schell, for one, remembered how well a similar strategy of encouraging design wins had paid off for one of his previous employers, Intel. One important way Intel had propelled itself to market share and dominance had been to get the company's chip sets embedded into their major partners' technologies. Bingo: design win. Everything Intel's partners built on top of that—personal computers, whatever—would be based on the Intel chips. Simple concept: Get your partners to use *your* core technology as *their* core technology.

The executive staff thought for a minute about what Barksdale had proposed and then someone said tentatively, "Uh, Jim, what about the board of directors? Will they go along with this?"

"I'm on the board of directors," Barksdale reminded them. "Don't worry about those things."

Barksdale told his executive staff that he needed them to help sketch in the details of his plan. He needed their feedback to decide how many sales the company could realistically expect to make, and he needed to know what deadline to set.

After the meeting, Mike Homer went to see Rulon-Miller over in the sales department. "How many do you think you can sell?" he asked.

Rulon-Miller, whose sales and product support staff now numbered more than seven hundred of the company's two thousand employees, said, "Look, I'm going to go see how many I've done in the past that look like these kinds of sales. Like when we sold the Navigator 3.0 product in conjunction with the mail server. We've had that before."

Next, Rulon-Miller extrapolated. He knew the worst thing he could do would be to set the bar so high his teams were doomed to fail; that wouldn't be good for anybody's morale. On the other hand, he wanted to challenge his staff, to rally them behind a single point of focus to achieve more than they thought was possible.

About 75 percent of Rulon-Miller's staff worked from field offices around the world, in places like Oslo, Norway, and Stockholm, Sweden, and Melbourne, Australia. If his deployed field operations were to make the design-wins goal, they would desperately need the full support of the rest of the company.

You'd be surprised how much a guy out there in the Oslo office relies on the people back in headquarters. In a single day, he might need to inform the finance department of a unique business model that's in place in Norway and ask for subsequent approval for an unusual pricing discount . . . then hook up with someone in the legal department to get approval to delete some obscure clause from Article 17 in a sales contract because the clause is illegal in Norway . . . then talk to an engineer about how a certain bit of code in a specific product is going to interact with software the prospective customer already owns.

With an incentive program to motivate the company's whole staff, Rulon-Miller decided it would be feasible to aim for a total of two hundred design wins by the end of the first half of 1997. Soon afterward, Barksdale announced an all-hands meeting, to be attended by everyone who worked for the company.

Netscape's staff had long ago outgrown not only the conference rooms at Castro Street, where Clark had convened the impromptu earliest meetings, but also the big empty warehouse of a building where Clark had announced, the previous year, his plan to take the company public. Come to think of it, there were no more empty buildings to meet in, anyway. Ed Axelsen's staff had seen to that. So once every six weeks, Netscape rented space at a nearby college, which had a comfortable auditorium that could hold five thousand.

After everyone settled into their seats, Barksdale climbed up onto the huge stage and said, "I want to tell you about a new program that I'm calling the two-for-two program."

The plan was simple: If Netscape managed to get two hundred design wins by June 30, 1997, every single employee at the company would get options to purchase two hundred shares of Netscape stock.

The plan was beautifully simple—and guaranteed to motivate everyone from the overseas sales reps to the secretaries, the janitors, and the shipping clerks to do whatever it took to help make those sales.

Think about how your department is going to help the sales teams. Think about landing the big deals—like the one Barksdale himself had personally closed with the big accounting firm KPMG Peat Marwick LLP. That particular deal was a huge design win, with KPMG planning to adopt Communicator as the standard software used by the eighteen thousand accountants and consultants in its 120 U.S. offices. The accounting firm was building a huge intranet called KWEB, to enable staff to keep up with customers, products, and strategies, and had been convinced to choose Communicator over both Microsoft's Exchange and Lotus Notes. In fact, the deal called for KPMG to phase out an older generation of Lotus software (cc:Mail for E-mail) over the next year as the Communicator products phased in.

The KPMG deal was exactly the kind of sweet sale Netscape needed to make because the accounting firm also planned to become a prime reseller of the software to its own corporate clients.

Barksdale had no compunctions about sharing details of the KPMG negotiations publicly; after all, the deal had been sealed by a handshake with Roger Siboni, KPMG's vice chairman. Where Barksdale came from, a handshake was as solid as a contract. "Roger told me I had the business, and that's all I needed," Barksdale said. One of Barksdale's unusual managerial qualities was a belief in sharing as much information as possible. When speaking with his troops, Barksdale liked to "inform, inform, inform." His strategy was to tell everybody on staff as much as you can about the business. He understood that the best way to enfranchise his employees, to make them feel responsible for the company's continued growth and success, was to share the proprietary information. Share the power.

To keep the staff informed, Barksdale said Netscape would publish a daily tally on its own company intranet. When you arrive at your desk in the morning, you can check your E-mail and get an update on the 2-for-2 program! See how many design wins we have already! See which sales team has gotten the most!

February 27, 1997: On the wall in the company cafeteria, a six-foot-high sign that looked like a big "design wins" thermometer was taped prominently near the condiment counter. The "mercury" in the thermometer had risen to show that Netscape had twenty design wins, with another twenty-five or so pending. *Think about how your department is going to help the sales teams.*

"The point is," Barksdale had told his staff, "I want everybody to feel like they're a part of this. When the sales force is out in Paris, and they call back to headquarters and say they need help to make a sale, I want the receptionist who answers the call to know how important it is to hook the salesperson up immediately to the engineer who's got the little piece of code that will make the difference."

Soon after the all-hands meeting, Barksdale E-mailed a little reminder to his staff: The website for the 2-for-2 program is up, here's the URL; go take a look at it.

May 5, 1997: The thermometer showed seventy-five design wins. *Think about how your department is going to help the sales teams.*

May 22, 1997: One hundred wins, including companies like Bay Networks, Chrysler, Cypress Semiconductor, KinderCare, Eastman Kodak, Prudential HealthCare, Chubb Insurance.

Netscape's sales benefited, as well, from the fact that the new intranet market was growing as fast—maybe faster—than the Internet market had been growing just months earlier. "Intranets have gone from newfangled idea to best determined practice in Fortune 500 companies in a year—which is unheard of," said

Bob Lisbonne, who headed Netscape's client marketing efforts. "We've not seen another technology be more quickly adopted by major companies."

June 30, 1997: Two hundred wins, among them Bell Canada, Blue Cross and Blue Shield of Georgia, Federal Express, Sprint, U.S. Information Agency, Knight-Ridder, Federal Reserve System.

Barksdale's 2-for-2 program had been successful. In the second quarter of 1997, the company sold $135.2 million in software—an 80 percent increase over the same period of the previous year, when sales had totaled a mere $75 million. And every employee at Netscape was richer by two hundred shares.

It was difficult, however, for the outside world to accurately assess how quickly Netscape was making significant inroads into the groupware market. That's because Netscape did not disclose key details about its sales strategies. Although Barksdale's policy within the company was to inform, inform, inform, his policy was also to withhold proprietary information from outsiders. For instance, the company wouldn't reveal how big its installed base truly was. Nor would Netscape say what percentage of those customers had paid for products or give the average price per seat for each new deal. Under Netscape's licensing agreements, customers generally didn't actually pay the company until after product had been shipped.

Meanwhile, groupware leader Lotus Notes had been proving to be a formidable opponent.

IBM, the new owner of Notes, had quickly moved to reposition the product as software that embraced the Internet. Companies that used Notes now were able to create websites with the product, and employees could use a web browser to access Notes. To tout the software's merits, four hundred IBM salespeople had been assigned to the newly reconfigured product. It had been inevitable that Lotus Notes would transform itself to take advantage of the Internet—because it was easy to do—and, in so doing, make its strengths apparent in a new market.

For one thing, its core technology embodied a valuable feature, called replication, that other groupware makers had not yet been able to match. Replication enabled a company that used Notes to maintain identical updated copies of documents on all its servers around the world. That meant that any employee, anywhere, could call up a document and see the current version—even if someone else in another location was also working with the same document.

For Netscape, landing those design wins had been expensive. The company had hired more salespeople, opened new sales offices, and continued to expand its presence overseas. Consulting fees, sales commissions, advertising, travel . . . it all added up. During the first half of 1997, Netscape spent $115 million on sales and marketing, expenses that accounted for 45.3 percent of total sales.

It cost a lot of money to make money. It was clear that if Netscape was going to continue to post quarterly profits, the company's groupware sales would have to continue to grow at a fast rate. And for that to happen, well, Netscape needed to outmaneuver Microsoft.

A Sweet Deal Goes Sour

At its annual meeting in Florida in August, KPMG Peat Marwick LLP wanted the man responsible for creating the big accounting firm's intranet to give the keynote speech, so in early June, KPMG vice chairman Roger Siboni called Jim Barksdale to invite him down. Barksdale accepted, of course. KPMG was one of Netscape's biggest and most important customers. But two months later, on August 7, the man standing behind the podium in Orlando didn't look one bit like fifty-four-year-old Jim Barksdale. Relaxed behind trademark "nerd eyeglasses," it was Bill Gates who delivered the speech to the company's employees.

If Gates looked a bit triumphant standing up onstage, it was probably because he had just wrested the KPMG account away from Netscape. It wasn't enough that Microsoft was eating away inexorably at Netscape's browser market. The Gates machine was now firmly focused on grabbing the groupware market as well.

Addressing the assembled accountants and consultants in Orlando, Gates acknowledged that Netscape had been far more nimble than his own company in recognizing the huge potential of the Internet. But those days were past. "It was a wonderful chance for me to go to the company and remind them, 'Hey, we don't have a guaranteed place,'" Gates said. "'We've got to take this Internet initiative and really surprise the world with what we can do.'"

Microsoft had surprised Netscape, as well.

It had been a big shock to Barksdale and his troops to learn—after Barksdale had made arrangements to fly to Florida—that Microsoft had slipped in under the radar and made off with one of the biggest, most lucrative accounts Netscape had ever landed.

That hurt. "It was a hard one," Barksdale said. It was bad for morale, of course, since Netscape's sales force had been working since the previous autumn to seal the KPMG deal. But beyond the immediate sting of losing tens of millions of dollars' worth of business—the loss had a pyramid effect, because Netscape had expected Peat Marwick to persuade the accounting firm's own clients to install Communicator software as well—this Microsoft victory over Netscape had ominous overtones.

It was the first time Microsoft had made off with a lucrative piece of Netscape's groupware business. Even more important was the clear signal that it would not be the last.

Microsoft had once again reminded Netscape—and the world at large—that it's impossible to outmaneuver the biggest software company on earth. If you go head-to-head with Bill Gates, you're bound to lose. Microsoft had won the KPMG Peat Marwick account with pure brute-force staying power, sweetening the deal until it had become virtually impossible for the accounting firm to refuse it.

That was terrible news for Netscape, whose business strategy relied on staying a step ahead of the giant at all times, making inroads into markets that Microsoft had not yet discovered. Once Microsoft caught on, it was only a matter of time before the game was over.

Microsoft had clearly discovered groupware.

Consider what happened in the case of the KPMG deal, as it was described in *The Wall Street Journal*. Roger Siboni had evaluated both Netscape and Microsoft not once but twice—in the fall of 1996 and again in the spring of 1997—and both times had concluded that Netscape's software was better and would be easier to implement, cheaper to install, and more flexible in solving the problem of linking all the different flavors of desktop machines that KPMG's employees used.

Yet when Siboni called Microsoft with the bad news, Microsoft simply refused to take no for an answer. Gates's top negotiators kept coming back to the table until they managed to formulate so lucrative an offer that KPMG couldn't walk away from it.

To seal the deal, Gates himself had cleared his calendar to spend forty-five minutes meeting one-on-one with Siboni in Redmond. Perhaps more important, Microsoft had agreed to make KPMG a partner in selling Microsoft's Windows NT operating system.

The partnership would benefit both companies, of course. For KPMG, which specializes in helping big companies install intranets, the deal offered the potential of lucrative consulting fees. For Microsoft, which didn't have its own in-house stable of consultants, the partnership promised to expand the sales market.

Microsoft also agreed to give KPMG early access to new software to enable the accounting firm to meet its self-imposed deadline to install its full intranet by June 1998. Then Microsoft opened up its wallet, agreeing to buy a 10 percent stake in a KPMG unit called Enterprise Integration Systems, which sold networking technology to corporations. In addition, Microsoft agreed to pay $10 million to fund a new KPMG unit, five hundred consultants who would sell services to Windows NT customers.

There was no way Netscape could have matched terms like that—but for Microsoft, what's an investment of a few million dollars? The Gates view: In the long run, if it builds business, it's worth it.

The loss of the KPMG account was devastating to Netscape. While Barksdale had been able to shrug off the eventual erosion of the consumer browser market fairly easily, this stung. This meant Gates's army was marching straight into the heart of Netscape's core business.

The Big E

The biggest problem, at 1 A.M., was finding a truck driver who was willing to help.

Come to think of it, wasn't this always the biggest problem for someone contemplating a prank that involves dumping something massive on someone else's lawn—and then getting out of there without getting arrested?

But the engineers from Microsoft were not going to be deterred by a little logistical problem. They'd had a few beers. The prank would be the perfect way to cap a long day of celebration. Officially, the Microsoft team was in town—at San Francisco's Fort Mason—to announce the launch, hours earlier, of Internet Explorer 4.0.

Unofficially, the engineers had come to town mainly to celebrate making their deadlines, crunching so much bug-free code, and turning the tide once and for all in the browser war. They'd just finished 4.0, which would be shipping factory-direct-installed on 85 percent of the personal computers in the world.

All day long, during the launch festivities, the engineers from Microsoft had been staring at their Big E—that's E for Explorer, of course. The car-sized wooden logo held pride of place as speaker after speaker tromped up to the podium and rallied the crowd.

Now, late at night, the crowd had dispersed. Only the engineers—and the Big E—remained. It would take about six guys to lift the thing, wouldn't it?

Somebody started calling around, looking for a flatbed truck, and before they knew it a driver was there, pocketing a few hundred-dollar bills, and then upsy-daisy, there goes the E.

They rattled south on Route 101, drunk on the beer but even more intoxicated by the savage thrill of the prank. It was the kind of

sophomoric gesture you'd expect the pep squad to pull the night before the big homecoming game. They got off the highway in Mountain
View, couple of quick turns, and they were on Middlefield Road,
trundling down the deserted street toward . . . there it was! Netscape
headquarters! Notice the big blue N on the sign.

The truck screeched to a halt by the fountain in front of the
main building, and they pushed the Big E right off the truck. It hit
the lawn with a deadened thud, and they burned rubber (well, they
approximated that gesture as much as a flatbed truck can, carrying
half a dozen software engineers, a driver, and a reporter from *Wired*
magazine).

When the sun rose the next morning, the Big E was clearly
visible out the front window beneath Barksdale's second-floor office.
Next to it was a greeting card with a picture of a cranky baby on it
and, inside, the note: *It's just not fair. Good people shouldn't have to feel
bad. Best wishes, the IE team.* It was pitiful, really, that the Microsoft
team was immature enough to stoop to such a low level.

By midmorning, a group of Netscape employees stormed the
company cafeteria to liberate the bigger-than-life-size Styrofoam model
of Mozilla that these days stood relatively unnoticed by the food line.
They hauled Mozilla outside, right onto the lawn, in front of the fountain next to the Big E, and made a sign for Mozilla to hold, trumpeting
the fact that Netscape still had a greater percentage of market share in
the browser market: NETSCAPE 72, MICROSOFT 18.

The Long Slide

In the first week after the launch of IE 4.0, more than two million
copies were downloaded from Microsoft's website. In fact, the software set a Microsoft record after one million copies were downloaded
in the first forty-eight hours after release.

The enormous popularity of IE 4.0 resembled nothing so much
as the reception that Navigator 1.0 itself had received in 1994.

Three years had passed since the night of Netscape's first public beta. In Internet time, it might as well have been an eon. It had taken Microsoft's software three years to catch up enough to threaten to overtake Netscape.

The current groundswell surrounding IE 4.0 left no doubt that Microsoft was making significant inroads in the Internet software market. Most of the computer makers installing Windows on new desktops had elected to include IE 4.0 on their new models. And the list of corporate customers who bought IE 4.0 to run on their intranets was growing as well, to include such big companies as Bechtel Corporation, Ernst & Young LLP, Nabisco, Spring PCS, Dow Chemical, and, surprise of surprises, Compaq Computer.

By September 1997, Microsoft's share of the browser market had also climbed inexorably to 35 percent, an upward trend that showed no signs of ending. To compete against Netscape's 4.0 Communicator, Microsoft had changed Internet Explorer in several significant ways. With its new features—which changed the way the Windows operating system itself worked—Microsoft didn't view the browser as a stand-alone application. Rather, Microsoft had taken full advantage of the loophole in the 1995 Justice Department consent decree and referred to IE 4.0 as an operating system upgrade, just one part of an integrated product.

What that meant, among other things, was that any Windows user who also wanted to browse the Web would find it massively inconvenient to try to run Netscape's browser.

CHAPTER FOURTEEN

The Once and Future Internet

On October 20, 1997, U.S. Attorney General Janet Reno stood at a Washington, D.C., podium in a plaid jacket and skirt and announced that the U.S. Department of Justice was going to court against Microsoft again.

"Microsoft is unlawfully taking advantage of its Windows monopoly to protect and extend that monopoly and undermine consumer choice," Reno said. "The Department of Justice will not tolerate that kind of conduct." The problem, Reno added, was that Microsoft's widespread practice of forcing computer makers to install its browser on every new Windows machine was illegal.

In fact, tying sales of the operating system to the browser was a specific violation of the consent decree that the government had negotiated with Microsoft back in 1994, Reno said. Under the terms of the old consent decree, Microsoft had agreed not to force computer makers that preinstall Windows in new machines to also preinstall other Microsoft software. By forcing computer makers to install the browser, Microsoft was improperly using "exclusionary and anticompetitive contracts" to protect and extend its monopoly, she said. The government had concluded that Microsoft's operating system monopoly gave the company unprecedented power to dominate other markets as well.

Violating the consent decree put Microsoft in contempt of court. Reno asked that the court impose a one-million-dollar-a-day fine on Microsoft "if it continues to violate the court order."

During their investigation of Microsoft, Justice Department lawyers had interviewed numerous computer makers who licensed Windows. The government learned that Microsoft had refused requests from at least three computer makers to remove either the Internet Explorer program or the Internet Explorer desktop launch button from the personal computers they sell. So the government also asked the court that day to order Microsoft to stop requiring computer makers to license Internet Explorer as a condition of licensing Windows.

Then Reno introduced the man standing next to her at the podium, Assistant U.S. Attorney Joel Klein, and asked him to say a few words.

Klein explained why, in the eyes of the government, Microsoft's practice of tying the operating system product to the browser product was anticompetitive. Klein pointed out that the browser was much more than just another Microsoft product. Internet browsers were a new kind of software that potentially could cut into Microsoft's operating system monopoly—if Microsoft failed to control the browser market.

"Browsers are potentially the kind of product that could erode Microsoft's operating system monopoly because browsers take computers beyond the desktop, where Microsoft rules, and into the world of the Internet, where no one is dominant," Klein said.

Judge Jackson had his work cut out for him. It would take him nearly two months to decide whether Microsoft was in contempt of the consent decree. In the meantime, Netscape's position in the browser market continued to slide.

Set It Free

One day in the fall of 1997, a Netscape engineer named Frank Hecker was reading some messages that his colleagues had posted to an internal company bulletin board. Hecker worked in Bethesda, Maryland, where his job as lead systems engineer was to provide technical support to the sales team that serviced Netscape's government customers. Barksdale would have been proud: The systems engineer was definitely eating the company's own dog food. As an employee who worked in an office on the other side of the continent, using the newsgroup was the best way to keep in touch with life in Mountain View.

Netscape was on the verge of losing the browser war. It was a depressing thought but an inescapable one, considering the way the market was changing so drastically. By tying its browser to Windows 95, giving it away for free, and making it virtually indistinguishable from Navigator, Microsoft would quickly come to dominate the browser business. Doom was—at long last—at hand.

But while Hecker was reading, he ran across a posting by Jamie Zawinski that excited him. Zawinski, working from his home in San Francisco for months, had some time on his hands and had used it to contemplate Netscape's plight: How had a company with such a bright future fallen so far so quickly?

Zawinski had posted a provocative idea: Since the client version of the browser no longer seemed to have much value in the marketplace, why not reveal its source code to the world? Why not make it truly free? Post the source code publicly so that any programmer anywhere could add to it or change it. To Zawinski, who as an old Emacs hacker and was used to "preaching the free software religion," the idea made sense on a number of fronts.

The concept was far more radical than the old idea of giving away the browser, which had meant merely distributing copies of the software for people to run on their computers. Instead, Zawinski was proposing that Netscape give away its *secret formula* for its browser. It would be like handing out free bottles of Coke and including the recipe, so you could cook up Coca-Cola at home. While that sort of largesse had been a traditional practice in the good-old hacker days of the Internet's youth, it had never been tried on such a scale in the commercial world.

After all, if a business gives away both its product and its recipe for creating a product, how does it make money? Where's the business?

The truth was that within the commercial world there was some successful commercial precedent for Zawinski's idea. For instance, there was the Apache project. The Apache web server was a popular product used by a lot of small on-line service providers and noncommercial sites, such as universities. The Apache web server started out with source code that already was in the public domain. Built on top of the original http server code that Tim Berners-Lee originally wrote, Apache had grown and improved, thanks to a legion of volunteer programmers on the Internet. Although the Apache software itself was free, it provided a business opportunity for consultants and support. A company called Stronghold sold a high-quality commercial version of the Apache product.

Then there was the Linux project. Linux was a free version of Unix written from scratch in the early '90s by a clever Finnish graduate student named Linus Torvalds. He got help with the project from a constantly evolving group of like-minded hackers around the world who wrote new features in their spare time; their work enabled the Linux code to grow into a robust, fully formed operating system that ran on almost any personal computer that has at least two megabytes of random access memory.

Torvalds copyrighted the fundamental portion of the operating system, known as the kernel, but made it available to anyone to copy, change, or distribute so long as other programmers agreed not to restrict future distribution and agreed to make all new source code available.

Despite the fact that the source code is publicly available—and free—a number of viable businesses have sprung up to distribute commercial versions of Linux and provide support for it, including Red Hat, a Durham, North Carolina–based business that sold CD-ROMs chock full of the operating system and all the tools one might need to run it. With zero marketing effort, Linux was steadily becoming more popular, and a huge cadre of volunteer developers was constantly updating it and making it better—which, in turn, increased its popularity. In fact, NASA used Linux to run some of the computers on the space shuttle. Computers running Linux also created some of the special effects in the blockbuster movie *Titanic*. At least five million computers around the world ran Linux. Was there a lesson here for Netscape?

The more Frank Hecker thought about the idea to give away Netscape's source code, the more excited he got. Hecker, who at forty-two had been both a programmer and a systems engineer for more than two decades, had worked for Netscape for nearly three years. That made him an old-timer, someone who could remember the excitement of the early days back in 1994 when it seemed that the company might really conquer the world, when the programmers were calling themselves the Doomed because they didn't dare hope they would be able to create a commercial version of a browser.

"I started thinking about the possibility of actually doing that in a systematic way," he said. "It seemed like such an interesting problem—especially trying to do this as a business proposition—that I decided to write it up as a memo."

As a systems engineer, Hecker was trained to view software from a customer's perspective: Why is this feature important to someone? Why would someone want to pay money for what I'm giving them? So he sat down to try to figure out why anyone would want to pay money to Netscape if the company was willing to give away the source code for its browser, the most precious thing it owned. Hecker wrote a twenty-page paper that not only proposed a business model for distributing the source code but also dispensed with various objections he believed might arise to such a plan. He thought of that part as the "We can't do this because of X" section.

While Hecker was writing the paper, he discussed the ideas in it with John Menkart, a sales manager who worked with him in Netscape's government sales group. He also got feedback from Zawinski.

Zawinski suggested that Hecker look at an interesting piece that discussed the success of the Linux project, an article written by Eric S. Raymond (who had edited the inestimable *New Hacker's Dictionary*) and posted on-line. Hecker was impressed by the ideas in the article, which showed that if a software program had enough "eyeballs" focused on it, the problems of spotting and fixing bugs became almost trivial. Product development could race along, with rapid revisions, without any of the traditional delays that plagued "closed" development of proprietary code.

In late fall, Hecker finished his paper, which he had considered a "spare-time project," and passed it along to Marc Andreessen for review. Andreessen was happy to get it. Although Hecker didn't know it at the time, Netscape's top managers had been discussing the very same possibility—giving away the source code.

It would be a desperate measure, but maybe they were desperate people. Browser sales had shriveled up; the stand-alone browser would account for only $12 million in sales during the fourth quarter of 1997, down from $52 million during the same quarter the year before. Barksdale and his team were casting around for something that would save the company.

The browser war had affected aspects of their business that went far beyond losing client market share. Netscape was having trouble completing sales to groupware customers as well. It was hard to pinpoint what the problem was, exactly, but it didn't look as if the company would meet its projections for the fourth quarter. Some big deals that Netscape had counted on closing before the end of 1997 were dragging on more slowly than expected. The customers didn't *say* it was because they were nervous about doing business with a company that Microsoft was running out of town, but that had to be a factor.

Although Andreessen had been defending the commercial viability of Netscape's browser publicly—at a speech in late 1997, he went so far as to draw a line in the sand and declare that Microsoft would not be able to grab any more market share—privately he had come to a different conclusion: "The browser business is a zero-dollar business."

But the browser was something that the Netscape brand was inexplicably associated with in the public mind. And even if it represented a shrinking portion of their business, the public beating it was getting was shaking confidence in its other products, in the company itself. Months ago, Andreessen had tried to reposition the company beyond the browser. Maybe he had gone too fast? Maybe it was time to go back to the company's roots. Andreessen thought the browser could still have terrific value to the company—but only if they returned it to the very Net they had helped to create. Would Barksdale agree?

Where's the Plan, Jim?

One morning in December 1997, the newest batch of enlistees in the great cyberspace wars, a few hundred of them, watched with anticipation as their wily general, Jim Barksdale, ambled up to the front of a rented hall in Sunnyvale. The day was a regularly scheduled indoctrination day for new employees ("N is for Netscape!"), although the events of the past weeks had been anything but typical. With its antitrust case against Microsoft, the government had been bearing down and playing hardball. Microsoft had responded with belligerence, and now the whole court case appeared to be headed for a showdown. The remarkable events made Netscape's new recruits wonder, What's going to happen tomorrow? Or next year? What did the chief executive officer of Netscape Communications plan to do now that the government was beating up on his rival? Barksdale had said repeatedly that he didn't want to be known as the leader of the resistance, but he had to do something. Netscape's stock price had been plummeting as Microsoft's Internet Explorer gobbled up more and more of the browser market.

If you could hear people think, you'd have heard a cacophony of doubt and skepticism in this room. Their concerns coalesced around the red-hot drama that had spilled out of the technology columns and onto the front pages of newspapers across the country: Was Microsoft killing Netscape? Could anything stop Microsoft?

"Everyone hates a monopoly unless they've got one," Barksdale acknowledged. Then he blandly finished his standard Welcome-to-the-greatest-company-on-earth routine. He led the newest inductees in a company cheer (*N* is for Netscape! *E* is for Everywhere! *T* is for *Team*!) after a short indoctrination with the Netscape corporate line: "Our purpose is to create and keep customers."

Obviously Netscape had excelled at the first part of that purpose; the company and its gangly group of college-kid programmers had effectively created the whole World Wide Web phenomenon, making the Internet a viable commercial enterprise. For a good two years after Clark and Andreessen founded the company, it had owned the Net.

But keeping customers? That goal appeared elusive. In the software industry, where a monopoly power like Microsoft dominated, Netscape hadn't been able to compete. Sure, the Silicon Valley start-up had made a glitzy show of changing the rules, and the rest of the industry had quickly adopted Netscape's more innovative strategies for creating and distributing products. But Netscape's attempts to diversify appeared stalled; the company seemed to be making only modest inroads into the crowded groupware market. Had Netscape run out of new ideas?

December Is the Cruelest Month

A few days after Barksdale rallied the new troops, the extent of Netscape's financial woes became evident. The company announced in late December 1997 that it expected to lose more than $85 million in the fourth quarter. In fact, the outlook was so dire that the fastest-growing start-up in history planned to lay off some of its twenty-four hundred employees. The news shocked Wall Street analysts, who had predicted a modest profit for the company.

Barksdale and his team tried to reassure investors, with Barksdale promising that Netscape had a real plan to return to profitability. He was able to explain disappointing fourth-quarter results by saying that revenues hadn't caught up with the company's dramatic recent growth and that sales deals had taken longer. It had been a miscalculation, along with bad luck and stiffer-than-expected competition from Microsoft and IBM. But what the rest of the world saw was Netscape sitting on the sidelines of the court battle, waiting for the government to force the schoolyard bully to play nice. Not so, Barksdale said. "The legal part of our strategy accounts for probably one percent of our overall strategy." He said Netscape had a plan to thrive in the shadow of the giant, to work with Microsoft—and even grow with it.

Outgunned, Netscape seemed to be waging a war with a single weapon: patience. The Internet software market would continue to grow, Barksdale pointed out. And just by being there, Netscape could grab a growing portion of that business. He likened it to the old days, when he worked for McCaw Cellular: "By the time I was in the cellular business, there were only two cellular licenses granted in every city," he recalled. "The 'B' carrier was always the incumbent telephone company, right? So by definition I was always competing against the incumbent telephone carrier." McCaw was in virtually every major city, including Los Angeles, San Francisco, Seattle, Houston, and New York. Not surprisingly, it thrived everywhere. "We had a forty to sixty percent share. All you had to do was show up and you got a forty share! That's kind of the way the law of large numbers works. Everything else being equal, the market splits.

"The number of connected users is growing at least fifty percent a year," Barksdale said. By "connected" he meant networked over the Internet, corporate intranets, and business-to-business extranets. All of them need (as in "will pay for") sophisticated software to function well. By the year 2001, that networked market was expected to be worth nearly $26 billion. "Would I take fifty percent of the new users next year? You're damned right." In fact,

Barksdale would be happy to settle for 10 to 20 percent of the whole market. Who wouldn't?

"There's a huge market for web advertising, commerce, E-mail, groupware, and application servers that's a wide-open space. Nobody has a great advantage. Nobody. All I have to do is get ten percent of that over the next three years and I'll continue as the fastest-growing company in history," Barksdale said.

In theory, Barksdale's idea sounded fine. But in reality? Rumors began to swirl—Netscape was on the verge of being bought by Sun . . . no, by Oracle . . . no, by Novell—as the company's stock price dipped even lower in the early weeks of 1998, to about $18 a share. That would have been the equivalent of $36 on the day of the IPO, half as high as it opened.

Had Netscape blown it? Had the company somehow made fabulous missteps that ensured its doom?

It was easy to ask such questions in hindsight. Had Netscape become the victim of its own hubris? Should the company have made a deal with Microsoft, back in late 1994, to license the Navigator code to Gates?

Look at what happened to Spyglass. Microsoft had paid nearly $14 million to Spyglass in 1994 and 1995, in return for the privilege of licensing the Mosaic code as a basis for the early versions of some of its browser platforms. But then two things happened that put Spyglass out of the browser business anyway. First, after Microsoft developed its own subsequent versions of Internet Explorer, that company no longer needed the Spyglass code. Second, and more damaging to Spyglass, was the fact that Gates announced at the end of 1995 that Microsoft planned to give away Internet Explorer for free. Within a matter of months, most of Spyglass's browser sales to other customers dried up. Doug Colbeth, the company's president, estimated that Spyglass lost nearly $20 million in revenues in a year.

By 1997, Spyglass had shifted into a new market, creating software that enabled digital devices—such as phones—to connect to the

Internet. No longer in the black, Spyglass lost $9.7 million in the fiscal year ending September 30, 1997. The company hoped to be profitable again—by 1999. Of course, Microsoft wanted a piece of that new software market as well.

Should Netscape have partnered with Microsoft, then? Maybe Barksdale could have figured out a way to structure a deal that would have better protected Netscape's long-term interests. The bigger question, though, is this: Why should Netscape—or any other software company—*have* to do a deal with Microsoft in order to survive? Shouldn't Netscape be able to stay in business and run its own company? Netscape had played as good a game as any competitor could hope to: The company had created an innovative and popular product; it introduced new business and marketing techniques to the industry; it changed tactics and broadened its product line as quickly as it could; and all its new software products were competently built and of use to the customers the company sought. Why wasn't that enough to ensure long-term success?

Those questions brought the issues squarely back to the Justice Department—and into the court of public opinion.

I'll Take My Ball and Go Home

On December 11, 1997, Federal Judge Penfield Jackson didn't find Microsoft in contempt of the 1995 consent decree. "Microsoft offers a plausible interpretation of what it considers to be an integrated product as the term is used." Jackson defined integrated as "a product that combines or unites functions that, although capable of functioning independently, undoubtedly complement each other." Microsoft, he determined, demonstrated "at the very least, the ambiguity of the term *integrated product* and has provided a reasonable explanation for its understanding that the consent decree did not preclude Microsoft's insistence" that computer makers package the browser with Windows 95.

In December, Jackson noted that the legal issues in the anti-trust case were so complicated they would take months to finally decide and appointed a "special master"—a preliminary fact finder to the case, Lawrence Lessig, a Harvard University law professor who specialized in the Net.

But his decision was a huge boon to Netscape. For starters, Jackson issued a temporary restraining order that forced Microsoft to stop bundling its browser with Windows 95 and barred the company from requiring computer makers to even accept its Web software. The preliminary ruling was a blow to Microsoft. Even so, Microsoft's reaction surprised many who had watched the case closely—and had to please Netscape. Instead of bowing meekly to the judge's wishes, Microsoft belligerently announced that it would comply by offering personal computer makers three bad choices: an outdated version of the Windows 95 operating system that was not bundled with its browser, a crippled version of Windows without the browser, or the current software package that bundled Windows with IE 4.0.

The two-year-old version of Windows 95 was vastly inferior. It was not compatible with updated versions of software from on-line services such as America Online. Nor would it work properly with newer versions of such popular software programs as the Quicken financial management program or groupware like Lotus Notes.

Microsoft insisted it could not comply with Jackson's order in any other way, claiming that newer versions of Windows 95 relied too heavily on the browser to separate the two without crippling the operating system. Microsoft's message to the government, and to the court, seemed to be: "Software is too complicated for you to understand. We know what's best and we told you once already—it's impossible to separate the browser from the operating system."

With that attitude, Microsoft might as well have issued a personal challenge to every computer user on the planet. Stung by the company's apparent arrogance, Internet users around the world quickly rallied. They posted on Internet newsgroups easy-to-follow instructions for deinstalling Internet Explorer 4.0 from PC hard drives. And Netscape got some mileage out of the public relations debacle: Microsoft's chief antagonist announced that, as a seasonal gift, it would "help out" Microsoft by posting deinstallation instructions on its own company website.

Even worse for Microsoft was how its legal strategy played out with the judge. A few days later, Jackson performed a public demonstration in his courtroom that made Microsoft look foolish. Was it really so impossible to remove Internet Explorer 4.0 from the desktop, as Microsoft's lawyers had claimed? With a few keystrokes, the judge erased the Microsoft browser from the screen of a new personal computer.

Microsoft had a lot of explaining to do. The American civil court system would have plenty of time to hear it.

Mr. Gates Goes to Washington

During the first months after the Justice Department's antitrust division announced its case against Microsoft, the sound byte coming out of Redmond was defensive to the point of being petulant. Initially, Bill Gates hung back and let his lawyers and senior staff people respond on the company's behalf. That strategy didn't work.

Even after the debacle in Judge Jackson's courtroom, Microsoft lawyers refused to back down, claiming that, sure, it might *look* as if you could remove the Internet Explorer 4.0 icon from the desktop—as the judge had demonstrated—but users who tried it would run the risk of damaging Windows. Indeed, in court papers, the company took a dig at Justice Department trustbusters, asserting that "poorly informed lawyers have no vocation for software design."

The whole thing was turning into a public relations nightmare. Yet the company continued to take a hard line, perhaps because Microsoft's stock quickly recovered any value it had lost after the government announced the antitrust case. "Sometimes you have to take positions in legal cases for a larger purpose, even if it does give you public relations problems," Microsoft's lead counsel, William H. Neukom, told *The New York Times*. Microsoft also filed for its own preliminary injunction, asking that Jackson's order be thrown out—along with the special master, Lessig, who the company believed exhibited anti-Microsoft sentiments.

"Every time Microsoft is confronted by a government authority, it reacts like a surly child," said attorney Gary Reback, who had written the August 1996 letter complaining to the Justice Department about Microsoft practices.

As the weeks ticked by, Gates himself decided to go on a public relations offensive.

Gates actually volunteered to testify before the Senate Judiciary Committee at a hearing scheduled for early March 1998. These were hostile waters to cross, as the richest man in America knew well: Senator Orrin Hatch, the Republican from Utah, was known to Microsofties as "the Good Senator from Novell"—a reference to the networking software company that was an economic mainstay in his home state. Likewise, Gates knew that Sun's Scott McNealy, a long-time Microsoft basher, would testify. So would Barksdale.

Hearing Room 216 of the Senate Hart Building has seen its share of drama, including Clarence Thomas's confirmation hearings and the Iran-Contra inquisition. But for sheer media mass—as measured by the number of still cameras (forty-one were counted)—Gates's first Congressional testimony surpassed all those historic events. Senator Patrick Leahy was so excited he took a picture of the photographers himself.

Barksdale began his testimony by asking for a show of hands: How many people among the two hundred or so in the gallery had personal computers?

"Raise your hands. Go on!" urged Barksdale. About a hundred people did.

"OK, if you use an operating system other than Windows 95, keep them up," Barksdale said, and every single hand went down.

"That, ladies and gentlemen, is a monopoly," Barksdale told the senators. Microsoft, he testified later, "has done everything it can think of to drive my company out of business."

Gates demurred. He maintained that Microsoft had every right to wage an aggressive campaign against Netscape, Sun, or anyone else. He pointed out that Netscape only began complaining about the Internet Explorer browser after Microsoft's browser started winning favorable head-to-head reviews. And repeatedly Gates stuck to his message: Microsoft was not a monopoly. In the topsy-turvy world of software development, his company could be upended overnight, he said.

The senators, though, were having none of it. For four hours they laid into Gates, examining every aspect of Microsoft's arrangement with computer makers and the degree to which his browser was tied into Windows 95. If Mr. Gates went to Washington hoping to win some political friends and buy some goodwill, it didn't work. If anything, his appearance would probably embolden the Justice Department, which had made no secret of its plans to widen its investigation into the Redmond colossus.

The Hail Mary Play

For Netscape, the trick, then, was to wage a war of attrition and stay alive—even try and thrive—as long as possible. At the end of January 1998, Netscape went public with the secret plan that Hecker, Zawinski, Andreessen, Eric Hahn, and others had been working on: The company would give away for free both the browser *and* its underlying source code. The goal was simple: Keep Microsoft from owning the Net.

They hoped to keep Netscape's browser on desktops around the world by allowing the tens of thousands of developers out there on the Net to modify it, tweak it, alter it—and, above all, improve it. In so doing, maybe—just maybe—Netscape would be able to block Microsoft's Internet Explorer.

It was a natural extension of the idea that began four years earlier with Andreessen, who had seen the browser as a kind of Trojan horse to get onto companies' servers, where the real money was. The more Netscape browsers out there, the more the brand name flourished, the more people were likely to actually pay for other Netscape goods and services. It was also a fundamental reshifting of the Communicator strategy, which had been an attempt to distance the company from its early identity.

Financial analysts greeted the announcement with some praise. Giving away the source code was a good move on two fronts, they agreed. It would encourage more developers to write Netscape-compatible software, and it also would enable computer makers who licensed the browser to create their own customized brands. For instance, if Compaq were to decide to put Netscape's browser back on its desktop, it could be customized to use Compaq's Web page as a default home page, increasing traffic to the computer-maker's site. A Compaq HELP button could be built into the browser. Preinstalled bookmarks, with Compaq's choices for hot sites, could be there as well.

Anyone could change the browser in any way. Developers were only limited by their own ideas.

Netscape's move had the potential to mobilize the increasingly dormant powers of the once-idealistic Internet to rise up and save the company. By putting the Navigator code into the hands of the public, Netscape could enfranchise programmers around the world in the battle against Microsoft. It was a risky gamble, though; Netscape couldn't deny that plenty of programmers had resented the arrogance the company had displayed when it was riding high.

But the opportunity was there, the potential to turn a corporate struggle into a political cause. That's because an active and grumbling resistance movement thrives, despite Microsoft's worldwide dominance over the bread-and-butter software applications that most desktop users rely on. The Net may have become a commercial commodity, but it still retains a strong core of philosophers (many of whom are crackerjack coders who write and then give away stunningly useful programs in their spare time for the sheer fun of it) who believe that software yearns to be free. Or at least yearns not to be Microsoft's. Their cause includes hackers from around the world—"hackers" in the old, best sense of the word—or as Raymond put it in his *New Hacker's Dictionary,* "One who enjoys the intellectual challenge of creatively overcoming or circumventing limitations."

In Washington, the federal government was trying to convince the courts that Microsoft had placed limitations on the software industry. On the Net, hackers already knew it.

Andreessen had easily convinced Barksdale to agree to give away the source code. "He went for it right away, after he saw that we had enough revenue from our enterprise market and from revenues off our website so we could afford to do it," Andreessen said.

Andreessen, who was familiar with this model of software development from his youth, made a convincing argument. The way he saw it, "We knew, from the past experience of things like Linux and Apache, that this kind of model can sometimes work. So the key was: When do you have business models that encourage rather than discourage this kind of thing? We are in a position that encouraged it and we believe it could be as big a step forward for commercial software as our idea of distributing commercial software on the Net was."

Andreessen had decided that Netscape's most valuable asset was not actually its source code, it was its audience. Netscape had a huge audience. That's because, since day one, Netscape had sent everyone who ran its browser to the Netscape Web page as a starting point. Netscape's page had been the default home base for people running the browser. As a result, millions and millions of people looked at Netscape's Web page every day, enabling the company to charge premium rates for advertisements that appeared there. "The value for us consists in having the audience, not in having the audience page," Andreessen said. "It's very much like a TV network model."

With the company pulling in revenues from ads on its home page, Netscape planned to abdicate revenues from the consumer market, relying instead on high-end corporate customers who would be willing to pay not only for groupware but also for a branded version of the client browser. Even though the source code would be publicly available, Andreessen reasoned that corporate customers would be willing to pay a fee to Netscape for support and consulting.

The key to the whole venture was that after Netscape made its code available for hackers to work on, à la Linux and Apache, it would take the improvements and add them to its branded source code. "Here is a base on which lots of developers will do lots of things. What we need to do is make sure we are constantly taking the best changes and adding them to our 'reference' source code," Andreessen said.

So on February 23, 1998, Netscape set up a central clearing-house to watch over and guide the process of putting Netscape's code into the public domain. Although the gatekeepers would be a newly created division of Netscape, their mission and methods would be anything but corporate. The people brainstorming on the project included charter members of the core group of hackers who had called themselves the Doomed, headed up by Tom Paquin. But what to call the new entity?

Mozilla.org.

The name harkened back to the precommercial release days, to the days of infinite promise. Mozilla.org would coordinate what it hoped would be the furious and frenetic activity of thousands of hackers who would collaborate and spawn something amazing. Mozilla.org's main function would be to make sure that updates were incorporated into the source.

Zawinski was the first to admit it was a bit like neighborhood kids putting on a Christmas play: "I've got this box of old clothes, and we can use my grandpa's barn!"

"Microsoft is much bigger than Netscape, so it can throw lots more resources at anything than Netscape can. But Microsoft is not bigger than the Net," Zawinski said. "It all sounds kind of far out and wacky. But the thing is, it can work."

Zawinski wrote a mission statement for Mozilla.org and posted it on the Web. It described how the group would "provide a central point of contact and community for those interested in using or improving the source code." Netscape would rely on Mozilla.org to make sure the browser code grew in a stable, coherent fashion. Mozilla.org would put together the changes to the source, provide technical assistance, and see that updates were posted quickly and regularly. They would keep bug lists and operate discussion groups and mailing lists.

They had a lot of work to do before March 31, 1998, the date they would release the source code publicly. Too much work. They'd never get it all finished. But did it matter? Happily, they rolled up their sleeves, sure in their hearts that they were doomed.

Acknowledgments

Because Netscape's story never stopped developing up to the moment when we turned in a final manuscript in March 1998, we could not have made sense of the relentless flow of facts without help.

Our editor at Atlantic Monthly Press, Anton Mueller, exhibited enormous patience and tact as he waded through various drafts of the book. How he sorted through it we may never know; we are grateful he did. Likewise, copyeditor Janet Baker greatly improved the manuscript.

Some material in this book appeared, in slightly different form, as an article in *Wired* magazine in April 1998. Our editors there, Kevin Kelly and Katrina Heron, raised important questions that focused the final portion of the book.

At Netscape, the company's public relations team, led by Rosanne Siino and Suzanne Anthony, opened the doors to give us access to anyone at the company we wanted to talk to, even when this project ate up a considerable amount of time. Jamie Zawinski's writings on his home page were often profound; he gave us kind permission to quote from his résumé and from his work, which can be found at http://people.netscape.com/jwz/. His recollection of events brought many of the scenes in the book to life.

We also are grateful to Dan Okrent at Time Inc. New Media for granting the time and space to work on this book; to A. Littman for explaining antitrust law; to Doug Frantz for once again steering us in the right direction; and to Marie D'Amico and Steve Capps, who provided shelter in California and cannoli in New York.

As always, we thank our literary agent, Mary Evans, who propped us up in so many ways on so many occasions that we would be embarrassed to list them here.

Sources

The material in this book came primarily from interviews we conducted with more than a hundred people, from observations we made firsthand, and from information contained in various court records and in documents filed with the Securities and Exchange Commission. To the best of our knowledge, everything in this book is true. None of the information in this book came from unnamed sources.

With the exception of Netscape cofounder James Clark, who declined to be interviewed for this book, the company's employees were generous with their time, granting as many follow-up interviews as we requested. Interviews were conducted in person, over the phone, and via E-mail correspondence during the past eighteen months. In addition, a spokeswoman for Dr. Clark sent us a copy of Clark's written responses to questions; we used that material in the same way we used interview notes.

Microsoft's founder and chief executive officer, Bill Gates, declined to be interviewed for this book. So did the company's chief lawyer, William Neukom. However, both made relevant public statements over the past few months that we incorporated. We relied, as well, on written statements and arguments that Microsoft employees and lawyers made in sworn court documents. In instances where we were unable to interview a particular Microsoft employee named in the book or mentioned by inference, we asked Claudia Husemann of Waggoner-Edstrom, Microsoft's public relations firm, to forward portions of the manuscript for a review of factual accuracy. We have incorporated their responses into the text in the same way we used interview notes.

For background material, we also consulted a number of books on related subjects and dozens of recent articles that appeared in magazines, in newspapers, and on World Wide Web sites. We also reviewed dozens of Netscape company press releases and employee home pages from 1994 to 1998, archived at Netscape's World Wide Web page at http://www.netscape.com and at http://www.mozilla.org.

Because a book is the sort of record that will sit on a shelf for years and years, so will any inaccuracies it may inadvertently contain. In an attempt to avoid mistakes, we asked many of the people we interviewed to review portions of the manuscript before publication for factual errors. We're grateful for those they flagged; any that remain are our own.

The following is a list of published sources we consulted.

Books

Burns, Joseph W. *A Study of the Antitrust Laws: Their Administration, Interpretation, and Effect.* New York: Central Book Co., 1958.

Carroll, Paul. *Big Blues: The Unmaking of IBM.* New York: Crown Publishers, 1993.

Cringely, Robert. *Accidental Empires: How the Boys of Silicon Valley Make Their Millions, Battle Foreign Competition, and Still Can't Get a Date.* New York: Addison-Wesley Publishing Co., 1992.

Freedman, Alan. *The Computer Glossary,* 5th ed. Point Pleasant, Pa.: Computer Language Co., 1991.

Hafner, Katie, and Matthew Lyon. *Where Wizards Stay Up Late: The Origins of the Internet.* New York: Simon & Schuster, 1996.

McKenna, Regis. *Who's Afraid of Big Blue?* New York: Addison-Wesley Publishing Co., 1989.

Malone, Michael S. *The Big Score: The Billion Dollar Story of Silicon Valley.* Garden City, N.Y.: Doubleday, 1985.

Manes, Stephen, and Paul Andrews. *Gates: How Microsoft's Mogul Reinvented an Industry—and Made Himself the Richest Man in America.* New York: Doubleday, 1993.

Mills, Daniel Quinn. *Broken Promises: An Unconventional View of What Went Wrong at IBM.* Cambridge, Mass.: President and Fellows of Harvard College, 1996.

Raymond, Eric S., ed. *The New Hacker's Dictionary.* Cambridge, Mass.: MIT Press, 1991.

Reid, Robert H. *Architects of the Web: 1,000 Days that Built the Future of Business.* New York: John Wiley & Sons, 1997.

Shurkin, Joel. *Engines of the Mind: The Evolution of the Computer from Mainframes to Microprocessors.* New York: W. W. Norton & Co., 1996.

Sobel, Robert. *I.B.M.: Colossus in Transition.* New York: Times Books, 1981.

Stross, Randall E. *The Microsoft Way.* New York: Addison-Wesley Publishing Co., 1996.

Wallace, James. *Overdrive: Bill Gates and the Race to Control Cyberspace.* New York: John Wiley & Sons, 1997.

Magazine and Newspaper Articles

Aley, James. "The Heart of Silicon Valley." *Fortune,* 7 July 1997.

Andrews, Edmund L. "AT&T Paying $12.6 Billion for Cellular Giant." *New York Times,* 17 August 1993.

————. "Big Payoff for High-Tech Gambler." *New York Times,* 17 August 1993.

Baker, Molly. "Technology Investors Fall Head Over Heels for Their New Love; Little Stock Called Netscape Is Lofted to the Heavens in a Frenzy of Trading." *Wall Street Journal,* 10 August 1995.

Bank, David. "Microsoft's Persistence Costs Netscape Dearly." *Wall Street Journal,* 13 November 1997.

Cassidy, John. "The Force of an Idea." *New Yorker,* 12 January 1998.

Elmer-Dewitt, Philip. "Mine, All Mine." *Time,* 5 June 1995.

Gates, William H. "Why the Justice Dept. Is Wrong." *Wall Street Journal,* 10 November 1997.

Gilder, George. "The Coming Software Shift." *Forbes ASAP,* 28 August 1995.

Gleick, James. "Justice Delayed." *New York Times Magazine,* 23 November 1997.

Gruley, Bryan, John R. Wilke, David Bank, and Don Clark. "U.S. Sues Microsoft Over PC Browser." *Wall Street Journal,* 21 October 1997.

Heilemann, John. "The Networker." *New Yorker,* 11 August 1997.

Hof, Robert D. "Netscape: How It Plans to Outrun Microsoft." *Business Week,* 10 February 1997.

Kaplan, David A. "Nothing But Net." *Newsweek,* 1 January 1996.

Keller, John J., and Jared Sandberg. "Who's News: Barksdale, Head of Wireless at AT&T, Quits to Join Internet Startup Netscape." *Wall Street Journal,* 12 January 1995.

Labaton, Stephen. "U.S. Tells Court Microsoft Breaks Antitrust Accord." *New York Times,* 21 October 1997.

Levy, Steven. "How the Propeller Heads Stole the Electronic Future." *New York Times Magazine,* 24 September 1995.

Lewis, Michael. "The Little Creepy Crawlers Who Will Eat You in the Night." *New York Times Magazine,* 1 March 1998.

Lewis, Peter H. "Official Quits AT&T to Run Netscape." *New York Times,* 12 January 1995.

Lohr, Steve. "Microsoft Digs In Against a 'Poorly Informed' U.S." *New York Times,* 24 December 1997.

———. "Microsoft Says U.S. Challenge Is 'Perverse.'" *New York Times,* 12 November 1997.

———. "Spyglass, a Pioneer, Learns Hard Lessons About Microsoft." *New York Times,* 2 March 1998.

Lohr, Steve, and John Markoff. "Why Microsoft Is Taking a Hard Line with the Government." *New York Times,* 12 January 1998.

McCoy, Charles. "Netscape's CEO Hits the Jackpot, Faces the Glare." *Wall Street Journal,* 10 August 1995.

Madden, Andrew. "The Good Ship Netscape." *Red Herring Magazine,* September 1997.

Markoff, John. "Six Tips on How to Earn $52 Million by Age 24." *New York Times,* 14 August 1995.

Perkins, Anthony B. "The Thinker." *Red Herring Magazine,* March 1995.

Pitta, Julie. "Investors Get Caught Up in Netscape." *Los Angeles Times,* 10 August 1995.

Rebello, Kathy. "Inside Microsoft: The Untold Story of How the Internet Forced Bill Gates to Reverse Course." *Business Week,* 15 July 1996.

Schlender, Brent. "Software Hardball." *Fortune,* 30 September 1996.

Sloan, Allan. "High Wired." *Newsweek,* 25 December 1995.

Steinert-Threlkeld, Tom. "Can You Work in Netscape Time?" *Fast Company,* 1995.

Swartz, Jon. "Microsoft Pulls Prank." *San Francisco Chronicle,* 2 October 1997.

Swisher, Kara, and David Bank. "Netscape Expects to Report Quarterly Operating Losses." *Wall Street Journal,* 6 January 1998.

Tetzeli, Rick. "Cool New Companies: Mosaic Communications." *Fortune,* 11 July 1994.

————. "What It's Really Like to Be Marc Andreessen." *Fortune,* 9 December 1996.

Online Articles

Lash, Alex. "MS's Netscape Envy Revealed." *C/NET at http://www.news.com,* 23 October 1997.

Nee, Eric. "Jim Clark: An Interview with Eric Nee." *Upside Online at http://www.upside.com,* July 1995.

Oakes, Chris. "What Redmond Integrated, and When." *Wired News at http://www.wired.com,* 10 November 1997.

Raymond, Eric S. "The Cathedral and the Bazaar." Archived at http://sagan.earthspace.net/~esr/

Wingfield, Nick. "Now Microsoft and Netscape Battle Over Lawn Ornaments." *Wall Street Journal Interactive Edition, archived at http://www.wsj.com,* 1 October 1997.